HOTSHOT

HOTSHOT

A Life on Fire

RIVER SELBY

Atlantic Monthly Press
New York

FIRST EDITION

Printed in the United States of America

This book is set in 11.5-pt. Abobe Caslon by AlphaDesign & Composition of
Pittsfield, NH.

First Grove Atlantic hardcover edition: August 2025

Library of Congress Cataloging-in-Publication data is available for this title.

ISBN 978-0-8021-4949-7
eISBN 978-0-8021-4951-0

Atlantic Monthly Press
an imprint of Grove Atlantic
154 West 14th Street
New York, NY 10011

Distributed by Publishers Group West

groveatlantic.com

25 26 27 28   10 9 8 7 6 5 4 3 2 1

For my grandmother,
who taught me to love reading and encouraged me
to fulfill my destiny as a writer.
Tally ho.

Every time we remember something, the memory itself changes. Thus, memory is inherently unreliable. Personal experience is subjective, interpreted through our individual perspectives and belief systems. Two people experiencing the same event will inevitably remember it differently. I have not embellished or exaggerated anything in the forthcoming pages. The autobiographical material in this book details my personal experiences, as I remember them.

Identifying details may have been changed to protect the identity of others.

Contents

Part VI: The Last Frontier (2010)

Introduction

Growing up, I never imagined that I would become a wildland firefighter, or any firefighter for that matter. I grew up in the eighties and nineties, when there were very few firefighters, wildland or otherwise, who weren't men. My single mom was a secretary. We moved often, sometimes over twice a year, and although I intermittently played basketball at the Boys & Girl's Club, athletics were much less attractive to me than reading and listening to music. I wasn't competitive by nature. In high school I was kicked off the volleyball team for smoking cigarettes. The only sports I enjoyed were swimming and exploring the small swaths of wildland that sometimes surrounded our apartments, or my grandparents' house in the Seattle suburbs. None of this, including my solitary life as an only child, pointed to firefighting as a profession.

I was nineteen when I began fighting fires. By then, I had been a tween and teenage runaway, a sex worker, and a survivor of violence inflicted by both strangers and people I knew, most notably my mother. Anyone eyeing my life trajectory would have guessed that I'd end up permanently homeless and possibly addicted to several substances. That did happen. That's the life wildland firefighting saved me from.

White and purple crocuses were barely puncturing the soggy ground when my friend Kelly suggested I try wildland firefighting.

It was the year 2000 and I was living in Eugene, Oregon, attending community college a few hundred miles south from where my mom and stepdad lived in Olympia, Washington. The world had survived Y2K but winter had tested my will to live—first my grandmother, my soul mate whose first name I shared and with whom I'd lived intermittently as a child, had died. My mother warred with her siblings over their respective inheritances; my grandfather moved into a sad little apartment, where he fell and sustained a head injury, resulting in memory loss. My life unraveled. Organization, calendars, homework, and mundane tasks had always been difficult for me, and I was constantly at war with myself over these inadequacies. Bulimia was my primary coping mechanism, along with drinking, drugs, and sex. A few weeks into my first spring quarter I stopped attending classes, telling no one. Short gray days and long nights only accelerated my sense of disconnection. For a while I worked as a hotel housekeeper, until too many no-shows got me fired. Then I worked fast food, cycling through McDonald's, Taco Time, and random mid-level indie eateries. After exhausting all opportunities for steady employment, I relied on the local Labor Ready for my paychecks, which mostly went to rent, alcohol, and drugs.

Kelly, along with her roommate Peter, was one of the few people who knew all of this, and the debilitating depression underneath. She was also an experienced former wildland firefighter. "It will distract you," she said, flipping through a photo album filled with pictures of herself from when she had worked on the crews several years ago. In them she looked happy, grinning in her orange hard hat. She must have expected me to say no, because she reminded me that I was already doing manual labor, lifting heavy things and surrounded by male co-workers, many of them older, in dire straits of their own. I didn't need much convincing. I would have tried anything. A week later I was hired. Two weeks after that I was on my way to New Mexico for my first fire assignment: The Viveash Fire. By 2010, when I left firefighting, I had worked two years on Type 2 contract crews, four as a hotshot, and one year as a helicopter crew member. Type 2 crews commonly clean up after a fire has burned through an area, whereas hotshot crews are classified as Type 1 crews and conduct initial attack, usually working in direct contact with active fires. Hotshots are elite firefighters with a more complex skillset than Type 2 crews, though they're often called "unskilled laborers."

Now I have my own album of fire relics, including a faded newspaper clipping about a famous actor's ranch house at risk of burning, along with a dirty Incident Action Plan (IAP) my first crew boss gave me for a keepsake.

I discovered a whole world of wildland firefighting—an entire subculture of mostly men who spend their summers crisscrossing the United States fighting forest fires, desert fires, grassland fires, palmetto fires. All kinds of fires, many of them in areas rarely traversed by humans. And I became part of it when we pulled up to the Viveash fire camp in the government-issued yellow school bus. Rolling into a fire camp for the first time is a bizarre experience for anyone who's had the privilege of never enduring a catastrophic disaster. It summons images of military outposts and refugee camps, but we were merely a ragtag group of misfits hoping to cash in on some overtime pay. Out of the twenty-one of us, seventeen had never once been on a fire assignment. We marveled at the bustling outpost, with its canvas tents for incident command, staff, logistical personnel, a first aid tent and field medics, a canteen, fresh gear and tools, showers, port-a-potties, fields of small multicolored camping tents, and a kitchen trailer large enough for a decent salad bar. The horizon, lined with ragged, sand-colored peaks, hinted at the mountainous terrain where the fire burned.

Sophisticated fire camps aren't erected until a fire is large enough to require more than a handful of resources. Fire sizes are rated according to the Incident Command System, with Type 5 fires being the smallest and Type 1 being the largest and most complex. This system isn't exclusive to wildfire response but applies to any large-scale emergency, including hurricanes, earthquakes, and pandemics.

Type 4 or Type 5 incident management teams consist of no more than ten people local to the area, maybe city or county fire along with a federal resource, depending on land jurisdiction. Someone assumes the role of incident commander. Many fires ignite and are extinguished without the need for an official fire camp, but if a fire grows in size the incident commander orders more resources, like fire crews, aircraft, and engines, and a fire camp is erected to sustain those resources.

The Viveash was a Type 1 incident. There were more than one thousand firefighters and personnel assigned. One of several large fires burning throughout the southwest, the Viveash was ignited by lightning, a common spring occurrence in the southwestern United States. The lightning storms are often accompanied or shortly followed by monsoons , but this year the monsoons were late. 2000 was a drought year and forests were parched and overgrown.

A few weeks earlier, the National Park Service had lost control of a prescribed burn in Bandelier National Monument, sixty miles east of us. The resulting fire, named Cerro Grande, exploded, threatening the town of Los Alamos and destroying a handful of buildings at the Los Alamos National Laboratory. Agencies rarely lose control of prescribed fires but the media pounced, as they always do, capitalizing on the public's understandable fear of fire. Despite burning through sparsely populated land the Viveash garnered an outsized response because it followed the Cerro Grande fire. It's a familiar cycle to me now—the way media attention dictates federal fire response—but I didn't think twice about it back then. We set up camp, nestled amongst several other Type 2 contract crews (confusingly, a separate system from the numbering of fire size), and I was supplied with a canvas pup tent and two sleeping bags along with some wool blankets to sleep on.

* * *

My first two weeks are imprinted in my mind because everything was brand-new. Each morning we rode the bus for over an hour, ascending a treacherous pockmarked ancient dirt logging road. Seatbeltless, we were jostled and bounced, sometimes raising our hands to stop ourselves from hitting the metal ceiling. We emerged sleepy-eyed from the bus, grabbing our packs from the open back door, breathing in exhaust from the tailpipe. The land around us was completely scorched; I'd seen nothing like it before. Bare, blackened trees with pointed, spindly limbs and black soil that felt strange underfoot, both spongy and brittle. The air smelled sweet and repellent, like a puttering campfire. Each footstep sent up clouds of dust and ash, coating everything, including my mouth and teeth, in fine grit, blackening my snot and saliva. Like all fires, the Viveash was parceled into divisions named using the NATO phonetic alphabet, from Alpha to Zebra. Some of it was bare as a moonscape, some was burned in a mosaic pattern, with patchy green and brown tufts of grass and baby pine trees with newly browned needles. The high-altitude aspen groves, naturally fire-resistant, stood out like shining islands carpeted in tall emerald grass, some of it tinged black. The bright white trees, their trunks lined with deep gray and black markings, were juxtaposed with patches of scorched earth, creating a surreal, discordant kind of beauty I'd never seen before, except in works of art. But we weren't there to admire the forest. We were there to grid.

Imagine a search and rescue team searching a forest for a missing person: They line up ten or fifteen feet apart from each other, pausing at any hint of evidence and moving at a crawling pace so they don't miss any clues. Mopping-up is like that. The searching is called "gridding," for its grid formation, each person or team responsible for searching square by square. Instead of clues left by a person, we looked for any residual heat, like smoldering roots or wisps of smoke arising from stumps and logs. We walked, and walked, and walked. Every day. For twelve hours a day. It was mind-numbing. I hid my watch in my pack because checking the passing time was torturous. Still, the job was good. I liked being away from civilization, where I couldn't get into trouble. There was no booze and no drugs. All those decisions in the outside world—I didn't need to make them anymore. Every night I fell asleep right away, and every morning we woke up at the same time to our crew boss George's gruff voice or the sound of a crew member's singing. My life had never been so stable.

One afternoon, George's radio flared with chatter of medics and heat exhaustion. Two hotshots were being flown by helicopter to the local hospital. I'd almost forgotten there was an active fire—on our divisions, where we'd been assigned to work, the air was mostly clear, and any noise of aircraft was far away. I thought of the hotshots working closer to the flames. A few days earlier I had seen my first hotshot crew. They pulled into camp, supposedly to shower, and emerged from their buggies while we were at chow. They descended and devoured. Their yellow Nomex shirts were black, brown, and striped with mysterious ghostly lines I would later recognize as sweat stains. Their faces, covered in grime, were nearly indistinguishable from one another. They were quiet, almost silent, as they ate. Big guys. Solid, strong guys with militaristic countenances. I watched my crew boss watch them, as many others at the chow tent watched them, with reverence. Then they left. When I asked George if those men were hotshots, he nodded. "I want to do that," I said. He shook his head, looking almost sorry for me. "You can't be a hotshot. You're a girl."

Wildland fire crews, and hotshots in particular, wouldn't exist as they are today without the New Deal, which was enacted in 1933 by President Franklin D. Roosevelt as an effort to counteract the Great Depression. The United States Forest Service (USFS) and National Park Service (NPS) were still young and underfunded; twenty-eight and sixteen years old, respectively. Both held jurisdiction over millions of public land-acres and neither agency had enough funding to keep pace with increasingly strict fire suppression policies. President Roosevelt wanted to reignite the country's passion for conservation while creating jobs for unemployed men who couldn't support their families. He created the Civilian Conservation Corps and erected segregated work camps, over two thousand of them over nine years. Hundreds of thousands of (mostly white) men planted trees, cut firebreaks around townships, built bridges, created state parks, and fought forest and brush fires. Non-white men had less opportunity to work. Much of the fire infrastructure that exists today was built during the New Deal, including fire lookouts and thousands of miles of firebreaks, many of which have been ill-maintained due to continued lack of funding.

By the mid-forties, cohesive fire crews began taking shape. One thirty-man crew in the town of San Bernardino, located in Southern California, specialized in initial attack. In 1946 they began calling themselves the Del Rosa Hot Shots. Two years later, the Los Padres Hotshots were established about two hundred miles north, near Santa Barbara. It makes sense that hotshots were born in Southern California, where the fire landscape collided with several population booms and set off what's now known as the light burning debate—an ongoing argument for and against full fire suppression.

Today, hotshots, also known as Type 1 fire crews, or Interagency Hotshot Crews (IHC), are federal entities under the banner of three agencies: the United States Forest Service, National Park Service, and Bureau of Land Management (BLM). Each separate agency has a unique purpose, but they are all inextricably connected. The BLM (created in 1946) is the youngest of the three agencies and primarily manages rangelands. Their trademark triangular signs are ubiquitous in arid regions of the United States, like the Great Basin. The NPS (formed in 1916) is the second youngest of the three, behind the USFS (1905). The Forest Service has the most firefighting resources, including hotshot crews. There are thirteen BLM hotshot crews. The Park Service has only two: one in Sequoia National Park and the other in Rocky Mountain National Park, in Colorado. Comparatively, the USFS has over a hundred hotshot crews under its jurisdiction, a reflection of its massive fire suppression funding and aims. Seven hotshot crews operate under the umbrella of the Bureau of Indian Affairs (BIA) and individual tribes, as well.

Most people have no clue what a hotshot is, but in the wildland fire community hotshots are held in high regard. Hotshotting is complex work. The requirements and safety standards are stringent. Crews must have, at minimum, eighteen people at all times. Because of the frequency of injury and job abandonment, most crews start each fire season with 22 people and end it with 18 or 19. Not only is the work physically and mentally grueling, hotshots must dedicate at least six months of their life to their crew, sacrificing time with family and friends, along with individual autonomy. For most, it's a summer job lasting a season or two. For some, it's an entire career.

Despite these demands, and despite the colloquial title of elite firefighter, hotshots weren't officially categorized as firefighters until the summer of 2022. Before then, the federal government called all wildland firefighters forestry technicians and denied them the benefits typically granted to nonfederal firefighters, like health insurance and retirement, as well as "portal-to-portal" pay, which keeps firefighters on the clock for as long as they're away from home base. There was no health insurance offered when I was a seasonal hotshot—all we had was worker's compensation, in case we got injured. Seasonal wildland firefighters are now offered temporary health insurance.

My pay as a GS-2 (the second-lowest rank of government worker) was under $12 an hour in 2002. In over two decades, that rate has budged by barely three dollars an hour. In California, I got a cost of living stipend, and if we were working on "uncontained" fires an extra three dollars (called "hazard pay") was tacked on to our hourly wage. For this reason, the gold standard for a "good" fire season is judged by how many hours of overtime are accrued throughout the season. If it's a slow season, a hotshot, the most elite of wildland firefighters other than smokejumpers (who jump out of planes into small, remote areas unreachable by vehicle), can make as little as seventeen thousand dollars for six months of work. Wildland firefighters define a good season as one that the public calls catastrophic. They don't make a living wage without catastrophe, but either way they sacrifice their summers, remaining within the required two-hour radius of their base, so they can respond quickly to fire calls. Federal hotshot crew members and wildland firefighters get paid, on average, about 33 percent less than wildland firefighters who work for state agencies. In 2023, a nonprofit advocacy group called Grassroots Wildland Firefighters worked with Arizona Senator Kyrsten Sinema and other federal legislators to introduce the Wildland Firefighter Paycheck Protection Act, which temporarily increased benefits and raised pay for nonseasonal (permanent) wildland firefighters by up to 42 percent while also increasing hourly pay for seasonal workers by two dollars an hour. While this is a solid first step, it's still not permanent as of this writing. Seasonal federal wildland firefighters still lack many benefits and protections, like subsidized comprehensive health insurance. Their base pay is now $15 an hour, which is the minimum wage in many states and cities.

Because of low pay rates, wildland firefighters want overtime, but too much overtime raises their risk of injury and exhaustion and extends time away from family, friends, and important social networks, often leading to a sense of disconnection from one's community and a jarring reintroduction when the fire season ends. Suicide rates amongst wildland firefighters are high, and likely underreported. In 2018, a survey found that 55 percent of wildland firefighters have exhibited suicidal behavior or ideation, compared to 33 percent of non-wildland firefighters, but consistent and reliable data regarding the mental health of wildland firefighters simply does not exist. Federal wildland firefighters sacrifice their summers and risk their lives for low pay because they love the job—this is true for most federal employees, many of whom could easily find work that not only offers more balance, but pays better, too.

I came into firefighting by happenstance. Like my peers, I also wished for more fires and overtime despite the accompanying exhaustion and pain. Had I not left the profession in 2010, I would have eventually gotten my wish—since 2005 wildfire occurrences throughout the United States have doubled, and fires in the western United States have at least doubled in size, on average. Large fires are burning longer and fire behavior is increasingly unpredictable. The National Interagency Fire Center has reported that the ten largest fires since 1980 burned after 2003. In the twenty-four fire seasons since 2000, twelve burned over eight million acres. The cost of suppression has also risen: Agencies have spent over one billion dollars each season for all except four years since 2000, with five of those twenty-one years costing over three billion dollars. This isn't only a western occurrence. In late autumn of 2024, historical fires burned throughout the Northeast, incited by record-breaking drought. Then, in January 2025, several fires ignited in Los Angeles. Spurred by the Santa Ana winds, the fires destroyed over 17,000 structures, many of them in the historically Black and working-class neighborhood of Altadena. January wildfires in Los Angeles are historically quite rare. Media outlets coined the word "megafire" in the 1980s, and scientists picked up the term in 2005. Any fire over one hundred thousand acres is categorized as a megafire, but in 2020, after California's August Complex fire burned over one million acres, someone in a comment section coined the term "gigafire." It stuck.

These changes are usually framed in terms of climate change, which has lengthened fire seasons and weakened ecosystems in complex ways I'll address in this book. But climate change is only one of many factors in what has become a profound shift in the fire landscape. The shift may appear sudden, but it's happened gradually. We can trace it back to 1492, when Europeans first began colonizing the United States.

There are many ways to reflect on the United States before and after colonization, but few people do so exclusively in terms of fire. I certainly never considered any connections when I was a hotshot. It wasn't until I started research for this book, years after I left firefighting, that I thoroughly traced the connections. Many narratives detailing the history of fire suppression in the United States cite the Great Fire of 1910, which burned over three million acres of land in the Northwest, as the beginning of fire suppression. It was a beginning of some sort, but not *the* beginning, nor was it the first catastrophic fire in the United States. Before the Great Fire of 1910, catastrophic fires followed logging from east to west, and debates surrounding fire suppression were happening well before 1910.

For thousands of years before colonization, both anthropogenic (human-caused) and natural fire were common and vital to nearly all North American landscapes. Although this book focuses on the U.S., there are many parallel narratives, particularly in Australia and Canada, of colonization's effect on the fire landscape. Europeans brought particular ideas and beliefs surrounding fire, agriculture, and land development, as well as insatiable and destructive appetites for natural resources. Most were oblivious to the sophisticated ways Indigenous people tended their land, including the use of fire as an agricultural tool. Fire was, and is, a sacred and essential part of the lives and cultures of many Indigenous Americans, and Indigenous cultures around the world.

Most ecosystems in North America evolved with the presence of fire on a seasonal cycle. The near-constant presence of smoke is commonly mentioned in the journals, logbooks, and narratives of early North American settlers and explorers. Today, there is extensive scholarship detailing Native American use of fire and early fire ecology—scientific (drawn from soil, tree-ring, and glacier datasets), anthropological, and historical.

For this book I have relied upon the work of fire historians, like Stephen Pyne; anthropologists, like M. Kat Anderson; scientists, like Robin Wall Kimmerer; and the work of at least fifty others who have done and are doing vital work in this field. I also relied upon archival documents and texts, recent scholarly datasets and articles published in academic journals, and interviews I conducted myself with current scholars, scientists, and past and present wildland firefighters, all in the interest of giving the reader the most accurate and up-to-date picture of what we know about the way fire and humans intersect. One thing that is inescapable is that the impact of colonization on ecological landscapes and Native Americans is both ugly and intimately interconnected with the history of fire suppression in the U.S.

I am an academic studying, among other things, the history of American colonization. This occupation feels as surprising to me as firefighting did. But no book can be the sole resource for understanding the complicated intersections of fire, history, science, genocide, ecology, or wildland firefighting. I encourage you to read more on these subjects and come to your own conclusions, which is why there's a list for further reading at the end of this book. In particular, I urge you to read the texts written by Indigenous writers.

This book is a memoir of the seven years I spent as a firefighter, and I cannot extricate my personal and emotional histories from that time, just as I cannot wrest fire history from the hands of its attached histories; nor would I feel comfortable, or honest, if I tried. I was a person as well as a firefighter, and my relationship to firefighting was fraught and sometimes destructive, as was my relationship with myself at the time. I struggled with bulimia, substance abuse, and complex childhood trauma. To help flesh out my memories, I relied on my own journals, interviews with past co-workers and friends, and visits to the many places I've lived or fought fire. Everything is true but recollections are subjective. My truth and memories are my own, meaning that others may, and likely do, remember things differently. Memory is a tricky thing—always shifting. I left things out when I was unsure, in service of the truth. This is why quoted conversations are sparse, only appearing when I could confirm them with others or lift them from my journals.

My mother's death is also a large part of this narrative, because it occurred in 2010, during my last year as a firefighter. Leaving it out or minimizing its impact is not something I was willing to do. My relationship with my mother is woven throughout this book. Her suicide profoundly changed my life, and I was back on the fireline a week after she died.

One thing I don't engage with directly in this book is my non-binary identity. I struggled to inhabit my roles of girl and woman, and their accompanying expectations, but that is how I thought of myself and how everyone knew me during my time as a firefighter. It took me forty years to reach safe harbor within myself and accept who I am. For this reason, I decided to use my former name, Ana—the name I was called for the entirety of my twenties—and have written the past as I lived it.

PART I
NorCal (2002)

Chapter One

Women Have Smaller Lungs

I first came to the town at the foothills of the Sierras in April 2002, driving all the way from New York, where I'd been working as a nanny for the last eight months. Hand-drawn cardboard signs speckled telephone poles, advertising produce, tamales, agua fresca and horchata. On both sides of the two-lane highway skeletal trees and shrubs sprouted from hard-packed dirt in uniform lines. Occasionally I passed a long, narrow steel irrigation unit sitting idly in an otherwise empty and seemingly endless row. Before those rows, and before the Spanish brought grazing animals and invasive seeds in the late eighteenth century, Tulare Lake stretched along the Central Valley for over one hundred miles north to south, from Merced all the way down to Bakersfield. The Tachi Yokut Tribe call Tulare Lake "Pa'ashi," which translates to "big water." Tributaries ebbed and flowed in seasonal cycles, breathing silt and nutrients into the receptive soil. Flocks of white pelicans, herons, and egrets feasted on plentiful fish and nested in verdant riparian forests. Grasslands were plentiful, and several varying and distinct ecological habitats existed throughout the valley. Many native tribes depended on the lake and its tributaries for survival.

In the mid-nineteenth century, settlers began diverting water to their crops in the name of government-sanctioned "land reclamation," one of many federal efforts to prevent Indigenous Californians from keeping their lands. Within decades Tulare Lake and its accompanying floodplain habitats were desiccated. Government agencies installed dams throughout the region beginning in the late 1800s. Tulare Lake occasionally returns and vanishes; in 2023 several atmospheric rivers temporarily filled the lake. Waterfowl returned. News outlets reported this as flooding, apparently unaware that the lake had once been a permanent feature of the landscape. The Tachi Yokut Tribe are currently advocating for the return of Tulare Lake as well as the demolition of several dams, in an effort to restore the surrounding land.

Despite having grown up in the West, I knew none of this history. The entire landscape was new to me. The summer of 2002 would be my third working as a wildland firefighter, but my first as a hotshot. The previous two seasons I'd worked on a Type 2 contract crew based in Eugene, Oregon. The job spanned from May to October, but contract work was unreliable, and I'd applied to over a dozen hotshot crews in the hopes of becoming a federal employee. I got three job offers in late January. One of the superintendents, a gruff guy named Phillip, warned me that I'd be the first woman on their crew in several years. He asked if I was up for that kind of challenge. The other two superintendents sounded confident that I could do the work. Hiring a woman wasn't unusual for them, and I wouldn't have been the sole woman on their crews, neither of which was in California. But I accepted Phillip's challenge—that's how I saw it then. I still sometimes wonder how things would have unfolded if I'd chosen differently.

The highway ascended east from the San Joaquin Valley into rolling hills greened by spring rains and gleaming in the unfiltered sunlight.

Vermillion lichen splattered jagged gray rocks, which punctuated the grass like uncarved gravestones. Oak trees reached their dark gnarled branches upwards as if striking the bright blue sky. Accumulated dead leaves and rotten acorns skirted their trunks.

My scribbled MapQuest directions guided me to the hotshot base, where I'd meet Phillip. After parking my car in the nearly empty lot, I paused to admire the hotshot buggies, emblazoned with the crew's name: *Solar Hotshots*. Hotshot buggies are customized heavy-duty trucks resembling ambulances. Typically the captain and lead squad boss sit in the front cab and eight crew members sit in the back. Ours were Forest Service green. The front cab doors sported the Forest Service logo and the sides were lined with various compartments for tools, chainsaws and fuel, a first aid kit, and other supplies. There were eight small tinted windows. For two years I'd wanted to be a hotshot and now I was here. All I had to do was hold pace with the men I worked with.

I followed yellow-lettered signs to the office and rapped on the door. Phillip's gravelly voice, familiar from my phone interview, called me inside and I walked through a cold, empty classroom, into his office. Within seconds he rendered me self-conscious, eyes trailing my body as if assessing me. He was giant: well over six feet tall and wide enough that the arms of his office chair appeared too narrow for his body. I tugged at my T-shirt's lower hem, submitting myself to his evaluation. He shook my hand with a grip so strong I nearly winced. I giggled when he released it, a nervous tic. I hated the sound of my giggle but it worked to defuse tense situations, especially with men. It said: *I am no threat! Don't mind me, sir.* Phillip smiled.

When I'd accepted the job, Phillip had arranged for me to live with David, one of the squad bosses. Now, while tracing a hand-drawn map he asked me if I needed money, waving away my refusal. "You do," he said. "Don't worry. I know you're good for it." He deliberately counted out $200, laughing as I tucked the money in my pocket. His full-throated laugh overwhelmed the small space. I giggled in turn, unsure if I was being made fun of. The loan, in my mind, secured my spot on the crew. I'd heard many stories of wannabe hotshots washing out in the first few weeks. Surely he wouldn't fire me if I owed him money.

David's apartment complex conjured memories of all the apartment complexes I'd lived in with my mom, with their similar floor plans and cracked linoleum floors and reserved parking spaces. The inside was sparse and depressing, decorated with a couple football posters. A plug-in air freshener barely concealed the sweet, yeasty scent of beer. David was unfriendly and unsmiling; he avoided eye contact, gave me a clammy handshake, and showed me my room. There wasn't much to unpack: photos and postcards, my writing notebooks, and perhaps my most noteworthy possession, my friend Peter's tattered journals, which I'd kept after his death from a drug overdose a year and a half before. I stacked them with my books in a corner. Sylvia Plath, Richard Wright, Rachel Carson, Emily Dickinson, Leslie Marmon Silko, Jack Kerouac, Barbara Kingsolver, Sharon Olds, and some Buddhist texts my grandpa had given me. The tattered volume of Emily Dickinson poems was inscribed by my grandmother. *So—Tally Ho, the inscription read. Carry on. Start writing and I will always be your biggest fan.*

At some point in my transient childhood I developed a ritual, taping posters and postcards and pictures to my walls and stacking my books along the baseboards. I liked being able to fit everything I owned into my car. Now I taped up a picture of me and my best friend Greta making kissy faces in the tall grass in front of her rural Oregon house. She was still in Eugene, in college at the university. A good student. I stuck up a picture of me and my nanny boss sitting together at Tavern on the Green, where she'd taken me and her kids for dinner during my first visit to Manhattan. More pictures: me and my grandmother from when I lived with her and Grandpa for a while.

Me on a fire, gazing out over the Siskiyous in Oregon, bright pink hair curling out from under my hard hat. I collaged half a wall, hung my jeans, T-shirts, and sweatpants in the closet and folded my two cherished wool sweaters, bought at the J. Crew outlet in New York, on the closet shelf.

When I was finished I paused in the middle of the room. David had gone out. I longed for a beer and a whiskey back, the warm bloom spreading through my chest. But that was dangerous in such a small town. One drink always led to another, and I might embarrass myself in front of a future co-worker. Food was the next best thing. I snuck downstairs, checking outside to confirm that David's truck was gone. In the kitchen I wrapped a cold corn tortilla around a thick slice of cheddar, chewing fast and without pleasure while watching the front door. I ate half, then chugged some Diet Coke before stuffing the other half in my mouth and rushing upstairs to throw up. I was only twenty-one, but I'd been bulimic for nine years; long enough for my body to think vomiting was a natural reflex. The act of purging was always followed by a rush of endorphins. Then shame. When David returned home I hid in my bedroom, hoping he wouldn't notice that any of his food was missing.

When I arrived for our first day of training, the parking lot looked like a truck dealership. Mini trucks, lifted trucks, shiny new trucks and beaters lined the chain-link fence, parked nose-out. More than a few had those naked lady decals: silhouettes of reclined women's bodies with giant breasts and tiny waists. They reminded me of the strip club in Eugene, with its bright pink fluorescent sign, the neon leg kicking up and down. I wondered if the men here were anything like the patrons who'd tucked their dollar bills into my underwear.

I entered the classroom to find rows of men sitting at tables and two standing up front, one of whom stopped mid-sentence. As I scurried across the room I was sure that I could feel the heat of their collective gaze. I resisted the urge to cower, keeping my spine straight. The man who'd been speaking wore leather fire boots laced tight to mid-calf. The tightened Velcro straps at the bottom of his moss-green fire-resistant Nomex pants made the pants balloon out like pantaloons. Everything about him was tightened like that: tightly cinched belt, gold crew T-shirt stretched across his wide chest, and his sleeves so taut against his huge biceps that they dug into the muscle whenever he bent his arms. "Chain of command," he said, picking up exactly where he'd left off, "is how we communicate on this crew." He smoothed his neatly trimmed beard, thick and black like shoe brush bristles. "We're your captains. A-Mod and B-Mod." He gestured to the other man, standing near the whiteboard, when he said B-Mod. "Owen," he pointed to himself, then again to the other guy, "Nickolas." We nodded in unison. "Our crew has four squad bosses and three lead firefighters. Plus Phillip, your Superintendent."

Owen told us that California hotshot crews are the most sophisticated, capable of working as a single unit, splitting into two modules (mods), or splitting into four squads (two to a module), all interlinked with their radios for communication. Lead firefighters defer to squad bosses; squad bosses defer to captains; captains defer to superintendents. Superintendents defer to incident commanders and/or division superintendents. I got the distinct feeling that Owen thought A-Mod was superior to B-Mod; he pointed to himself whenever he said A-Mod, but he had stopped gesturing to Nickolas when he said B-Mod. Nickolas, standing against the wall, was disheveled and lean, almost scrawny, his eyes magnified by his thick square-rimmed glasses. Neither of them were much taller than me. Owen droned on about the importance of chain of command, telling us the Supt. (pronounced "soop") and captains were busy with important things. Nickolas rolled his eyes. Someone behind me snickered. I'd already filled a full page in one of the blank notebooks left for each of us on the tables, lest I forget anything he said.

As he paced the narrow aisle between tables Owen tossed out terms like "pay grade," as in, first-year hotshots couldn't discern whether something was important enough to require a superior's attention; this was "above our pay grade." If we thought something was wrong we should tell a lead firefighter or our squad boss, preferably the former. The captains and Supt., Owen said, were paid the *big bucks* to deal with complex issues. Mundane crew stuff was below their pay grade. Owen cracked a smile as he said this. But it was true; they really did make big bucks, all of them making at least six figures, while most of us would make a little over $30k in a good year, with overtime.

"Most of you will work harder than you ever have in your life," Owen said. He called physical training PT and said we'd be doing two-a-days. PT would determine who deserved to be on the crew. After two weeks of classroom learning and PT we'd be available for fires. I nodded along, as focused on him as I was on the eyes I could feel on my back.

The crew was homogenous; at least half of them were local and, except for two guys from a small town in Georgia, nearly everyone from California. Not San Francisco or Los Angeles, like I'd imagined, but smaller, more conservative towns. I'd always thought of myself as being able to get along with anyone. I got along with the men on my contract crews, for the most part, often befriending the older men who were married or had girlfriends but also bonding with the guys my age. The guys on Solar Hotshots, with their gelled hair, fresh shaves, and pungent Axe Body Spray force fields, were all my age or only a few years older. Each of the guys tried to sound tougher than the next as they introduced themselves. I contemplated whether I should simply say "Type 2" or specify that I had worked for a contractor, something the feds looked down upon. Almost all of us were new to hotshotting, a red flag I noted but didn't dwell on. Yearly turnover is now common on hotshot crews because of stagnant wages, but back then spots were coveted. High turnover signaled crew unrest.

Right when I'd perfected my introduction Owen pointed at me. "Ana," he said, "is the first woman we've had on the crew in years." Silence. Painful, face-scalding silence. I shrunk in my seat, flopping my short curly hair over my face. "Treat her with respect," he continued, now pointing at everyone. "Women have different capabilities than us. Their lungs are smaller, but some women have more endurance. Ana may not be able to do everything you can do, but if she does, she'll be working twice as hard."

Nickolas was grimacing. Some of the guys audibly shifted in their seats. Others nodded their heads sympathetically. The speech didn't surprise me; I'd long ago internalized the idea that I was categorically weaker than men, despite being much stronger than some of the guys I had worked with. But he'd singled me out as other. Special, but less capable. I didn't ask myself if what he'd said was true; I was grateful he'd acknowledged me at all, and given me a benchmark. All I had to do was work twice as hard. It didn't occur to me that was not a measurable criterion.

The following day Nickolas issued our gear. When it was my turn, he stacked two pairs of Nomex pants and two yellow button-up Nomex shirts on a shelf. "Switch these out on fires," he told me, meaning I should get replacements at fire camp, where they let you trade in your nasty Nomex for freshly washed or brand-new ones. He handed me an empty line pack. It was different from the ones I'd worn on the contract crew, with a lower center of gravity and made from durable material. The hip belt had several pockets for water bottles and one shoulder strap had a loop for our CamelBak nozzle. Then he gave me items to fill it with: an MRE (Meal Ready to Eat), Nomex flight gloves (for helicopter rides), clear plastic safety glasses, earplugs, a CamelBak water reservoir, an IRPG (Incident Response Pocket Guide), four cheap water bottles, and a weather kit. He placed a baseball cap on my head, gold and embroidered with the crew name and insignia, and gave me two gold crew T-shirts along with a small waterproof notebook for jotting down what he jokingly called *important fire things*.

There was more. A red hard hat, a fabric belt with a noisy metal buckle, and a fire shelter, which I stuffed into the large rectangular pocket sewn into my line pack's hip belt, right below the pack. It would chafe my ass the entire season, and every season thereafter.

Everything was either in my pack or piled on the table. How would I carry it all? Nickolas watched me panic for a moment before producing a big red duffel bag identical to the one I'd seen in David's bedroom. He grinned and I let out a sigh of relief, opening the bag wide so I could stuff everything inside. "Everything has to fit in there," he said. "I don't know how it works on the contract crews."

"It's the same," I said, and then paused, looking up. "I think."

I zipped the red bag and asked him if there was anything else. He began listing everything I should pack in my red bag: no less than fourteen cotton inner layer socks and seven wool hiking socks. "Make sure," he said, "to switch out the cotton socks daily and the wool ones every other day, or you'll end up like the guy who got gangrene on his foot and had to be flown out by helicopter. You don't want to lose your foot, right? Pack fourteen pairs of clean underwear. A fuck-ton of wet wipes. Buy more crew T-shirts to wear under your Nomex, because Phillip makes us wear them 24/7. He doesn't like white T-shirts; thinks they're unprofessional. Pack moleskin for healing blisters and a safety pin for popping them. Alcohol wipes and Neosporin, in case we're spiked out. Reading material, for waiting." Spiking out meant we were flown out to a remote location where we'd camp, totally self-sufficient. I'd never done it.

"You wear contacts?"

I nodded.

"Colored?"

I shook my head.

Nickolas squinted at me skeptically. "Take out your contacts when you can," he said. I couldn't help but lean in as he told me another horror story about a firefighter who never removed his contacts. "The guy got a bacterial infection," he said, his voice lowered confidentially. "You should have seen his eyes." Nickolas squinted and pretended to pop an eye out. I laughed for the first time in several days.

Finally Nickolas handed me a tent, sleeping bag, Therm-a-Rest, and small nylon pouch containing a sleeping bag cover. "Phillip doesn't like tents," he said, gripping the pouch so we both held it at the same time. "Put this over your sleeping bag at night to keep it dry. Because of the dew."

"Thanks," I said. "I will." We smiled at each other and for a moment I was hopeful. I lugged my gear to the buggy. The interior was lined with eight forward-facing seats, four on each side, all equipped with suspension like those in long-haul rigs. Each seat had its own cubby for personal belongings as well as a metal cage for our hard hats. Two long compartments lined the ceiling. This was where we stored our line packs and red bags. Both the cubbies and upper compartments were lined with nylon snap-down netting to ensure nothing fell out while traversing rough dirt roads. A few of the guys were there, putting away their gear. I recognized Gunnar, a short but muscular guy who'd snickered as Owen gave his speech about women's differences. When we made eye contact he immediately pointed to a seat in the back. "Bitch seat," he said, laughing. "You get to take out the garbage." I noted the plastic bag hanging from the rear door handle and dropped my line pack on my seat, dumping the rest of my gear in my personal compartment and topping everything with my red bag, which I'd take home and fill with supplies. The vibe wasn't friendly, but I hadn't expected a warm welcome.

There wasn't a women's bathroom so I used the handicapped one to change into my gear: Green Nomex pants and a crew T-shirt. On the contract crew I'd worn a white T-shirt underneath my Nomex, but

Nickolas had been clear that that wasn't an option here. I put my belt on, keeping it loose so the shape of my body was obscured, then turned sideways to pick myself apart in the mirror. *Too fat.* I ballooned the T-shirt out as far as I could while keeping it tucked in. A wave of self-loathing coursed through me. I squeezed the flesh of my belly, hard enough to leave bruises, before removing my sneakers and replacing them with my leather fire boots. Before leaving the bathroom I tied the laces tight. My distorted reflection followed me wherever I went.

The next morning, Owen gathered the crew near the edge of the compound, beneath a prominent hill peppered with manzanita bushes, in preparation for our first PT hike. We would line up in the exact order we'd learned earlier in class, called "tool order." I was behind Gunnar and in front of Max, who also sat next to me in the buggy, in the other "bitch seat." Tool order varies slightly from crew to crew, but the overall makeup is the same. The superintendent leads, followed by A-Mod captain (Owen, in this case), then squads one, two, three, and four. Nickolas, who captained B-Mod, took up the rear, ensuring that no one got left behind. Each squad also had a tool order: the squad boss, then two sawyers (called saw partners), followed by a couple diggers and the "clean-up" tools like shovels and rakes at the rear. We were called by the names of our tools. Saw. Shovel. Pulaski. McLeod. The crew hiked without our superintendent, which was unusual, although I didn't know this at the time. Phillip almost never hiked with the crew, because he either wasn't fit enough, had too many injuries, or simply didn't want to hike.

I'd been assigned a Pulaski and a monkey paw; a small rake with its handle chopped short, which fit through an elastic loop sewn on my pack. Owen had offered me a shovel but I'd scoffed and convinced him to trade me for a Pulaski, a much heavier tool. The Pulaski's metal head has an axe on one side and adze on the other; its handle is about three feet long and often composed of fiberglass. A lightweight shovel, with its long wooden handle, would have required less brute strength and prevented me from having to bend down so much. But I wanted a Pulaski. Not because I was one of the shortest people on the crew, with a low center of gravity, but because I wanted to prove myself.

Owen shouted for us to get into tool order. We all lined up behind him; four squad bosses, three saw teams with their thirty-pound saws resting engine-down on their shoulders, hands wrapped around the sheathed bars, and the tools, then Nickolas. We held our tools by their handles as we hiked, sharp edges facing down in case we fell. We sped up the small mountain Owen called Mini Hill, pausing to tiptoe over a low fence pole and mess of barbed wire and then running to catch up. The ground ascended so steeply that I could easily touch it with my hands; the hill was short but intense, about a thirty-minute hike. Someone behind me coughed and I hoped they were struggling as much as I was. My neck burned with the sun's heat. My legs cramped. Gunnar's boots disappeared and I gave up on trying to control my breathing. After about fifteen minutes Owen shouted "Free for all" and several people rushed past me. Hank, a scrawny guy from town, materialized, his pace only slightly faster than mine as he passed me. I coughed, tasting copper.

"Come on, Ana." It was Nickolas, who was bringing up the rear. I was in last place. His voice was calm. "Don't stop," he said. "Put one foot in front of the other." *One foot in front of the other.* I repeated it silently. I was so slow. I couldn't breathe. I paused, almost stopping. "Keep going," Nickolas said. My bones felt like iron weights.

"It's all mental," he said. "Your body can do anything." I cleared my mind of everything except *one foot in front of the other.* What would the guys think of me? One foot in front of the other. What if Phillip fired me? One foot in front of the other. Why was I doing this to myself? One foot in front of the other, until I crested Mini Hill's red dirt peak and tall metal tower. Gunnar stood beneath it, laughing with a sawyer from A-Mod. Hank's bare head dangled, his hard hat a few feet away as if he'd folded over and flung it off. I wondered how far ahead of me he'd been. Kieran, one of the Georgia boys, high-fived me. "You did it," he said in his southern accent. "That was a tough one." This would be the first of many times I felt grateful for Kieran's kindness.

The rest of the week we divided our time between PT and class time. I dreaded PT because I kept coming in last. Each time it happened I spiraled about my place on the crew, but Phillip told us someone always has to be last. There were a couple people who traded off each season. "It's okay to be last as long as you're not too far behind," he said. "Just find someone to beat, so you can take turns."

I didn't want to take turns being last. I wanted to be stronger. Each day after work I hiked alone, loading my pack with extra weight. When I crested the top of Mini Hill I always paused, watching the sun melt into shimmering honeyed light, painting the landscape gold. Was this, I wondered, one of the reasons they called it Gold Country? What had this place looked like before European contact? This was something I asked myself often, having grown up in Washington, a state transformed by the logging industry. To me the gold rush conjured images of bearded white men panning for gold in the local rivers: pioneers and prospectors. Like a piece of gold plucked from a river, the images only represented one piece of the whole story.

Chapter Two

Acorns & Gold

On Saturday morning I hiked Mini Hill and showered before setting off to find Mark Twain's cabin, marked by a small sign I'd passed several times. The cabin, more like a dilapidated shack, was tucked at the dead end of a well-maintained dirt road. I peered through the hollow windows at a lone desk. It was a reconstruction, the placard said. Only the brick chimney and hearth had survived the years since Twain's occupancy in 1865, when he had gathered material for "The Celebrated Jumping Frog of Calaveras County" and *Roughing It*, his popular travel narrative.

Only a half mile north from the cabin, alongside the two-lane highway, was a historical placard documenting the former site of a ferry transport established in 1848 called "Robinson's Ferry," which carried livestock and timber across a river that was eventually dammed to create the New Melones Reservoir. I was surrounded by towns with names like Chinese Camp, Jamestown, and Douglas Flat. Historical markers on the shoulders of side roads and highways documented the gold rush years and Spanish mission period, positioning these histories as quaint stories or triumphant tales of settlers.

But people occupied this land long before the missions and the gold rush. The ecological signs of their absence would have been impossible to ignore had I known what to look for. The gnarled oak trees that visually fascinated me had once been food sources. Many Indigenous Californians, including the Me-Wuk, used fire to increase acorn yields and prevent pest infestations, reducing underbrush after each harvest while also encouraging new grass to sprout. They harvested the fallen acorns and tapped down ripe ones with special sticks, catching them in handmade baskets woven from plants like willow, dogwood, and deergrass, whose flexible young shoots they also cultivated with fire. They knew each plant as intimately as they knew themselves.

Giant oak trees, along with old-growth ponderosa and sugar pines, had long ago been harvested in response to the population boom of the gold rush. Not too far away, in the San Joaquin Valley, farmers grew foreign crops of alfalfa and almonds fed by irrigation systems shuttling water from distant reservoirs. This increases the salinity of local rivers, threatening aquatic life along with both agricultural and public water availability. The oaks that remained were surrounded by brown-and-black acorns left to rot.

I paced in a half-circle around Twain's cabin, imagining his time there. My vision of him as a writer imbued the whole place with mystery. Had I known why he came west, I might have reassessed my admiration. Like nearly everyone who went to public school in the U.S., I was taught the quaint, mythologized stories about Christopher Columbus, the pilgrims, and their supposed friendship with the Native Americans. I'm a direct descendent of someone who came over on Columbus's ships, and a descendent of the Puritans who first colonized the Northeast, both on my father's side. My mother's lineage includes easterners from Ireland, Germany, Ohio and Illinois, many of whom sought new opportunities on the Oregon Trail.

Maybe this is why I thought colonization came from the east instead of the Pacific and Mexico. The Spanish first encountered the present-day U.S. via Baja California in the 1530s, and then from the Pacific Ocean in 1542, when Juan Rodríguez Cabrillo sighted California from his ship. He'd spotted smoke—a constant presence not only in California but throughout the United States, according to many explorers and colonizers. And people. When Cabrillo and his men sheltered in the Channel Islands, off the coast of Southern California, they battled with the Island Chumash, leading to Cabrillo's death from a gangrenous battle injury. In 1579 (thirty-seven years later), Sir Francis Drake ported in what's now known as Point Reyes, just north of San Francisco. The Coast Miwok, who clearly lived there, were so friendly that he named the place Nova Albion (New England). In his diaries he misconstrued the friendliness of the Coast Miwok as a land offering, like many European explorers and settlers encountering hospitable Natives throughout the pre-settlement U.S.

Early North American explorers adhered to the Doctrine of Discovery, set forth by Pope Alexander VI in 1493, declaring all lands uninhabited by Christians terra nullius: no man's land. According to the Doctrine of Discovery, the people who lived there couldn't claim land as their own, because they weren't Christians. This was a deadly rationalization.

From 1579, when Drake departed California, to the 1760s and the initiation of the Spanish mission system, California, and the people who had lived there for over ten thousand years, were left alone. They spoke a hundred different languages and countless dialects, mirroring the biodiversity of the California landscape itself, to which they were intricately and profoundly connected. Because of California's topography—its mountainous terrain and varied ecosystems—there was little conflict between tribes, many of whom had established trading routes and intertribal commerce. Of course, it wasn't California yet. Hundreds of small, independent settlements and enclaves nestled in forests, deserts, grasslands, marshlands, coastal and river communities. There was no quintessential California Indian, but when the Spanish established their first mission in 1769, they perceived these diverse individual bands and tribes as a monolith.

Competition for colonization was fierce. The Doctrine of Discovery dictated that colonized land belonged to whichever European country could populate it the fastest. The Spanish were lagging behind the English, who had already taken much of the Northeast. To maintain dominance, they expanded their missions northward, from their first mission in current-day San Diego to the northernmost mission in Alta California, now known as San Francisco, building everything on tribal lands. This wasn't stealing, according to the Spanish, but a benevolent kind of land trust. The Spanish wanted to convert Indigenous Californians into productive Christians. Only then would they grant them citizenship and return their lands. Initial intentions for the missions may not seem terrible at first glance. Missionaries still exist today, as does religious conversion, and the Spanish trained tribal members in trades, like brickmaking, leatherwork, and methods of European agriculture. The message from both Spanish and Mexican governments was: Work hard, get baptized, learn Spanish, and develop proficiency in these trades. Then you'll get your land back in better condition than it was before. There was a fundamental difference in perception here: Land was a commodity to the Spanish, but according to Indigenous Californians, land was autonomous, alive and occupied by sentient plants and animals. To own land was inconceivable. Belief systems differed from tribe to tribe and within tribal subgroups—but their understanding of nature was predominantly kincentric; everything was interrelated and without hierarchy. Plants, streams, and creatures were treated with the same familiarity and respect as any close relative. Harvesting, sowing, burning, and hunting were all practiced with a sense of reciprocity and respect. Their agricultural practices were scientific, honed over thousands of years. Did the Spanish understand this at all? There's little indication they did. Although some Spanish Franciscans acknowledged the sophisticated cultures, religious practices, and agricultural practices of local tribes, most thought of Native Californians as "wild beasts." But Indigenous Californians saved the Spanish from death many times over, generously sharing their knowledge of local plants, both medicinal and edible, as well as various life-saving practices. The Spanish created their own linguistic taxonomy for these plants, many of which are known today by the same Spanish names. How could the Spanish (and other settlers) accept help without admitting their own ignorance? Their sense of religious superiority prevented clear-sightedness, enabling them to rationalize land theft, slavery, and murder. We need not look far to see similar modes of rationalization in the modern world.

Contrary to their noble purpose, missions were nightmarish labor camps, comparable to any Gulag or Holocaust-era prison camp. Tens of thousands tribal members died and were killed throughout the state. Infections and disease spread because of cramped and unsanitary living conditions. As populations dwindled, Indians became more dependent on the Spanish for housing and sustenance. Grazing animals quickly destroyed Native lands and crops. The Spanish separated children from parents forced into servitude and sold them to white families. Many tribal members tried escaping, seeking refuge with other tribes who had not yet been colonized. If caught, they were tortured in medieval ways, executed, or both. Others fled and disappeared, choosing starvation over mission life. Sexual abuse of children was commonplace. Priests raped Indigenous women. Felipe de Neve, who later founded the town of Los Angeles, was one of many who criticized these brutalities, comparing the lives of Indians to those of slaves. Another critic, a padre who was upset that Indians were kept in stocks and flogged, complained to the Viceroy. He, like nearly all dissenting voices, was removed from the mission system and forced to leave California.

Over fifty thousand Indigenous Californians had died by the early 1800s, when the mission system began its dissolution. Their lands weren't returned but parceled off and sold to settlers. Treaties were made and broken on a whim, never in favor of Indians, who were increasingly dependent on the elusive and inconsistent kindness of the newcomers to survive. By 1845 all missions had been secularized and the Californios, a mix of Spanish and Mexican families, ruled over Indigenous people in California. They kept Indians on their rancheros as indentured servants, slaves, or peons. Surviving Indigenous Californians did everything they could to adapt and survive, leveraging their skills and secretly maintaining their cultural heritage. Indians who converted to Christianity and learned Spanish were typically treated better than non-converts, though they were still subject to abuse and indentured servitude. Residential schools became the norm, and Indian children were stripped of their families, culture, and native languages. Despite this, parents and families did everything they could to keep traditions alive.

And the land? Although fire suppression had yet to begin in earnest, the lives of those who had tended the land were fatally disrupted, undoing millennia of ecological balance. Fire had been applied with precision; now it was only used by settlers, who burned to produce grass for their grazing animals, whose hooves decreased soil aeration and degraded native species. The land and its inhabitants suffered, but the impact was invisible to the untrained eye. Newcomers mistook the resulting overgrowth for wilderness and abundance.

Mark Twain came to California in 1865. He was about two decades late to the party: Gold was struck in 1848, near a place called Sutter's Mill. But he wasn't seeking gold. Understanding why he came, what he was looking for, and what he found can help us understand why so many came first to the United States and then west, and how their perceptions of Native Americans inform the present day.

Twain came west in search of stories. He wrote of seeking "real Indians," like the ones portrayed in James Fenimore Cooper's *The Last of the Mohicans* and Longfellow-Taylor's *Song of Hiawatha*. In his book *The Vanishing American*, Brian Dippie defines a cultural shift in perceptions of Native Americans occurring in the thirty years between 1830 and 1860, beginning with the publication of *The Last of the Mohicans* in 1826. Dippie argues that, prior to the 1830s, dominant perceptions revolved around assimilating Native Americans into white culture, but as whites migrated west during the 1830s and 1840s, violence towards Native Americans escalated. The California Gold Rush brought upwards of 300,000 settlers to the state. In 1850, the California legislature enacted the Act for the Government Protection of Indians, which allowed whites to remove Indians from stolen land now owned by settlers. Indians not employed by whites were deemed "vagrants" and sold at auctions to whites who enslaved them. Native American children could also be indentured to whites. There were no options for appeal. Native American testimony was explicitly written in the act as invalid against whites. State and federal government paid vigilante groups to "exterminate" Indians. These laws weren't repealed until well after the turn of the twentieth century.

Mark Twain's grandparents had settled in Missouri, on Native American land, and were consequently raided. But by Twain's day, Native Americans in the Midwest had already been stripped of their cultures and forced onto reservations. Twain was disappointed by the Indians he encountered in California. He saw them as degenerate, mostly unintelligent, and uncivilized. This is partially a personal failing on his part, for there were other white writers, like Bret Harte and

Anthony Benezet, whose views were more nuanced, but it was also a mainstream white narrative: Racism cultivated by texts like those previously mentioned, which flattened Native Americans into the clichéd paradigm of the Noble Savage. Incoming settlers relied on this trope to rationalize land theft.

Homeless, starving Indians, dependent on settlers for their basic needs, shattered Twain's ideas of what he called "the noble red man." In the white American consciousness there came to be two Indians, and only two. The noble, who surrendered their land willingly, and the savage, who refused to leave.

My hotshot crew was located in a county whose name is loosely translated as "Cluster of Stone Dwellings," or "Many Stone Houses," in reference to the jagged rock outcroppings I'd admired upon my arrival. The region is also called The Motherlode. Many of the tribes there—the Me-Wuk, Wá·šiw (Washoe), Northern Valley Yokuts, Nisenan, and Konkow Maidu (amongst others)—resisted Christian conversion during the mission system, and were therefore more vulnerable to the Californios, who came after. White settlers called them "diggers" because they often subsisted on tubers, but the name clearly had racist connotations. These tribes had created a landscape that John Muir called "Edenic." But Muir, like Twain, had difficulty reconciling the Indians he saw with those he'd imagined. He didn't like their modern clothes, so much like his own, and was disappointed that they weren't more integrated with nature. In *The Mountains of California* he writes lovingly of animals and plants that had long been cultivated by Native Californians, but of the Mono Indians he writes that "they were mostly ugly, and some of them altogether hideous." To him, "they seemed to have no right place in the landscape." He made similar observations about other encounters. Muir knew that the Mono had been forced off of their land but seemed incapable of empathy. California Indians were at that point almost entirely dependent on white people, who often wanted them dead or disappeared. Muir himself wrote that he "was glad to see them fading out of sight down the pass." Both Twain and Muir would come to understand their own reactions as problematic, and both experienced ambivalence regarding the state of Indians after settlement. But neither would ever fully realize how much the land needed its people—its kin, and the care they had long provided.

After looking at the cabin I got into my car and drove aimlessly for hours. There was so much I didn't know. I was just a hotshot. I couldn't see that the landscape needed cleansing by the flames I was supposed to extinguish.

Chapter Three

Deploy

"Firefighters must never rely on fire shelters. Instead, they depend on well-defined and pre-located escape routes and safety zones. However, if the need for shelter deployment should ever arise, it is imperative that firefighters know how to deploy and use the fire shelter."—*Six Minutes for Safety*, National Wildfire Coordinating Group publication

I'd first heard the term "Shake n' Bake" applied to fire shelters back on the contract crew. The guys on Solar Hotshots used the same gruesome nickname, but as a verb. As we drove up into the foothills for our final day of training one of them said we were "going to Shake n' Bake." The nickname rendered death abstract; a joke rather than a possibility. None of us wanted to believe we would ever have to use a fire shelter for protection, but they have saved over seven hundred lives since the 1970s. Fire shelters resemble flimsy silver pup tents: layers of silica and aluminum strong enough to protect us from ambient heat, direct flames, combustive heat, and toxic gases capable of killing someone on the first inhale. In the 1950s the Australians came up with a bell-shaped structure that, over time, researchers elongated and shrunk closer to the ground, where breathable air is most plentiful. The adhesive layers separate above five hundred degrees Fahrenheit, exposing whoever's inside to temperatures that can exceed fifteen hundred degrees. Fire shelters are a last resort, deployed when there is no other choice. During any wildland firefighting operation winds can change in an instant, rapidly shifting a fire's direction or increasing its intensity. If firefighters haven't maintained a clear escape route and safety zone, or have somehow been cut off from these, they're caught in what's called an entrapment. If the fire is actively overtaking them, and they must deploy their shelters, this is called a burnover. Entrapments and burnovers are immediately investigated by the jurisdictional agency, who must follow federal guidelines for investigation.

Since the '90s, approximately fifty firefighters have died while using a shelter.

Phillip had us swap our silver shelters for tarps modified into practice shelters. We drove up into the foothills and donned our line packs. After a short hike we began digging fireline, half-working, ears perked for the drill. Jonah, my squad boss, had told us it would be quick because Phillip was there, and Phillip hated being on the fireline with the crew, especially when it was so hot out. The chainsaws had only been buzzing for half an hour when Phillip yelled for us to RTO. We all stopped working, reversed tool order, and headed back towards the buggies single file, taking our time until he yelled, "Fire's coming! Get going! Get hiking!" Then we sped up. I stayed close to Max, who was usually behind me. Owen's voice boomed "Fire's behind you! Drop your gear! Keep your shelter!"

I unbuckled my line pack, fumbled for the back compartment, and tugged at the Velcro opening, struggling to extract the bulky practice shelter. Intellectually I knew it was a drill, but my body was panicking. Time slowed as Owen screamed for us to *get going, get moving, the fire is coming!* Finally my shelter popped out. I tucked it under my armpit and abandoned my pack, keeping my Pulaski. "Deploy, deploy!" Owen's voice boomed. I was momentarily paralyzed. Drop my shelter to clear the space, or hold my shelter and clear the space? I dropped it, frantically sweeping away crispy pine needles and dried leaves, then tossed my Pulaski, unfurling the shelter and grabbing the upper straps before sticking my boots into the bottom corners and collapsing into the dirt, where I pressed my face into the cool ground. The shelter was dark and quiet. A few feet away plastic rustled. Phillip screeched: "Fire's here!" The sound of rustling plastic crept closer until the straps of my shelter lifted. I clamped my hands and feet down hard.

In a Lessons Learned training video we watched a firefighter recount his deployment in a burnover. He'd forgotten his gloves and the skin of his hands "slipped right off." All around him the fire roared like a freight train. Quiet came, but he knew it wasn't over. He was in the fire's eye, and he said it was like the eye of a tornado. I've heard this description by many survivors, likening wildfires to more familiar weather events. A fire needs three elements: fuel, heat, and oxygen. Fire breathes oxygen, inhaling cool air from below and expelling a hot, moist mixture of carbon monoxide, carbon dioxide, toxic gases, and small particles upwards. With dry-enough conditions and plentiful fuel, the fire's rising heat (called a smoke column) quickly expands in size and strength, destabilizing the surrounding atmosphere and creating its own weather system, called pyrocumulus. A pyrocumulus is essentially a cumulonimbus (thundercloud) created by fire. The air condenses as it rises, and because it's hotter than the surrounding atmosphere this can cause lightning, created when cooler air collides with warmer. Unlike cumulonimbus, pyrocumulus systems can float smoldering embers, called firebrands, aloft, sometimes for over a mile, and expel downdrafts along with lightning, exacerbating and increasing fire behavior while simultaneously starting new fires. The ember wash descends like a swarm of fire-bearing locusts. In 2002 powerful fires like these were not necessarily rare, but they weren't commonplace, either. The number of fires throughout the United States has doubled since 2005, and in several U.S. regions, including the West, fires are burning at a much higher severity.

As we lay in our shelters, I couldn't help imagining the freight train sound of a fire roaring over us. Faces, most of them from glossy black-and-white photos, cycled through my mind. During my first fire season I'd read every book I could find about wildfire, all deconstructing "tragedy fires," as they're called in the fire world. *Young Men and Fire*, written by Norman Maclean, was the first, and my favorite. An investigation into the 1949 Mann Gulch Fire in Montana, the book offered a minute-by-minute narrative of the fire, its change in wind direction, and the second fire ignited by crew boss Wag Dodge ahead of the flame front, which saved Dodge's life but may have killed some of the men he was charged with protecting. *Young Men and Fire* painted its subjects, nearly all smokejumpers, as heroes. I read it compulsively, constantly flipping back to the glossy center pages and staring at the photos of the men in their gear.

During my second year on the contract crew, in 2001, four firefighters died in Washington State, on the Thirtymile Fire. Caught in a canyon during a fire's blowup, they deployed their fire shelters but were killed by asphyxiation. Three of those who died were below the age of twenty-two. Six years after the event, John Maclean, Norman's son, published *The Thirtymile Fire*. In 2013, nearly an entire hotshot crew, nineteen men in total, died after deploying their fire shelters on the Yarnell Hill Fire, in Arizona. Their crew was called the Granite Mountain Hotshots. That happened less than three years after I had stopped fighting fires, which meant I was enjoying my summer—an impossibility for any hotshot. For two years I'd avoided news about wildfires, but here was this crew. These men. Nineteen lives. Although there were multiple investigations into their deaths, book deals, a film, few people asked why they were there in the first place, when fire behavior was so unpredictable. They sacrificed their lives but the fire kept burning.

And their fire shelters? Apparently the fire was too hot.

After several minutes Owen yelled for us to get up. Few people spoke as we refolded our practice shelters, put our tools away, and refilled our waters. I quietly observed, wanting to see if anyone noticed me. Other than the instructive exchanges with Jonah and Nickolas, I hadn't spoken to anyone all day.

On our way back to the hotshot base Owen opened the rectangular window that separated the front cab from the rest of the buggy so he could tell us we'd been called to a fire. I'd never seen him smile before. Suddenly everyone, including me, was buzzing in their seats. My anxiety vanished. It was happening! We weren't officially available until the next morning, so Owen instructed us to get a good night's sleep. "We'll meet at 0700," he said, feigning a stern expression. "Don't be late, and drink lots of water."

Chapter Four

A New Country

Nearly all the guys showed up groggy-eyed the next morning, clearly hungover, chugging giant to-go cups of gas station coffee. The weather was cool and clear. I felt revived. Awake. Riddled with anxiety. By the time we were on the road several of the guys were whooping and chattering with excitement. Because it was only mid-May, which was early in the season for a fire call, we were avoiding what everyone called "base work": Weeding, cleaning, and general monotonous busywork overseen by Phillip. But the buggy was divided between the younger celebrants bouncing excitedly in their seats and the older crew members like Jonah, my squad boss, and Jason, a sawyer and a lead firefighter, who sat impassively, foreheads lined with subtle traces of annoyance. I knew that Jonah's kids were both under three years old, the youngest not one year old. Later he'd tell me about how he didn't want to repeat what had happened with his first. He'd missed her infancy. Jason was divorced and shared custody of his daughter.

There was a television rigged onto a shelf and Daniel, Jason's younger and less experienced saw partner, had started a movie: *Platoon.* My headphones, practically an extension of my body since childhood, dulled the overwhelming noises of the world around me. When we pulled into a gas station three hours later, David told us we had ten minutes. I'd been squeezing my legs together for the past hour and a half and sprinted to the bathroom. This was one of my first lessons: Don't drink so much water. The guys were encouraged to pee in bottles because stopping slowed us down. I'd never be able to pee in a container while inside the buggy.

In my Nomex pants, wearing my gold crew shirt and baseball cap, my heavy leather boots with their laces tied loose around the ankles clomping on the scuffed linoleum, I was no longer a girl, or a woman. I deserved respect. This is what I'd wanted. Most people greeted us curiously, trying to deduce why we all wore the same outfits, but I could tell when someone knew we were hotshots because they looked at me like George had looked at those hotshots on the Viveash Fire. One gray-haired man, clad in country jeans and work boots, gave me a conspiratorial nod. Another thanked us for our service, as if we were soldiers headed to war for our country. Since developing breasts at twelve, I'd reluctantly accepted men's assessments of my body, their eyes lingering on me in ways that made me cross my arms over my chest, or self-consciously tug at my clothes. Eventually I saw myself primarily through their gaze, as a girl, as a woman, and as an object of attraction. Being treated with respect and admiration was an entirely different sensation. Instead of wanting to make myself smaller, I felt more powerful.

This didn't translate to my newbie position on the crew. My duties involved untying the trash bag from the metal bar on the back door and stuffing it into any available trash can. Max's younger brother Adam and I took care of the Supt. Truck, washing the windshield together. We emptied Phillip's trash and checked the fluids. In my own life I avoided oil changes, but these little chores instilled a sense of purpose in me, and Adam was genuinely friendly. He was on B-Mod but I wished he was on A-Mod with me.

* * *

In the buggy everyone dug into bags of chips, sodas, candy, and chewing tobacco. The guys chewed Skoal and Copenhagen. Gunnar opened his canister of mint Skoal as Daniel took a big wad of Copenhagen and held it in front of Gunnar's face. "Too much for you, huh?" Yanking out his lower lip, Daniel shoved the wad in and smiled, mouth bulging. They examined each other's gumlines to see whose had receded the most. I resisted rolling my eyes. We pulled back onto the freeway, the buggy stifling hot and stinking of chew, corn chips, and energy drinks. I opened my window, cursing Phillip for not letting us crank the air conditioning. Our bodies needed to acclimatize to the heat, he'd said, using one of his many pet words.

I couldn't stop thinking about what had happened before we left, when Owen told us to change into our clean crew shirts so we looked professional and reminded us that baseball caps were mandatory in public. "Don't fuck around outside of the buggies or base," he'd said, echoing a motto Phillip had already repeated several times: *Perception is reality.* "Don't do anything you don't want printed on the front page of the newspaper."

He'd recited the speech, one I'd hear tens of times over the next couple years, because a hotshot crew south of us had been temporarily suspended. Apparently they'd plastered posters of naked women inside their buggies and left their door open. A Forest Service employee, a woman, saw the posters and reported the crew. The crew was at fault, but many of the guys were obsessed with the woman's conduct. To them she was a meddling shrew, probably unattractive and single, clearly infringing on the crew's rights. Any crew should be free to decorate as they see fit. It was her fault for looking inside. This revealed a double standard. I didn't comment. Phillip had already expressed his opinions about affirmative action, to me and the crew. I wouldn't have been hired without it. Despite my two years of experience, I was somehow an interloper. This weighed on me. I didn't know the facts:

that the woman, an archaeologist, had taken photos of the naked women covering the buggy's interior. After reporting the incident, a proliferation of death threats forced her and her son to leave Region 5. But there was no escape—she left the Forest Service soon after, due to a hostile work environment.

Earlier in the week we had all watched an ancient sexual harassment video. "We're required to show this to you," Phillip had said, telegraphing his lack of respect. In the video men hit on their female office mates in various ways. Some were scenarios I'd already witnessed and even participated in, like people talking about women's bodies and sexual acts in the work environment, or making dirty jokes. Raunchy jokes, I had learned, were one of the keys to dispelling any tensions about me being a possible snitch, and I had some memorized from working on the contract crew. Other scenarios, like the quid pro quo or sexual propositions, I had yet to witness.

The video became a running joke. Some of the guys play-acted sexual trade offers and inappropriate touching, pretending to grab or slap at each other, wrists limp, repeating "Stop" and "You're harassing me," in lispy, high-pitched voices. I always hung back, plastered on a false half-smile or laughed half-heartedly when they did this, trying to hide my repulsion from them and from myself. When the guys had discussed the suspended crew, they said that anyone choosing this profession should know what to expect. Can't deal? Quit. I'd heard this many times before, and internalized it. Any resistance or judgment on my part when it came to their behavior could potentially undo my place on the crew.

I had chosen a man's job and, in that first year, I accepted everything that came with it. It was a perfect fit. Every new school of my itinerant childhood had come with a new social hierarchy, and I learned how to be whatever kept me from sinking to the bottom, though I usually ended up there. I wanted to be accepted into this crew. To be a real hotshot, and earn the respect of the men who surrounded me.

Chapter Five

The First Burn

B ouquet Canyon, located in the Angeles National Forest, is one
of the many Southern California canyons where fires burn too
often through lands that are out of sync with their adapted fire cycles.
We always drove in the same order: Phillip's truck up front, then
A-Mod's buggy, followed by B-Mod. Our buggy groaned and swayed
as Owen navigated giant potholes and jutting rocks, inching along for
twenty minutes before finally stopping. When David yelled "Gear up,"
I jumped into the narrow aisle, squeezing between everyone else. This
was the first of thousands of times I'd unsnap the webbing from the
metal compartment above my seat, yank my line pack out and sling
it onto my shoulder before grabbing the thin metal rail near the back
door of the buggy and hopping down the two steps to the ground.
My boots were laced tight. I pressed my red hard hat onto my head,
tightening the dial so it fit snugly, and pulled my gloves on. All the
metal compartments on the outside of the buggies were hanging open;
I grabbed my yellow-handled Pulaski and monkey paw from the tool
compartment and asked Kieran to slip the rake into the loops on my
pack. Someone handed me two aluminum MSR canisters, one gas,

one oil, and I stuck them in their proper compartments on my hip belt, one on each side.

Phillip was leaning on the hood of his truck, giant hand curled around the IAP, ready to give us our first briefing of the season. We all gathered in front of him. The growing fire was on its second day of active suppression, transitioning to a more complex Type 2 incident command team. We needed to stop it from getting big enough for a Type 1 team by lighting a new fire along the road, which would theoretically burn into the main fire, consuming all the fuel in the main fire's path until both were starved of fuel and extinguished.

After the briefing, Phillip sent Kieran to get a drip torch from the bed of the Supt. Truck. These thick aluminum cylinders, with their bulky metal screw caps and curlicue tubes, are the most commonly used ignition devices. Turn a full drip torch sideways, and fuel drips through the wick, which is attached to the end of the curlicue. The fuel, called "burn mix," is gas and diesel mixed to burn at the perfect pace and temperature. Gas alone burns too hot and too fast. Diesel, too slow.

"Light it," Phillip said. Kieran tipped the metal cylinder sideways until fuel soaked the wick and dripped onto the dirt road. Raising it up, he lit it.

Phillip gestured to a patch of scraggly brush and yellow grass, barking "Lay it down there." Kieran poured out a thin stream of flames; for a moment it looked like he'd flung a long, glimmering necklace adorned with crackling jewels over the brush, whose leaves quickly shrunk away before combusting into black smoke. I was mesmerized. Squad Three lined the road facing away from the burn. Nickolas told them to keep their eyes on the unburned area, called the green. Sometimes shifting winds can parachute firebrands into the green, igniting spot fires. One errant spot fire can burn an entire town, threaten lives, and cost millions, if not billions, of dollars. We never burned without eyes on the green.

I prepped several additional torches on Owen's orders, unscrewing each canister with my gloved hands and releasing the vents so the fuel could flow freely. Then I lined the torches along the road's shoulder. Before I could ask for another task, Owen called me back to the Supt. Truck and told me to fill more torches using the three twenty-liter jerricans sitting near the truck's two-hundred-gallon water tank. I grabbed one of the fifty-pound jerricans and lugged it to the edge of the truck's bed, hopping down before setting it on the ground. The guys were watching. Whenever I looked up I found at least one pair of eyes on me. I glanced at Sky, the only first-year firefighter on our crew, and envied the casual way he leaned on his tool, how unselfconsciously he daydreamed. Adam, who was helping me, unscrewed the cap from the jerrican and replaced it with the flexible metal pouring tube Phillip called a "donkey dick." We both poured the mix into the torch using a funnel. The repetition was soothing: unscrew cap, fill cylinder, screw cap tightly, release vent, set down in dirt. Burning was less predictable. These men hadn't earned my trust, nor I theirs. The fire's plume, previously light gray and driven sideways by the wind, was now black and mushrooming skywards, indicating an unpredictable plume-dominated fire.

Knowing I would be burning any minute activated my fight-or-flight response: a breathless, mothlike fluttering in my throat that I'd long ago learned to ignore. My insides screamed; I kept moving. Jonah placed me as the final burner, alongside the dirt road. Gunnar was next, fifteen feet into the proposed burn area, and Daniel was fifteen feet farther in. Jason was the farthest, with the second radio. I could see them all through patches of tall brush and oak. This was my squad. Already one of them, Gunnar, disliked me. He wanted my spot on the road, bringing up the rear; I didn't understand why.

A permeating smell of minty Skoal asserted Jonah's presence. "Always carry a lighter," he said, handing me his blue Bic. "Jason leads the way. Keep eyes on him. Don't get ahead of any of those guys,

because your fire will cut them off. You can trap them. Stay behind
Gunnar. Once Jason starts, things are gonna go fast. Keep up. Got
it?" I nodded and lit my torch. Voices droned through Jonah's radio.
Helicopters and occasional tankers sounded like giant insects buzzing in the distance, closer to the main fire. I tried to listen; Jonah's
radio was tuned to our crew channel and air attack, which allowed us
to communicate with tankers and helicopters, but there were several
other channels being broadcasted, including specific channels for each
division, weather channels, and intercrew channels. When Phillip gave
us the green light Jonah took my tool, stepping back but staying close.

A pilot flying over us would have seen what looked like a necklace of
glinting red beads bordering the brown dirt road, each burner a bead,
three surrounded by brush and white grass, plus me, straddling the side
of the road and our burn area. Phillip's truck was ahead of the crew;
Nickolas and David were trailing us in the buggies. If anything went
wrong, we'd jump into the buggies and head back down the road. I
had unanswered questions (What if the other side of the road caught
fire? What if the winds shifted and increased suddenly?) but didn't
dare ask them. That was above my pay grade.

Jason started seesawing his torch up and down, releasing and pausing, assessing the fuel's flammability. How fast did the oak leaves
catch? And the grasses? What about the thick stands of chaparral?
The fire's behavior dictated how fast we burned, and how much fire
we needed. Too much fuel and we'd lose it. Not enough and the main
fire would keep burning and jump the road. Slowly, almost timidly,
Jason started moving ahead, metering out bursts of fire, making sure
everything burned hot enough, but not too hot. Flames bloomed
behind him as he walked.

A shimmering veil of rising heat warped the air until it resembled
distorted glass. Daniel started his own fire, then Gunnar. Jason's smoke
billowed towards the main fire. Daniel's fire blew into Jason's. Once

Gunnar was fifteen feet ahead of me, I glanced at Jonah. He nodded once, decisively. Time for me to start. This singular purpose, and the risk involved, narrowed my concentration in a way I'd never experienced. I poured flames into the grass, imprinting perfectly round black coins whose edges immediately overflowed and distorted like dynamic Rorschach blots. Trembling flames leapt across the grasses and climbed up into the brush. Grass, a fine fuel, dries quickly and can catch fire easily. Brush typically takes longer unless its leaves are coated in flammable oils, like chaparral and poison oak. Anything burning underneath something, or burning uphill, preheats the fuel above, increasing flammability. The land sloped uphill from me, so I walked slowly, laying down short lines of fire, staying well behind Gunnar. Stands of oak and chaparral hissed and whooshed into flame-bodies, flushing my cheeks.

A strong gust of wind coaxed my fire towards Gunnar's. The wind paused and the fire stopped short, momentarily righting itself before another gust blew it into Gunnar's fire, like a strong exhale. For all the years I worked in fire, I would observe this rhythm, so much like my own breathing. The fire was seeking oxygen. It seemed to breathe like any other animal, popping, whistling, crackling, and sighing. Jason yelled from the inside that it was getting hot. Gunnar struggled to keep up. Now I understood his anger—my spot on the road's shoulder was free from obstacles and easier to navigate.

"Speed up!" Jonah yelled. We jogged, the fire's hot breath at our backs. Behind us it consumed the canopy of brush and oak trees, pulsing out ribbons of black smoke with its swirling orange fingers. This was more action than I'd seen in two years on the contract crew. Now I knew why no one had announced an official escape route or safety zone: Everything was perfect. Phillip's voice came over the crew radio channel: "Let's see if that gets air attack's attention!" He wanted slurry—a red gooey mixture of nitrate fertilizer, ammonia, and water often dropped from large tankers and helicopters to prevent the fire from establishing in the green. When the retardant's moisture dissolves, salts in the fertilizers dry to a fine powder capable of slowing the fire's progression.

In many ways a wildfire is like an animal running from a predator, swerving unpredictably with changes in wind, fuel type, and/or topography. The fire's head is like its front legs; its flanks, usually less volatile, run parallel to the head; but if the wind shifts a fire's flank can easily become the head, driving the fire in a new direction. This happens sometimes without warning. Phillip wanted slurry on the main fire's flanks because the wind would shift with early evening cooling. Get control of the flanks, and the head of the fire would have a harder time shifting with the wind. Instead, it would run into our burn and flicker out. One load of slurry can cost over two thousand dollars.

My gear bounced on my hips as I jogged. When my drip torch ran out Jonah handed me a new one and I squeezed my hip belt as tight as I could, no longer worried about my appearance. "Want to switch out?" Jonah asked, gesturing to everyone on the road. I shook my head and grinned. If I wanted to get stronger, this was the way to do it, I thought, surprised that I was holding pace with the guys. When my torch emptied again it was almost dark. Max replaced Gunnar. Jonah gave me another torch. After another hour or so we all switched with David's squad.

This may have been the exact moment I fell in love with being a hotshot. Burning was like entering an alternate dimension. My shirt was drenched but I hadn't noticed myself sweating. The drip torch became an extension of my arm, fire a liquid expelled by my body. There was no pain. I'd been totally focused, consumed like branches alchemized from solid to smoke. I was cleansed.

Phillip yelled something about Gatorade in his cooler, winking at me while tossing us our bagged lunches. We shoved sandwiches into our mouths, barely chewing, and chugged Gatorades. When I saw the guys rubbing their fuel-soaked gloves in the dirt I copied them, rubbing until the dirt had absorbed most of the fuel. We must have looked strange: all of us bent down, caressing the dirt road with our gloved hands as if in prayer, or worship.

It was our turn to watch the green with our backs to the fire. We kept our headlamps turned off. You'd think the darkness would complicate things, but embers and flames show themselves more quickly at night. As David's squad burned we inched along with them, staggered about twenty-five feet apart. The fire's heat was so intense that we untucked our Nomex neck shrouds from inside our helmets. They hung down like yellow mullets, keeping our necks from blistering.

Daniel and Jason were on my left, talking about girls. I could only hear scraps of their conversation. They repeated the phrase "fucking hot" so many times it began conjuring unwanted memories and questions. For as long as I could remember, I'd wanted to be fucking hot. Jason said it again: "fucking hot," and I wondered if they were talking about me. I was so accustomed to this constant chatter about women, equating their worth to their appearance. On the contract crews, at the strip club, in magazines and on television. Now here. I wanted them to be talking about me, and at the same time, I couldn't do my job without being reminded that I, like all women, was a sexual object.

Memories cycled through my mind in quick succession—my mom calling me fat; the kids at school making fun of me for being fat; losing weight for the first time and finally being seen; the hyperkinetic sensation of being desired; the power of someone's extended eye contact; the forcefulness of wanting to be wanted. So many people had told me I was fucking hot, or said, "you're so fucking sexy" as they pulled my clothes off or while we had sex. A lot of those people had been strangers. All that time I knew that the invisibility of being fat was still there, waiting. That my so-called beauty was not about me at all, and that being fucking hot kept me sick.

Our line shifted to the right and I returned to the present moment, barely realizing I'd been away. These reveries were constant, like self-loathing daydreams. I refocused my attention towards the dim auburn light cast by the fire and chastised myself for caring who thought I was hot. *Stop caring what people think of you and do your job!* Taking my weatherproof notebook from my shirt pocket, I wrote my first words of the season, which weren't about important fire stuff. Be nice. Be quiet. Work hard. Then I sketched a circle with a dot in its center, a symbol I'd constructed from a passage in the *Tao Te Ching*. Stay in the center of the circle. Bend like grass. Stop feeling things so deeply.

There were two of me, each at war with the other. One part craved invisibility. The other wanted to be the hottest person at the party.

Chapter Six

Mop Up

We woke the next morning in a ball field, scattered in a semi-circle. Hotshot crews sleep anywhere—fields of grass, public parks, patches of forest off the side of the road. This wasn't unusual for me; I spent part of my adolescence sleeping under bridges and on sidewalks, narrowly protected from the elements, and I remembered that as I awoke. All of us were out in the open, sans tents, instead sleeping on 8x8 tarps with insulated silver bottoms called space blankets. Tents took too long to set up, according to Phillip. I had briefly mourned the loss of those four flimsy nylon walls, my only opportunity for privacy, and dragged my sleeping arrangement away from the group's circle until Owen scolded me back.

I pulled my pants, damp with the morning dew, into my warm sleeping bag, forcing them on as my teeth chattered. Everyone was shivering. Some of the guys hawked loogies and blew snot rockets as we all rolled up our gear.

Someone tossed two boxes of MREs on the ground. Originally invented as a food ration for soldiers, MREs come in matte brown plastic bags, twelve to a box. The guys descended and fought for their favorite flavors. Because MREs are meant to last at least seven years, the food is highly preserved, and my "omelet" was like yellow rubber in texture, flavor, and appearance. Nauseous with sleep deprivation, I forced myself to eat, knowing I needed the calories. We had worked around sixteen hours the day before, counting the drive, and slept for about six. On the drive back up to the burn we must have looked like soft little animals, all of us half asleep and curled into various shapes.

Our burn had gone so well that the fire was almost officially contained, and Phillip was acting as incident commander. When a fire is 100 percent contained its perimeter is secured with dozer line or fireline, but the interior may still be actively burning. Sometimes it makes more sense to check the burned perimeter by hand rather than constructing more fireline, which is called *cold-trailing*. If it's declared cold, the perimeter is secure. But the interior must be fully extinguished before a fire is declared 100 percent controlled. Meeting this qualification means checking inward from the fire's perimeter, extinguishing hot spots, and, as the National Wildfire Coordinating Group (NWCG) says, burning out unburned fuel on the fire side of the fireline, eliminating chances of reignition. This last part, while understandable, is a perfect example of how fire policy focused on eradication is shortsighted. It inhibits the mosaic pattern of burned and unburned land that wildfires would otherwise establish, often leading to larger and hotter fires over time.

If a fire burns slow enough and hot enough through a landscape, consuming not only the fine fuels like grasses and shrubs, but also heavier fuels like large brush and trees, its aftermath resembles the sterile, pockmarked surface of the moon. The land is black; the trees like charcoal statues, limbs burnt to spiky protrusions; the bushes are whittled down to sharp black fingers poking up from black earth. It's natural for some land to burn this way, but if all the land burns uniformly, it will grow back uniformly. The next fire will follow the same

pattern, and the next. Time between fires shortens. Trees stop growing. Desertification ensues, and the landscape transforms. In Southern
California, the largest of fires are usually repeat burns tearing through
the footprints of previous fires. With each burn the footprint expands,
priming itself for the next fire, which will inevitably come too soon. This
phenomenon is worsened by uniform burning. If patches of unburned
fuels are left alone, they'll burn on different timelines, and often less
severely, greatly reducing the chances of large-scale desertification.

Hotshot crews specialize in initial attack (IA), but mopping up is also a
big part of the job. It can be a godsend when there aren't any other fires
because crews still get sixteen-hour days and, if the fire isn't contained,
hazard pay. Phillip had arranged for us to stay on and mop up just for
that reason. We parked, unloaded, tooled up, and broke into squads.
I volunteered to carry a piss pump and Jonah heaved the yellow bag
of water onto my back, holding it there while I struggled to thrust my
arms through the thin straps. I was accustomed to these water-filled
backpacks, which added around forty-five pounds of weight to my
thirty-five-pound line pack, but I also wanted to prove myself. Hank
and Max took the other ones.

Jonah led Jason, Daniel, me, Gunnar, and Max into the burn and
we followed like little ducklings, boots slipping on loose soil until we
reached the burn's edge along a ridgetop. I bounced up and down,
repositioning the piss pump's weight onto my fire pack, so its thin
straps wouldn't cut into my shoulders. An inversion layer of residual
smoke covered the sprawling valley like an ugly blanket and hung
midway up the foothills. Inversion layers are good for fire behavior
but terrible for air quality. Warm air traps layers of cool air in valleys
and foothills, preventing wind events and dampening flames. This
usually occurs in evening and morning but can sometimes last days,
obscuring sight enough to prevent aircraft from flying. We were high
enough for clear air; the expansive sky beamed blue. Jonah pointed

out the Supt. Truck, parked on another ridge. Phillip's binoculars glinted from the cab's window. "He'll probably take a nap soon," Jonah half-joked. "His little Supt. bitch will do all his work for him." This is what he called Owen: Supt. bitch. Anyone who got stuck riding in the cab with Phillip was Supt. bitch. After spitting out a wad of Skoal Jonah told us to be careful. "Last year, Owen and Phillip went through everyone's shit in the buggy, like we were criminals. They're ruthless."

We lined up fifty feet apart from each other. The delicate woven root systems were incinerated, reducing the once voluminous brush to pointy bare black branches. There were no leaves or grass, except for tiny patches that had escaped the heat of the fire.

Max yelled "gridding" and we started walking. The word traveled down the line, until I heard Jonah yell "gridding" and saw him crouch down to cold-trail the edge of the burn, checking for heat with his bare hand. I remembered the Viveash, with its islands of spotty burns and beautiful aspen groves, the soft, white bark of the trees and how it peeled away so easily, revealing smooth, slimy trunks the color of green apples. Here everything was black and brown, its beauty hidden from me whether burned or unburned, not like the New Mexico mountains or the variegated green Pacific Northwest. That kind of lush, large-scale beauty was more obvious than the subtle intricacies of Southern California's Chaparral mountains and foothills. I kicked away the top layer of burnt soil, revealing blackened rocks and brown dirt. It all looked dead to me, but I'd learn later that many of the plants were fire-adapted. Many species of Chaparral shoot out serotinous seeds activated only by fire's heat. Others, like chamise, sink their root systems several feet underground, or form subterranean root burls, both of which resprout after fire.

"Ana," Daniel said. "Water." I hiked over and plunged my Pulaski into a circle of white ash. The surface resembled solid ground, but white ash often signaled burned or smoking root systems, sometimes called stump holes. It only took me a few seconds of digging to reveal the smoldering root wad. I split the roots away from the center with my ax, then pried apart the root's center with the adze end of my Pulaski. His chainsaw was useless—ash and dirt would ruin its chain. He took the nozzle of my piss bag and pumped water into the hole as I scraped the orange embers away from the wad, squishing them into the ground. The charcoal always gave a satisfying crunch. If we left these embers smoldering, a gust of wind could float them into the green and start a new fire.

We worked wordlessly, accompanied by the enthusiastic squeaking of the nozzle and scraping sounds of my tool. Daniel had a naked lady sticker on his truck. I thought I could feel him watching me. Maybe he was, but my internal gaze was the most exacting.

Daniel picked up a root wad with his bare hands, holding it gingerly before nodding to confirm it was cold. I excavated all the underground tunnels around the hole to ensure everything was extinguished. Occasionally he sprayed a squirt of water, and occasionally I paused to rebalance the perpetually leaking bladder bag on top of my pack. My pants were soaked.

This work consumed our morning and early afternoon. We scooped and stabbed our tools into roots with burning orange hearts, excavating them, crushing them into the ground. The most stubborn embers got suffocated with a mud mixture. The pulsing sun warmed the heat-absorbent black soil until it felt like we were tiny creatures marooned on an increasingly uninhabitable planet. Black crows floated on the smooth air currents, cooing and clicking. We untucked and re-tucked our sweaty shirts so the air could dry our skin with its hot breath. My feet ached and burned. A helicopter dropped a load of cubees—soft plastic containers of water enclosed in cardboard boxes with flimsy handles. We balanced them on our thighs, topping off each other's CamelBaks and water bottles, then piled the empty containers back on the net, to be picked up and discarded by helitack, adding to the mountains of waste created by fire season each year. By midday our water was hot enough for tea. Only my CamelBak, stuffed in my backpack, stayed remotely cool. I saved that water for last.

Around one p.m. Jonah told us to "hooch up" and wait for the early afternoon heat to coax smoke from the ground. We constructed shelters (hooches) near the top of a ridge. I ended up with Max, who immediately told me about fucking someone in a port-a-potty. The story was self-deprecating. I told him about stripping but left out the heroin. "Oh, cool," he said. "One of my friends is a stripper." Most of his friends were girls. I had a radar for people who were, as I would have put it, as fucked up as I was. We became friends. As far as I know he never told anyone what I'd confided.

When I couldn't hold it anymore, I went to find a spot to pee, walking past Daniel and Jason, who ignored me, and then Jonah and Gunnar. "I'm going to pee," I said. Jonah wished me luck, but there were days that the guys wouldn't leave me alone about this. They nicknamed me Pee Spot. Paranoid that someone would spy my bare ass, I huffed over the ridge and into the green, where there was more cover.

We stayed there for a few long days. Nothing was going to catch fire. Any heat was sheltered deep underground, hundreds of feet into the black. Still, I dug into every white ash imprint, pausing and feeling for any emanating heat with my hovering bare hand. In the absence of heat I lowered my hand into the cavern once occupied by roots and shoots and felt the rough edges, now transformed to charcoal bits. The white ash had a silken texture but its particles were abrasive enough to scratch glass and cracked my fingerpads no matter how much lotion I used. We breathed it in constantly. I didn't dwell on the possible health consequences of exposure. According to the California Department of Public Health, people exposed to ash should wear, at minimum, N95 masks. We sometimes tied bandanas over our mouths and noses in thick smoke, but never had masks, nor could we have worn them while working sixteen-hour days. We were always hacking and coughing; my mucus was always tinged black and sometimes red.

I knew smoke was unhealthy, but recent research has revealed that wildfire smoke in particular transports bacteria and fungi, with highest concentrations nearest to the fire. Wildfire surface temperatures can be equivalent to volcanic lava, but many organisms are capable of surviving this heat. The American Society for Microbiology reports that wildland firefighters are often exposed to Valley fever, a toxic fungal infection. One study conducted after California's 2020 wildfire season found an increase in Valley fever occurrences due to the presence of wildfire smoke.

Wildland firefighters are also at an increased risk for many types of cancer due to smoke inhalation. In 2022, after years of pressure from advocacy groups, Congress finally granted federal wildland firefighters eligibility for preemptive cancer coverage. But they neglected to include several types of cancer that affect female bodies, including ovarian, breast, uterine, and cervical cancer. This, despite including testicular and prostate cancers. After pushback, the Biden administration included these cancers in preemptive coverage, but this was nixed when the administration changed hands, along with any funding for further research. A lack of research regarding cancer development in wildland firefighters has contributed to the historical lack of coverage. A 2019 study found that wildland firefighters are 35 percent more at risk for lung cancer than the general population, and 14 percent more likely to develop cardiovascular disease. Fifteen percent of wildland firefighters are women, but female cancers have not been studied as of the date of this writing. The Firefighter Cancer Support Network found that nearly 75 percent of all line-of-duty firefighter deaths can be attributed to various cancers.

Fewer and fewer white spots produced warmth as each day passed; we spaced ourselves farther apart, covering more ground. Whenever someone yelled "hold" to work on an elusive spot we had to stand still, waiting for the shouted "moving" which signaled that they were finished. Gravity weighed me down until my entire body ached. My pack felt like a thousand pounds; my skin itched; throbbing hips protested my cinched hip strap. I ignored it all. Everything I wore left its imprint—divots, blisters, chafed and bleeding flesh.

On our last night I sat sockless on my sleeping bag, examining my feet beneath the park's floodlight. Layers of ash and dirt covered my legs down to my boot line, where my bright white ankles were marred with raw skin and blisters, front and back. This was White bite, named after the brand of boots we wore, whose thick leather bit into our ankles. I popped the blisters before sticking on layers of moleskin that inevitably sweated off the next day, which only caused more blisters. My Nomex pants were so stiff with ash, dirt, and sweat that they practically stood up on their own. I still missed the privacy of a tent but had stopped putting on and taking off my pants in my sleeping bag. Each night I stealthily yanked them off—silencing the metal belt buckle with my hands so no one would look at me—and slid my naked legs, gray with ash and dirt, into my sleeping bag. They rubbed like sandpaper against the nylon.

Sometimes when I took my boots off the pain in my feet got so intense it became almost pleasurable, like plunging them into a searing hot bath. I'd moan, then catch myself, embarrassed. I felt as if almost anything I did would be construed as sexual, as if I were always being assessed in that way. The guys talked about sex all the time: how much they missed it and how horny they were.

Being the sole woman was more complicated than I had predicted. I missed women. The previous August I had worked alongside a former sorority sister with a blonde bob and unshakeable self-confidence. Girls like her intimidated me—the perpetual new kid watching them from afar, braced for their cruelty. But Molly was kind and arrestingly funny. She sat shotgun while I drove the crew van south from

Eugene, making jokes and playing DJ so I stayed awake. On the fire she proved herself tough and hardworking—a badass with a talent for fast comebacks. When she got an infection from a bad case of poison oak the crew felt hollow without her.

I thought of my grandmother, of the women in New York: my employer who encouraged me to write; and her neighbor, a girl my age who told me to take a poetry class. There was my best friend, Greta, and Sera, Peter's ex-girlfriend. My dance partners at the strip club, who shared their body spray and cheap, sparkly dresses. I thought of the women I'd kissed and slept with, but not the women I'd betrayed for men's approval. Not the brothers or boyfriends I'd slept with because it temporarily filled some bottomless pit inside me. Despite any positive experiences with women I still believed they were untrustworthy, that they gossiped and tore each other down. There wasn't enough in the world for women, and whatever we got we had to hold it close, protect, and defend.

I also didn't feel like a woman myself—I had never been good at being a girl, or a woman, and grew up fearing the wrath of girls, then women, because I failed to conform. There was some indecipherable encoded system I never learned. Perhaps this is why I rejected the other crews and instead chose the land of donkey dicks, piss pumps, and silence. In the buggy the guys talked over and through me. Phillip threw around the word *pussy* as casually as anyone else says "and." I felt invisible, but if it was invisibility, it was not a refuge. It was not private. Everyone could see me. They all knew I was there, but it was their world. It was not unlike my experiences of homelessness: always trying to assert my right to exist when others wished me gone.

Lying on the grass, I gazed up at the black, nearly starless sky, and knew I was alone. It was a familiar feeling.

Chapter Seven

Hopping Fires

The Ten Fire Orders:

1. Keep informed of fire weather conditions and forecasts.
2. Know what the fire is doing at all times.
3. Base all actions on current and expected behavior of the fire.
4. Identify escape routes and safety zones and make them known.
5. Post lookouts when there is possible danger.
6. Be alert. Keep calm. Think clearly. Act decisively.
7. Maintain prompt communications with your forces, your supervisor, and adjoining forces.
8. Give clear instructions and be sure they are understood.
9. Maintain control of your forces at all times.
10. Fight fire aggressively, having provided for safety first.

—*NWCG Incident Response Pocket Guide (IRPG)*

The only lull in our season had come directly after our first fire in mid-May. For two weeks we wrung our hands about base pay, worried that the season's initial spark had already fizzed out. The crew alternated gym workouts with brutal hikes and a couple trips to the local high school, where we speed-walked the stadium track and ran up and down the metal bleachers in full gear, without tools.

After work I always loaded my pack with extra weight and scaled Mini Hill, letting my breathing get ragged and ugly. The terrible voice in my head that told me I'd never be good enough finally had something to aim for. I envisioned passing everyone on the crew, until one morning I finally passed Gunnar and Hank. Gunnar growled and pumped his arms hard and called me a *fucking bitch* under his breath. This would happen on every PT hike until the end of the season: his cursing, the tantrums on top of Mini Hill, chucking his hard hat like a misshapen frisbee. I told myself his rage was funny.

Hank was different. We exchanged high-fives back and forth depending on who passed who. I congratulated Gunnar a couple times, but he ignored me so I stopped trying.

Colin was on Saw Team One. I kissed him while we were both in the hot tub at a crew party. He was monologuing; I was hypnotized by his freckled lips and the water pooling in the hollows above his collarbones. He kissed me back and we left the party, shushing each other as we stalked like robbers around the back of his house, me in my sweatshirt, wet tank top, and underwear, carrying my jeans. Kieran and Eric, his roommates, were still at the party, but we crept to his bedroom as if we needed to hide. I thought it was a one-night stand and was surprised when he asked me out for breakfast the next morning, far enough away from town that no one would catch us together.

On hikes, Colin was always one of the first guys to the top, propelled by his long legs, one giant hand wrapped casually around the yellow shield guarding the blades of his Husqvarna chainsaw, the other swinging with each step. According to him the crew hiked too slow. We spent every night together during those two weeks on base. He told me Gunnar was mad I was still on the crew. "Too bad, Gunnar," I said, whisper-laughing so Eric and Kieran wouldn't hear us from the living room. I always parked my Saturn a block away and knocked on the sliding glass door that opened directly into his room. Some mornings we showered together in his bathroom. He didn't make me feel nauseous, like so many men did when I got too close to them.

Colin declared his love after only a week when we were lying in bed. "I don't want you to think I'm saying this because of the sex," he said, and I told him I loved him, too, thinking it was true. I loved his masculine body and his strength and wanted to toss out my old self and become the person he thought I was. Colin said he had prayed for a woman all winter. I'd never been the answer to anyone's prayers.

I told him about the stripping, my heroin addiction and Peter and running away and being homeless, not even keeping my bulimia secret, which I rarely shared with anyone. He squeezed me, as if these things made him like me more, but he never asked questions, except to ask if I'd been tested after using needles. My past, he said, was okay with him. And my bulimia? He wanted to help me get better. "Just tell me when you feel like throwing up," he said, "and I'll help distract you." I nodded, knowing that would never work but wanting to believe it could. Compared to myself I thought he was flawless and totally wholesome. He opened up about his family, the closeness he had with them, his dog and their house and the expanse of wilderness behind it, his plans to travel to Central America, his love for reggae music and the Bible, and his friends. I figured he couldn't understand a lot of what I'd been through. I wanted to be stable and confident, like him. At work we ignored each other. We both thought it best to keep our relationship a secret.

On May 31st we were called back down to Southern California. The fires blend in my memory, but their names are listed on the yearly timesheet I kept: Arrowhead, Copper, Borel, Copco, Wildwood, Crestline, Artesian, and Louisiana. Some, like the Louisiana, were large enough for a fire camp. Others, like the Wildwood and Crestline, lasted only a shift or two. We bounced between the Angeles and San

Bernardino National Forests and slept wherever we could. One night, after a grueling day shift bled into darkness and we had exceeded our work/rest ratio because of imminent danger to structures like houses and businesses, we bedded down in a large patch of dirt, only to be awakened by our captains screaming for us to load into the buggies. I remember thick smoke and the increasingly loud sound of crackling brush, the heat of approaching flames. The fire had been several ridges away but was now heading towards us, spurred by a wind shift. I suppressed the fear pummeling my throat. We shoved our things into the buggy before hopping in ourselves, quickly gearing up for an impromptu extended night shift, having slept only a couple of hours.

If you've seen pictures of nighttime volcanic eruptions, you can imagine an active wildfire in the Southern California darkness. The fire's head, sometimes spanning hundreds of feet, spits giant flames as it chugs forward, leaving an expanse of simmering orange, black, and yellow in its wake, barely shrouded in smoke. Night shifts were advantageous for catching a wildfire because of higher humidity and lower temperatures, but this is becoming less true as climate change raises overall temperatures; parched and weakened plants are primed for burning at faster rates, even at night.

I'm sure Phillip would have preferred we fight these fires with more fire, but the weather was too unpredictable, so we constructed fire-line instead. The guys turned "initial attack" into a verb: we were IAing. On the Arrowhead fire, in the San Bernardino National Forest, I quickly learned how crews navigated tightly woven chaparral, which was impenetrable and sometimes taller than fifteen feet. First, Phillip flew over the land in a helicopter, dictating the path of the fireline to Nickolas and Owen. Nickolas, following GPS coordinates, marked the planned path with bright pink flagging. Each module would begin constructing fireline in different locations, with A-Mod working towards B-Mod.

David parked the A-Mod buggy on a dirt road, which we'd use as our anchor point to prevent the fire from looping around our unfinished line and trapping us. Our fireline doubled as an escape route. Phillip was watching the fire and would warn us of any danger. Because of the thick brush, we needed to establish a saw line: a thin, quickly cut line leading to B-Mod's starting point, eventually to be widened into a fireline. Owen guided the saws. When cutting line, saw teams alternate between sawyer and swamper, switching roles each time the saw runs out of fuel. Whoever is running the saw at any particular moment is the sawyer. The other half of the team becomes the swamper, clearing whatever the sawyer cuts and transferring it to the green where it will hopefully remain unburned when or if the fire burns to the fireline. In thick brush some crew members will drop their tools in favor of swamping because of the overwhelming amount of vegetation.

Kieran revved his saw and cut a large chest-height hole into the brush, then stepped aside so Colin could jump in to yank the mass of brush out of the hole. The hole allowed Kieran to get the bar of the saw all the way into the brush. From there he cut upwards from one side of the hole, lifting the saw above his head, rotating the saw so the tip swooped and sliced through the top layers of brush and then repeating this on the other side, sawing upwards again and then down towards the ground before stepping back again so Colin could grab the giant clusters of brush. The saw weighed at least thirty pounds. Kieran made it look easy, but sweat quickly darkened his yellow Nomex. When Colin turned towards the road holding a massive clump of brush I took it from him and threw it onto the other side of the road, away from the fireline. We "chained" it across, passing armfuls of brush to each other so we didn't have to run across the road. Colin and Kieran disappeared into the brush, leaving a narrow, claustrophobic saw line in their wake. Jason and Daniel, my squad's saw team, began widening this into an actual fireline. We stayed behind with them while David followed Saw One, accompanied by his squad.

Jason and Daniel started cutting and Max, Gunnar, and I swamped the brush across the road. Once the road was too far away Jason cut holes into the side of the fireline that would hopefully stay unburned, and we stuffed them with excess brush, because the vegetation was too tall to throw anything over. Throwing this fuel onto the burn side would increase the fire's heat, making the fire more likely to leap into the green, creating what's called a slopover. But at the same time, the excess brush we loaded into the green side would dry out and increase the next fire's severity. I thought about this as I bear-hugged the brush and forced it inside the holes, first with my body weight and then with my gloved hands. The bundles scratched at my exposed skin. Whitethorn, a native species and one of the first plants to establish itself after fires, stuck me with its spikes while the intertwining poison oak wept its oils onto my clothes. I would only notice the scratches and oak rash later, I was so focused. My mind quieted, lulled by a singular goal. My earplugs blocked out everything but the dull drone of the saws and my labored breathing. We grunted and yelled with frustration, pulling and pushing at the brush, all of us in our own worlds while working as a team.

I loved constructing fireline. I scraped my rake over the line to clear leaves and sticks, or someone else would yank it out of my pack and do it for me while I was swamping. My endurance surprised everyone, including me. I may have lacked brute upper body strength, but I could swamp for longer than many of the guys. Whenever Jonah asked me if I needed to switch out with someone I always shook my head. Sometimes he pulled me out anyway, worried I wasn't conserving my energy, lifting his hand vertically towards his mouth. Drink water. I'd drink some water, annoyed, and reclaim my rake so I could scrape the line.

*   *   *

Over the next few days I got in the habit of giving Max my rake so I could swamp. Sometimes Jonah forced us to switch, pissing us both off. Max enjoyed leisurely raking the line. I hated standing around while other people were working.

Afternoons are typically when fire activity picks up the most, colloquially called "the heat of the day." They scorched the landscape, evaporating humidity and encouraging the fire to torch. Flames tore through the brush, racing up hillsides before pausing along the ridgetops and slowly backing downhill. The heat and steep topography caused squirrely and unpredictable winds to weave through the ridges and valleys like ever-shifting river currents. We dug and scraped and cut, hoping to create a barrier strong enough to stop the flames from following the wind. Sweat soaked our shirts and stung our eyes. We shoved food into our mouths whenever we could. I was amazed at how each hillside, canyon, and ravine supported different ecosystems.

Sometimes we emerged from the oppressive brush into a tranquil ravine, bathed in the shadows of oak trees, where daylight filtered through the hovering smoke and shone like milky gold. Bronze, silver, and copper leaves glimmered on the ground. Wisps of water caught the sunlight and strung it through the canyon. In the evenings cottony smoke occasionally blanketed itself in the valleys below the bony ridges, submerging the bodies of the mountains as if tucking them in to sleep.

The days melted into one another. We worked until dusk then loaded up, resting our heads on sweatshirts or contraband pillows as the buggies swayed and rumbled down the dirt roads. I was usually a light sleeper, but we all slept hard on those drives, waking only when David yelled, "Chow!" We lined up in tool order and waited patiently, our boots scraping the metal stairs leading to the kitchen. We sat as one unit under the food tent. Any woman I saw, I smiled at. Some smiled back. Some glared. Most of the crews had no women at all.

Many of the men stared, trying to catch my eye. I usually donned a blank expression and avoided eye contact with them, honoring some unspoken rule. After chow I speed-walked to the row of port-a-potties, punctuated at both ends by gray plastic sinks. Inside, the port-a-potties were dense with stale heat and, if they were cleaned recently, a plasticky floral smell, unpleasant but preferable to the pungent stench of those in need of cleaning. These were my only moments of privacy, and I sought them out as often as I could.

Chaparral is full of poison oak, and my skin burned from the residual oils. I slapped myself with my hands, because scratching sent me into an oakgasm—a kind of unstoppable scratching fit which was pleasurable at first but only led to broken flesh and intense stinging. My belt line, the backs of my knees, my inner elbows, and my neck and face itched the most. A lot of us had it, some worse than I, so I didn't complain, but I craved the cure—steroid pills that could only be prescribed back on base. The medics in fire camp couldn't prescribe medication. Everyone offered me interim solutions. Nickolas suggested Gold Bond and I squeezed the powder down my shirt, rubbing it on my neck and face. There's a fun picture of me and a couple of the guys, taken while we were on a night shift. My face is bright white with powder, but I'm smiling. I was happy.

We were strongly discouraged from using the in-camp showers because sleep was more important. When I started itching from poison oak I gave in and showered, trading my dirty Nomex for clean, something anyone could do at fire camp. The guys made fun of me and Eric, who also had oak, for our bright yellows. Eric rubbed his shirt in loose dirt before putting it on. Everyone said a bright yellow shirt was the mark of someone who wasn't working enough. I'd assumed that swapping out Nomex wouldn't be an issue; no one on the contract crews had cared, but apparently wearing the same disgusting Nomex for as long as possible was yet another sign of strength and commitment.

According to federal guidelines all wildland firefighters need to follow the work/rest ratio, which splits each twenty-four-hour period into three eight-hour segments and requires one hour of rest for every two hours worked. Ideally this results in eight hours of sleep, but it never panned out that way. Phillip wanted sixteens and this meant late-night tool sharpenings and twilight dawn wake-ups, sleeping through the camp noises: engines rumbling and port-a-potty doors slamming and whispers and shouts of conversation. In between assignments we slept anywhere. On the side of a road along a chain-link fence, the wind sweeping through a line of pepper trees that kept me awake with their whispering song; along a hand line adjacent to a smoldering fire that had already burned through, waking as no-see-ums hovered and landed around my nose, lips, and eyes. In several fire camps. A city park. A school football field.

Maybe some of the guys slept well, but I didn't. I was usually awake when Owen's voice announced another workday. As the days wore on I stopped wishing for a tent and instead longed for just a pillow, another object Phillip banned for no apparent reason. I lay in my sleeping bag, my body pulsing with residual adrenaline. Whenever I closed my eyes I heard the buzzing sound of chainsaws, radio feedback, the clink of tools in the dirt, and the sound of helicopters and aircraft. I thought peripherally of Colin, and wondered if he was thinking of me. I tried not to scratch my poison oak. I dreamed of fire.

We spent six days alternating digging line with clearing the dozer line on the Arrowhead Fire. In the early morning, we unloaded and hiked to wherever we had stopped work the day before, or followed the path of another crew's line to its end so we could extend or finish it. Sometimes we tied our line in with dozer line, then hiked the ugly scars littered with flammable branches and brush, occasionally bending down to toss the debris into the green until we reached another section and started our line again. As we hiked the dozer line, clouds of dust made us cough and spit. With each incline I was forced to inhale through my mouth, which filled with grit so thick I had to rinse it away with water. The soil crumbled under our feet and we'd slide down, cursing as we tried to gain traction. Going uphill, I often veered off the dozer lines to seek a better path, if one was available.

Dozers are considered a front-line tool, but their lines wreak havoc on soil and plant life, turning the soil dusty and unstable like a sand pit. Everything in the path of a bulldozer is destroyed and upended. Uprooted brush and small trees are left half-buried in the disturbed soil. Seeds are spread from one ecological zone to another without discrimination. Newly loosened soils muddy rivers and watersheds, destroying aquatic life and ecosystems. In areas with layered, duffy soil, bulldozers are even more harmful. Their blades slice into the soil's delicate fungal networks and connective root systems, severing communication and increasing ecological fragmentation. Dozer lines remain long after fires are gone, and studies show that they're less hospitable to native plants. Over time, within their fifteen-foot track, new, often non-native plant life will grow, visibly different from the surrounding vegetation, and often more flammable.

They're also less effective than one would think, especially in thick fuels. Although smaller dozers can be surprisingly nimble, all dozers are top-heavy and have limited terrain capacity, often cutting line ineffectively while also putting dozer operators in danger. Because they move slowly, it's dangerous for dozer operators to cut line close to the fire itself, so they usually cut indirect line, which leaves swaths of unburned land that is later ignited by crews.

I began to understand why the guys constantly made fun of Phillip. He supplied our Emergen-C powder packets, protein bars, and kipper snacks, but dipped into his generous offerings more than we did. None of us wanted to ingest warm, oily fish bits while covered in dirt, ash, and sweat, yet the kipper tins inevitably dwindled, vanishing about halfway through our fourteen-day roll. Phillip could swipe several at a time with one giant hand. He mentioned them constantly, as if he'd bought them for us with his own personal money, and not taxpayer dollars.

On a fundamental level the job of a hotshot superintendent is to keep the crew physically safe. Superintendents are a conduit between their crew and all other personnel. They count on their captains (or their assistant superintendent) to pass information down through the chain of command. Some superintendents barely speak to lesser crew members, while others constantly engage with the entire crew. Crew culture is set by the superintendent, which is why some hotshot crews are more diverse, inclusive, or hospitable than others.

On most days our crew had two meetings: the morning briefing and the after action review (AAR) in the evening. The briefing is meant to define work objectives, establish communication (including radio frequencies), and outline the day ahead. The AAR is, according to the National Wildfire Coordinating Group, "a professional discussion of an event." The NWCG highlights the need for open communication, respectful disagreement, and equal ownership leading to improved outcomes.

When Phillip led these meetings he reclined in the dirt or lay his torso on the hood of the Supt. Truck. He was mercurial. Did the camp have food that adhered to his diet? Good mood. Had the incident commander failed to see the virtues of his ideas? Bad mood. No matter what, he talked. In the mornings we didn't care, because his talking ate into our working hours, but in the evenings, when we were exhausted, Phillip's AARs could be torturously long. During his bad moods he singled me out, referring to the crew as "guys" before looking at me and saying, "and girl." Sometimes he mentioned my dyed hair, my work ethic, or told me to smile. He also picked on some of the guys. A loose, untucked shirt or bare head was cause for ridicule. "Look at that bagger," he'd say. While I didn't know what a carpet-bagger was, it was clearly an insult. He commented on people's weight and congratulated me on my loose pants, asking everyone if they had noticed my weight loss. The muscular guys garnered his admiration while he prodded the skinnier ones to work out more.

Phillip seemed to foster competition and imbalanced power dynamics, which he then exploited for his own entertainment. Colin and Kieran, as Saw One, were the gods of the crew while Gunnar and Max were failures because they couldn't hike with the extra weight of a chainsaw. About 10 percent of the information he gave us was pertinent—the other 90 percent was rambling insults, details of his fad diet, musings on the especially hot women he observed in leadership positions, and stories about his own prowess as a firefighter and a man.

I despised Phillip, and sought his approval, and despised myself for seeking his approval. He had put me in charge of timesheets because "girls have the best handwriting." This isolated me from the rest of the crew. Every week or so I sat in the air-conditioned cab of his truck filling out the paperwork while everyone else worked in the heat. Sometimes he insisted I ride with him for no apparent reason, making me Supt. Bitch. I gripped the door as he spewed stream of consciousness thoughts, clenching my jaw so hard I gave myself headaches. When he asked for my thoughts about my peers it felt like he was saying: *You're special. You know things, and I will take that into account.* I wanted to be special. A good worker. At the same time, I divulged as little as possible about my peers, navigating my loyalties by feigning ignorance, keeping my answers vague, nodding or shaking my head depending on what I thought he wanted to hear. Sometimes he shouted "Bullshit," or prodded me for more information. When he agreed with me, I felt smart. When he disagreed, stupid. He compared me with previous women from the crew. "Dumb as a rock, but a sweetheart," he said about one, and "I bet she slept with every guy on the crew."

He mentioned how one woman intentionally flashed the crew when she peed outdoors. I took note and policed myself, hoping not to end up in one of his future stories.

Owen parroted Phillip, constantly reminding the crew that women were weaker than men; not to expect as much of me, although I worked as hard as anyone else, if not harder. He dissected and analyzed various women using old assumptions repeated by generations of firefighters and still being repeated today. This woman knew someone or was related to someone who got her into a leadership position. That woman didn't deserve her post. So and so doesn't have women on their crew because they just make life harder for everyone. Intention aside, Phillip and Owen's behavior worked as an intimidation tactic, marginalizing me from my peers.

I didn't know that California, categorized by the U.S. Forest Service as Region 5, was under its second consent decree, enacted in 2000, which called for increased oversight based on a class action lawsuit representing over 6,000 women who, in that region alone, had experienced sexual harassment, assault, and reprisal. This was the Donnelly Consent Decree (DCD). It lapsed in 2006. Preceeding the DCD, the Bernardi Consent Decree (BCD) was enacted in 1971 and ended in 1995. According to legal testimony, the region "fomented an attitude that unqualified women were taking men's jobs" in reaction to the BCD, whereas conditions improved during the DCD. I was, at the time, working under improving conditions.

When Phillip asked me who I had my eye on, I always shrugged, annoyed. He warned me away from sleeping with anyone on the crew by sharing private details about my peers: who cheated on their girlfriend or wife and who was terrible in bed.

"You know," he'd say, "girls shouldn't be hotshots. I know you don't want to hear that." He said this more than once, always with a wink. Girls, he said, screwed with the crew's equilibrium. I started to think I

was personally responsible for any crew conflicts or any negative attention I received. I was grateful for any kindness from my crew members
and secretly believed that everyone shared Phillip's views, including the
guys who treated me with respect, like Jonah and Nickolas.

Hank, a hard worker, was also targeted by Phillip, who said he was
too scrawny and clumsy. Sometime in June I started feeling superior
to him. We were both near the bottom of the crew hierarchy, but
he had friends whereas I was still an outsider. I told several of the
guys about how he struggled when his rake pinned him between two
burned bushes, how his legs had spun cartoonishly. Never mind that
my downhill hiking consisted of repeated, purposeful falls. Hank
eventually asked me why I was gossiping. I apologized and said I
didn't know. "It's okay," he said. "Just don't do it anymore." That was
the first time someone had ever called me out directly, without ill
intent. I never said a bad word about him after that and counted him
as someone I could trust.

Chapter 8

The Place of Flowing Water

Watch out situation 11: Unburned fuel between you and the fire

The Nüümü (Owens Valley Paiute) word for the Owens Valley is Payahüünadü: The Place of Flowing Water. Owens Lake was once a turquoise gem fed by mountain streams flowing from the Sierra Nevada mountains. Owens Valley was inhabited by the Nüümü and Newe (Shoshone) people for thousands of years. Both tribes were interlinked through shared cultural exchange and intermarriage. They migrated seasonally within the region, inhabiting lower elevations near Owens Lake and its feeding streams in the warmer months, where they subsisted on several species of ducks, grebes, and geese, as well as shorebirds who thrived in the shallow waters and mudflats. Because the tribes had intimate knowledge of seasonal migration patterns, their methods of hunting and egg collection were sustainable. The Paiute and Shoshone harvested and processed meat via smoking, drying, and roasting, repurposed bones for needles and fishhooks, and converted skin into containers and pouches. They also incorporated feathers into bedding and clothing as well as ceremonial dress and arrows. Egg harvests, occurring in spring, were conducted with careful consideration for continued population growth and sustainability. Many tubers and other edible plants were also cultivated by hand-irrigating the land surrounding Owens Lake. In the mid-1800s miners and prospectors arrived, followed by settlers who destroyed crops and fenced off land. While many tribal members were forced onto reservations hundreds of miles away, some returned, reclaiming their land. Through a series of broken treaties the U.S. government forced tribes onto reservations again in the 1930s, cheating them out of promised water and land rights. This was after several prominent developers scammed the residents of Owens Valley into supplying water to Los Angeles. Without this water the city wouldn't exist as it does today. Now the valley is arid, resembling a desert. Many tribal members are currently fighting for access to their homelands while also advocating for ecologically sound stewardship.

We were called north from Southern California to the Inyo National Forest. The forest, adjacent to Owens Valley, is home to the bristlecone pine and consists of over a million acres of land and nine wilderness areas. It was established by Theodore Roosevelt, primarily to support the Los Angeles aqueduct. Two of its wilderness areas are named after men whose associations with the area still define how many people experience the outdoors: early twentieth-century Western landscape photographer Ansel Adams and nineteenth-century naturalist and conservationist John Muir. There is also Mount Pinchot, named after the first superintendent of the U.S. Forest Service, whose aggressive fight for fire suppression continues to influence land policy.

The Birch Fire started on July 1, 2002, about fifteen miles north of Bishop. Its cause was later blamed on malfunctioning power equipment managed by California Edison. In 2010 the company settled a $2.8 million–dollar federal lawsuit, but never acknowledged full responsibility. We were one of twenty-six hotshot crews called to the fire, along with sixty fire engines and seven helicopters. We were not far from Tom's Place, a small outpost community originally established in the 1920s, at about seven 7,000-foot elevation. Several towns had already been evacuated.

The main fire started in the mountains. Thick, dry stands of brush, ponderosa, lodgepole, and Jeffrey pine trees, sage, and grasses lay like a lake of fuel between us and the fire, heightening the need for caution. There were fewer roads, trails, and firebreaks here than in Southern California. Sending burners with drip torches too far into the unburned fuel risked entrapment and increased our chances of accidentally starting an entirely new fire. The incident commander, along with Phillip and several other hotshot superintendents, decided to use flare guns to start a fire farther in, which could pull more easily into the main fire.

We set up along a narrow dirt logging road. Juan, one of the B-Mod squad bosses, opened an Army green metal box and loaded the flat metal flare gun and hiked interior from the road, his squad high-stepping behind him, through dense brush. I heard him yell "firing" several times. Each exclamation was followed by the gun's pop as it sent a flare deep into the woods. About three hundred feet away from us flames leapt upwards, whooshing and crackling before arcing towards the hillside. Phillip's plan was to clear the hillsides of fuel, stopping the main fire. The wind picked up slowly, drawn towards the fire's heat, and B-Mod began burning, the wind lifting their fire away from the road and towards Juan's.

I stood against the bush chinquapin, a brushy shrub that inhabits the forest floor beneath the looming pine trees. Its deep green leaves were thick and waxy. Delicate yellow pom-pom flowers hung like ornaments, swaying with the heat of the fire, which was only fifteen or twenty feet away. I watched the roadside fire establish itself, then turned away to look for stray firebrands. The narrow road gave us no refuge from the fire's heat. I pulled my shroud down. Chinquapin leaves sweated with flammable oils, threatening to ignite. Max, who was fifteen feet away from me, yelled that it was getting hot. Our eyes met and confirmed each other's fear before we quickly looked away, mutually ashamed. Our buggies were far down the road, and there was no safe black where we could go if the fire crossed the line. I stared at the leaves until they blurred, and I was overcome with the familiar sense of watching myself from far away. The pop of the flare gun startled me back into my body. I folded my fear up tightly, plastering it into the back of my mind. It was useless here.

For our nine days at the Birch Fire the crew camped in our tents—at real campsites—for the first time. The feeling of crawling into that single-person nylon structure each night was intensely satisfying and as close as I could get to being alone, free from observation. I had stopped stretching in the open after Colin had proudly told me that some of the guys watched me when I stretched before bed, as if I were a prize he'd won. This had only increased my self-consciousness. I hadn't realized how tense I was during my stretching ritual until that first night in the tent, when I poured my torso over my legs and felt my entire body soften for the first time all season. Each night I stretched for a solid hour, cycling through the yoga poses I'd first learned as a teenager, silently inhaling and exhaling. The constant observation, which I'd first thought was all in my head, had severed me from parts of myself. In these moments I remembered that I was a person who existed in my own right, not just as a *girl* firefighter.

There was no fire camp, so a local diner hosted us for breakfast each morning. Paying local restaurants is sometimes less expensive than hiring a contractor to run a fire camp kitchen. I usually sat with Max or Kieran, but navigating seating could be treacherous because there were certain guys I needed to avoid—the ones who either ignored me and talked to everyone else or sat in awkward silence until I left the table. Colin and I never sat together. I had a couple friends on

B-Mod, including Martin, a seasoned hotshot in his thirties. Martin had sustained a head injury in a car accident when he was twenty-three and had mild brain damage. He would never work as a lead firefighter, sawyer, or squad boss, but his work ethic was unbeatable. We often had long theological conversations, musing on the origins of Buddhism and Christianity, and he told me about his life before firefighting. I had been raised Buddhist and Martin was a practicing Catholic. He was parental towards me, and kind. But Martin was terrible company at breakfast. He ate fast, head down as he shoveled hash browns and scrambled eggs into his mouth, pausing for messy gulps of orange juice. Still, I preferred sitting with him to some of the others. Jonah always sat with Phillip and Owen because he was the most recent Supt. Bitch, at Phillip's mercy until another poor soul was chosen. Being Supt. Bitch was both a marker of status and a form of torture.

Every morning, we had the same middle-aged server. She was sweet, with graying hair and nervous, darting eyes. It was always painful to see Phillip interact with women, but he was especially aggressive towards her, ordering her around and demanding special adjustments to his meals. After the first few mornings I watched her flinch at the sound of his voice, but her face remained unchanged, always with the same impassive expression. I got the impression she'd seen much worse than the likes of him. Even when he called her a bitch from afar, loud enough for her to hear, she remained neutral. She was especially nice to me. Maybe we both felt sorry for each other.

Restaurants were slippery territory for me because of my bulimia. Feeling full was intolerable but I was so disconnected from my body I never stopped eating early enough to avoid it. Sometimes I threw up silently in the women's bathroom, keeping some of the food down so I'd have enough energy for work. Before the restaurant trips, my bulimia had mostly been in check. Maybe it was those evenings in my tent, alone, being present in my body, that triggered me. Or maybe that time alone emphasized the pressure I felt outside of my tent. This crew couldn't offer me security or acceptance, but I thought I could earn it. It would take me another year to understand that most of these men would never see me as someone who belonged there as much as they did.

Hundreds of years ago tribes regularly burned the dense brush surrounding their homes and villages to keep them safe from fire, but fire has been suppressed there for over a century, as it has throughout most of the continent. This has led to larger fires like the Birch. Because of the fuel buildup and the distance between our crew and the main fire, our methods on the Birch resulted in extreme fire behavior. The fires we ignited with our flare pistols ripped up the hills, burning the fuel at high severity and killing almost all the trees, including the pinyon pines, which are fire-adapted. Even some fire-adapted plants are vulnerable to high-severity fires.

Nine years after the Birch Fire, two ecologists conducted a field analysis of the land. Few new trees had grown, and the burned plots, as opposed to the unburned ones, were overrun with cheatgrass—an invasive, highly flammable grass that sheds its stalks each year, layering the ground with an ever-increasing abundance of dry tinder. The cheatgrass was especially prevalent on the hills, where the fire lit by our pistols burned the hottest.

But there was something else: Some of the burned land, nine years later, despite the severity of the fire, was host to a more diverse crop of native herbaceous shrubs, unlike the unburned, whose shrubbery was less diverse and composed of more invasive shrubs. Both unburned and burned land had similar brush density, but fire, although severe, created more plant diversity. All plants burn in their own unique ways. Heterogenous plant habitats help promote a healthy fire mosaic and can lessen the impact of future fires. In contrast, homogenous habitats tend to burn uniformly. This makes them vulnerable to type conversion, a process in which overlapping incidents of severe wildfires transform landscapes. Forests can morph into more flammable shrublands. For thousands of years anthropogenic fire prevented type conversion and many ecosystems thrived with low-severity fire regimes, while some thrived with high-severity regimes with longer time intervals between burns. Repeated and frequent high-severity fires can decimate tree populations and eliminate the protective overstory, inhibiting new seedlings from sprouting because of the lack of shade. This becomes a feedback loop wherein the landscape adapts to and promotes high-severity fire, which is exacerbated by climate change.

The ecologists who conducted this study offered some land management recommendations, like increased prescribed fire, reseeding of specific native plants with properties competitive with cheatgrass, native seed collection, and minimized grazing. These are all Indigenous methods of land tending, interrupted shortly after contact with Europeans and settlers.

Chapter Nine

Oregon

B y mid-July the country was at a preparedness level 5, meaning that over 80 percent of the nation's resources were committed. We were called to the Monument Fire in Eastern Oregon, adjacent to John Day, a small town where I was stationed for one month the previous summer. When we drove through John Day I remembered the demolition derby and the local John Day crew—I had helped one of the guys prepare his car for the demolition derby, and we all attended the county fair, screaming at him from the sidelines as he demolished his car. Those had been country boys like some of the guys I worked with now, but so much more laid-back. So much more fun. Not hostile, like some of my co-workers.

I reminded myself that I got along with men. There was something about the hotshot crew itself, the performance of it, similar to the military in its rigid conformity. The guys loved watching war films, like *Platoon*, *Full Metal Jacket*, and *Saving Private Ryan*. Our crew itself was like a platoon. Phillip, equivalent to a platoon leader, handed down orders to the captains, who gave them to squad bosses, or squaddies. In the Army, platoons are split into squads, and squads are split into teams, equivalent to our mods and squads. We used "strategy" and "tactics" to fight fires, like soldiers did in war. Each crew member was expected to conform to the crew's culture, just as soldiers must conform to their platoon's culture. The grunts—the ones without a title like lead firefighter, squad boss, or captain, like me—remained mute when it came to thoughts or opinions. We weren't supposed to initiate communication with the captains or Phillip, who had ultimate authority over our lives and behavior.

This is no accident. The first national parks were governed by the U.S. Cavalry. Military training occurred in national parks during World War II. The military was also deployed in Oregon and California when Native Americans resisted displacement from lands that are now governed by the Park Service, Forest Service, and Bureau of Land Management.

The Spanish came by ship to Oregon in the 1500s—they were the first Europeans to arrive there, where more than sixty tribes and bands had lived for thousands of years, speaking at least eighteen languages (probably more; written accounts were mostly left by settlers and explorers). Oregon and California hadn't yet been separated into two states. There was no border, and many Northern California tribes were also Southern Oregon tribes. Tribes and bands were intimately connected to their land, its microclimates and flora and fauna, in a way most white settlers never would be. Food and game were abundant. Salmon ran all the way from the ocean to the Malheur River in Eastern Oregon, something that is now almost inconceivable.

England's Captain James Cook arrived in coastal Oregon in the late 1780s and the allure of abundant sea otters and beavers drew British fur traders to the territory. They edged out the Spanish, established numerous forts, and transformed the lives of many local tribes from a subsistence culture to a market economy. Europeans also spread disease, weakening tribal communities. Indigenous people throughout Oregon, like those of California, migrated seasonally, and settlers exploited this. Beginning in the early nineteenth century, British and

American troops began occupying Oregon. White settlers, enamored by the storied Lewis and Clark expedition, squatted and eventually settled on Indigenous land, encouraged by the federal government. In their eyes, tribes were wasting valuable resources in land ripe for agriculture. Christians established missions throughout Oregon during this time, and like the Spanish missionaries in California, Oregon missionaries saw themselves as benevolent overlords, bestowing Oregon tribes with sophisticated agriculture and religion. Violence ensued. Tribes defended their land and were punished, often with death. In his book *Possessing the Pacific*, Stuart Banner details the federal government's failure to protect Oregon tribes. Many tribes were forced into treaties, surrendering their land, and moved onto reservations. Children were stolen from parents and sent to residential school. This caused much tribal conflict and initiated cultural genocide.

Before the arrival of Europeans and American settlers, meadows and grasslands populated much of Oregon. Lush green grass was maintained by fire in order to draw elk and other herd animals; the absence of trees improved sightlines for hunters. After each year's elk hunt tribes burned the meadows, keeping trees at bay. Trees are thirsty, siphoning water from the soil. With unchecked growth water supplies dwindle. The use of fire was multifunctional, encouraging new grass while also producing pliable shoots for basketry and building materials. Budding spruce roots, sedge, beargrass, tule, reeds, willow, dogbane, and fern are all used for basketry, which is both an art form and a utilitarian essential for many Indigenous groups across the United States. Baskets and containers are often dyed with various natural materials, like lichen, to produce intricate designs.

Berries, particularly huckleberries, were also burned on timelines tailored to each berry's growth cycle, usually occurring in late summer after harvests. Although settlers burned in Oregon well into the mid-1900s, these burns were in service of livestock grazing, not land tending. With the disappearance of Indigenous fire, open prairies transformed into dense, flammable forests overgrown with brush. This was an ecological occurrence across the United States as it was settled—townships and villages sprouted on sparsely forested land formerly maintained by the frequent burning of prairies and grasslands. Grasslands converted to forests, and forests, which had become so scarce in Europe, became a symbol of the land's health rather than a sign of deterioration. Increased tree cover transformed the landscape.

Some of Oregon's largest fires occurred in the nineteenth century with the advent of clear-cutting. The Tillamook Burn, which started in 1933, burned over 350,000 acres. Historian Stephen Pyne argues that the fire burned for eighteen years, with new fires igniting each year in its footprint and each successive fire further degrading the land. In 1949 reseeding began. It continued for two decades. In 1979 the Tillamook burn area became the Tillamook State Forest.

When we were called to Oregon in 2002, the Biscuit Fire, Oregon's largest post-1900 fire since the Tillamook, had ignited four days before we arrived. It was expanded by thousands of acres (almost doubling its natural size) through burning operations, although no structures were threatened, and the region included many fire-adapted native species. The area, which is considered "mixed-conifer," supports a fire return interval of 45–80 years. This doesn't mean that one fire burns every 45–80 years but rather that many small fires regularly burn in mosaic patterns, leaving some patches unburned and some burned. When the Forest Service decided to burn extra land to allow the fire to meet various barriers, like hand-dug firelines, roads, and dozer lines, they interrupted the natural mosaic pattern the fires would have assumed, increasing the severity of the fire as well as its size. They spent over 150 million dollars on suppression, but the fire wasn't declared contained until December, by which time it had made its way across the California border. Many large fires, especially those in forest ecosystems, burn until the snow falls, despite aggressive suppression efforts.

The Monument Fire, where we'd be working, was east of the Biscuit Fire, near Unity, in a more arid ecosystem. Ponderosa fuel type up high, pinyon/juniper at mid-elevation, and sage in the high desert, which is the lowest elevation. The Burnt River Valley, where the town of Unity is situated, is over 4,000 feet in elevation despite being the flattest and lowest landscape around. Much of Eastern Oregon and Washington is high desert. Unity is on the east side of Malheur National Forest, less than two hours west of the Snake River, which traces Idaho's western border. We angled up from the valley, along switchback dirt roads and into the shelter of the mountains, armed with extra fuel, cubees of water, and rectangular cases of MREs. Although there was an established fire camp, the drive to the fire was so long and the camp so crowded that it was better for us to spike out, retaining our independence as a crew. We were in for more burning.

Everyone constructed camp, surrounded by a haze of gauzy gray smoke that obscured the waning daylight. David built a warming fire as the sawyers bucked a tree for sitting logs. Once they settled, standing and sitting around the warm orange glow, I found a place to sit and write in my journal. Some of the guys teasingly called it my diary. *Are you writing about me in your diary?* I did write about them, all of them, but not in the way they imagined. I tried to parse each day, to understand my place on the crew and in the world.

Cold, high-elevation nights called for the tangible shelter of our tents. Each morning Owen and Nickolas rustled our tents and told us to get up. More and more, I was startled from a deep sleep, groggier than earlier in the season. Some of the guys needed to be yelled at or shaken awake. My body carried the past two months of sixteen-hour days like dead weight. I craved sleep more than anything else and hated waking up to frigid mornings. My sleeping bag was filthy but so cozy, unlike my stiff, cold Nomex pants. We hadn't showered for seven days and wouldn't shower for seven more. My entire body prickled with grime, legs layered with ash and dirt, hair an unbrushable tangled mess. Every morning, I switched out my sleeping shirt for a dirty crew shirt bleached with whitish sweat lines matching the straps of my pack. I first donned clean cotton socks, then a pair of wool socks stiff with old sweat and dirt or, on alternating days, luxuriously clean ones. My leather boots had pinched hard red calluses into the fronts and backs of my ankles. Calluses and blisters marred my heels, toes, and the balls of my feet. My big toes were numb and would never regain full sensation.

We milled around like zombies, all of us looking haggard beyond our years, until Owen poured us strong hot coffee from Phillip's percolator. For breakfast we had MREs. We also had them for lunch and dinner. After that, we brushed our teeth and got to work.

Every day we poured streams of burning fuel mix into the thick undergrowth composed of half-fallen dead trees, brush, and plant litter. There's a picture of me holding a drip torch while the dry, spindly trees behind me crown. Crowning is what happens when fire fully consumes a tree, including its crown, and these trees crowned quickly and easily because of their poor health. Trees that crown are more likely to die in fires—this is why trees like redwoods are so fire-resistant. Their lack of lower branches prevents fire from climbing into their vulnerable crowns.

Two and a half months in, burning, once exciting, was now mundane. I no longer needed a funnel to pour fuel mix into the canisters, and I wasn't scared of laying a line of fire down right next to me. I high-stepped over the forest floor, almost running to keep pace with the fire. It felt like an obstacle course, choked with brush and small trees, ladder fuels that carried flames upwards, causing crown fires and incinerating the canopy. The ground, a crunchy layer of parched needles, scraggly brush, and fallen branches, dried by months without rain, crunched beneath my feet. This accumulated matter increased the fire's intensity, so even the most resistant trees would likely die. All of it lit up magnificently, its heat parching my skin. My face was blackened by soot and dirt, but my upper lip was clean. I obsessively wiped it because the guys had made fun of me for my trademark black soot mustache.

Phillip encouraged us to torch the landscape, because it prevented the land from reburning when or if the main fire came through. Back then I was happy to be in the woods and grateful for a paycheck. Privileged to be traipsing through nature, even when it was burning. But I cringed sometimes, setting little trees on fire, knowing I was leaving a moonscape of torched land in my wake. I thought we were doing something useful because the land clearly needed to burn, but creating a moonscape in these forests is the opposite of a fire mosaic. It increases invasive plant populations and takes longer to regenerate. So much land burned so completely only leads to more land primed for burning with more volatility in the future. We never considered regional fire regimes, or what would foster long-term forest health. This is the traditional mode of wildland firefighting: a self-perpetuating feedback loop that encourages larger fires and ultimately weakens the ecosystem. The end point is desertification.

Martin was almost two decades older than me but had reached a ceiling as far as pay grade on the crew. On a recent fire, David laid into him when he hadn't answered a nearby radio despite the voice on the other end squawking for someone to pick it up. When Phillip joined in, Martin's face flushed until his cheeks and chin burned red. He often seemed paralyzed by indecision.

I saw an intelligence in Martin, despite what others said. Our friendship was a refuge for me, a space where I also felt seen as intelligent and interesting. We both shared a penchant for conversational pauses, gathering our thoughts, and must have appeared to be sitting in silence when we were mid-conversation. He always waited for me to speak instead of interrupting; he was the only one who did. Sometimes

I trailed him with his forgotten PPE (personal protective equipment), discreetly handing him a pair of his dropped gloves or forgotten safety glasses. Now that I know I'm autistic, I wonder if he was, too.

My adrenaline crested and fell like waves throughout the day. I got fourth, fifth, and sixth winds. Phillip took advantage of the lengthier Oregon daylight, making sure we got lots of overtime. Near the end of the roll, we were snapping at each other constantly, all of us exhausted from the days made longer since we spent what would usually be our driving time working instead. Phillip continued to pull me off the line so I could write out the timesheets. By now, I dreaded spending time with him. "Girl," he once said, "you look like you're getting skinny." He spoke to me intimately, as if we were close friends. Each time he said *girl* I cringed. The word sounded like an insult. His nickname for me was "Fake Red," because of my dyed hair.

This fire, like the Biscuit Fire, was manned by the National Guard. After burning for many days we worked with military personnel, clearing more fuel breaks, sawing trees and brush, and chaining the stumps, branches, and clumps of brush from hand to hand onto the other side of the fuel break, where we hoped the fire would not burn. Fire dozers were also everywhere: small ones cutting fireline and large ones heaping the flammable materials we'd thrown across the break into piles reaching six feet tall. These piles were commonly slotted for off-season burning, but most of them would be neglected along with the fuel we had thrown across the fuel break, only to increase the power of successive wildfires.

The way we torched the trees and immolated the landscape that may not have burned at all without us—it almost felt like a show of force. The government spent millions of dollars for an increased burn area with a reduced fire mosaic, but there weren't enough funds to properly manage the land after the fire. The money, which could have gone towards prescribed burns and other land management, was now spent, released from the government coffers for the "emergency." Of course, wildfires can be emergencies, but stewarding the land in which they burn could lessen their severity. That simply can't happen without adequate federal funding.

On our last night, day twenty-one, we drove into camp for demobilization; paperwork and processes above my pay grade. We raided the government-funded supply caches, grabbing cases of water bottles and Gatorade, which we carried on our shoulders back to the buggies. Phillip and Owen always reminded us to take as many as would fit into the buggies and Supt. Truck.

Everyone exchanged their dirty Nomex for clean, showering for the first time in three weeks. The shared women's shower stall was all mine, one of the few benefits of being a minority at fire camp. Gingerly I removed my stiff dirty Nomex. I had long ago run out of clean socks and underwear. My wool socks retained the shape of my foot, reinforced by residual salt. Grime lined my hairline. My hair was matted with salt, dirt, and ash.

I stared at my body in the mirror. I saw it as an object—an unruly body, different from the women I saw in magazines, film, and television. I hated the characteristics that marked it as a woman's body. Turning sideways, I pressed the flats of my hands hard against my breasts, imagining myself without them. Free of them. My hands were dark against my pale skin, knuckles creased with black soot. I had no understanding then of how to shift the way I saw and categorized myself.

In the woods, away from everything, there were moments of freedom from my social obligations as *woman*. As *girl*. The men I worked with carved me out, separating me into a divergent category. But I wanted to be of them. Not one of them, but among them and unobserved like I assumed they were. I thought they were free from scrutiny but some of the men must have felt like outsiders, too, especially

Hank, who was teased for being scrawny, or Juan, whose beer belly was constantly pointed out. Not even Phillip was free. I didn't ridicule his size, but most of the guys called him fat and conflated his size with laziness, not taking into account how decades of hotshotting had destroyed his body, just as it would destroy our own bodies, if we stayed long enough.

These nuances escaped me back then. I only looked in the mirror and hated myself for being too big. My belly, one of the only parts of my body mostly free from grime, was soft, pale, lined with stretch marks. Even as a child I had imagined this part of me different than it was. I stared at my blackened legs, their skin fully obscured by layers of sweat-salt, ash, soot, and dirt. Most of the hair on my legs had been rubbed off by my pants. Some would never grow back.

In the shower I let the hot water pummel my face before soaping my body and washing my hair. I was alone for the first time in three weeks, rediscovering my unobserved body. I'd forgotten that I had a body at all, or a self independent from the crew's perceptions of me. With them I was so focused on how I was *supposed* to be, *supposed* to act, that it felt like I was losing any real sense of who I was, or who I wanted to be.

We bedded down in a field at fire camp. An Oregon hotshot crew nearby popped their tents as we laid out our space blankets. I watched them, counting out four women. Maybe five. I had never seen that many women on a hotshot crew, and imagined how my life would be different if I were on that crew. Would I be freer? Surely not, I thought. I had been taught that the presence of women only led to complications, and it would have been too painful to imagine otherwise. Despite my overwhelming loneliness, I didn't try to talk to them.

Chapter Ten

San Francisco

When we arrived home for a precious three days off I drove to San Francisco. The sight of the Golden Gate Bridge recalled a road trip I had taken with my mother when I was ten or eleven. I was hazy with Dramamine and she nudged me awake as we approached the bridge's giant tangerine arches. In San Francisco we ate clam chowder from sourdough bowls and visited Ripley's Believe It or Not. That week was our first vacation. It was one of the only extended periods of time in which I felt close to my mother or saw her happy or free. I felt responsible for her lack of freedom because she said, in her worst moments, that her life would be better without a child holding her back. Years later my mom told me she charged everything to a stolen company credit card—that we needed the temporary escape.

I came back to San Francisco when I was sixteen. It was three years after my mom had married my stepdad, Vern, and one of many times I had run away from home, both before and after their marriage. I wanted to escape them for good, their drinking, fighting, and constant criticism. They told me I ate too much, that I was fat, and installed a lock on the outside of my bedroom door so they could punish me by locking me in.

I started huffing inhalants like paint thinner when I was thirteen, snorting meth at fourteen. Then, at sixteen, I shot up heroin for the first time. When we moved to Olympia in the middle of my sophomore year I found the bad kids and spent a summer selling LSD downtown, on roller skates. People called me Rollergirl, like the character in *Boogie Nights*. I stopped coming home. I wanted to destroy myself.

It was early September, a month after my seventeenth birthday, when I hitchhiked my way down to San Francisco, flitting in and out of truck cabs and passenger seats, sometimes performing sexual favors for money. Somewhere north of San Francisco I got stuck on a low-traffic on-ramp. Night came. After several hours a white man in a gold Cadillac pulled up beside me and offered to take me to San Francisco. I got in. My stomach dropped when he passed the turn for San Francisco and kept going.

I'm not sure exactly where he took me, likely somewhere in Sonoma County, or how long he kept me there. There were kids around—all younger than me. After a while he stuck me in a dirty trailer far from his house. There was no food, but there were several plastic jugs of water, and a little pitbull puppy. The dog's owner, a guy with a mullet and a Trans-Am, showed up a couple days later and asked me what the hell I was doing in his trailer. I told him everything and begged him to take me to San Francisco. He would only take me to an on-ramp. I kept looking out the back window for the gold Cadillac. I could tell he was paranoid, too.

I got picked up by a white-haired man in a light brown van with a miniature pony in the back. He bought me McDonald's and dropped me off in the city. His kindness saved me from believing the entire world was an evil place.

During that time in Sonoma I once asked the man when I could go to San Francisco. We were at a gas station. "You think you can't leave?" he snarled. "Just go." But I was paralyzed. That's what I remember most clearly, more than him raping me, though I know that happened, too. Him telling me I could leave. The paralysis. My shame.

In San Francisco I slept on the streets until I met a couple guys who offered to take me to the farm they lived on in Mendocino County. We all hitchhiked there together.

All these memories trailed me as I walked through the city, down to Fisherman's Wharf and to the Haight, where the guy with the pony in his van had dropped me off. I remembered peering into the restaurants filled with patrons in fancy clothes and feeling as if they lived in a world totally inaccessible to me. Hunger gnawed at my insides, but I never considered going back home. It wasn't until I'd been on the farm a few months that I called my mom collect. She begged me for the farm's address, and sent me a letter promising she would go to therapy, that I could get emancipated. She apologized for how she treated me as a child. *I taught you not to trust.* I still have the letter, one of the few remnants of my childhood. I believed her, so I went back. Nothing changed.

Now I was here in the city with more money in my bank account than I knew what to do with. I could eat anywhere I wanted, but I got clam chowder in a sourdough bowl, like my mom and I had done. I drove back home, where we were once again called to a fire.

Chapter Eleven

McNally

From mid-July to late August we were spiked out on the McNally fire, which eventually burned over 150,000 acres in the Sequoia National Forest. Near the end of our first couple weeks, my grandfather died, so I went home briefly for his funeral. When I came back the crew was on mandatory days off, and Eric and Kieran threw a party at Jason's house. For most of the party I chain-smoked cigarettes with Adam, Max's younger brother. We stood together on the back porch. After a while he kissed me. I pulled away immediately, shocked at the kiss itself but also at how much I wanted to kiss him back.

"I don't understand why you're with Colin," he said, lighting another cigarette. "He's such an asshole."

He hated Colin? This stunned me. I thought everyone liked him. Apparently, some of the guys thought he was an asshole, like I sometimes did. I wished I had known that earlier.

By the end of the night everyone knew Colin and I were together because I got so drunk that he had to carry me to his Jeep. We spent the night in a hotel. I told Colin he could have left me at Jason's; I would have slept on the couch or floor rather than exposing myself to scrutiny. He didn't understand. "It's not a big deal," he said. And

it wasn't—not to him. But it was to me. And things did change
after that.

After mandatory days off the crew got sent back to the McNally. Jonah
didn't come with us. He had quit. I was devastated. His replacement
was a guy in his forties named Howard, who briefly worked on the
crew the year before. Colin said he was an old hippie, that we would
get along. When I complained about losing Jonah, he told me to be
positive. I was too negative all the time, he said. So, I tried to remain
hopeful.

We spent half of our first days back at a helicopter base. All federal
land management agencies are designated a select number of helicopters for search and rescue and wildland fire. During fire season they're
either kept on their home base or stationed at makeshift helibases
depending on fire locations. Helicopters are assigned helitack crews
for loading, unloading, and maintenance. The Kernville helitack crew
divvied us into groups dictated by the weight of our bodies and gear,
calibrated for safe flying. We separated all of our tools, Dolmars (a type
of gas can), MSR canisters, line packs, and red bags into groups, along
with boxes of MREs, cubees, bath-in-a-bag, and extra sleeping bags
for the colder high elevation nights. I gathered my squad's tools and
secured their sharp edges with fiber tape before taping them together
in groups of five. As we donned our safety gear and pulled down the
chin straps of our hard hats for flight, a timid helitacker read the flight
rules from a laminated card while nearly blinding us with his pristine
yellow Nomex shirt. I heard one of the guys whisper "helislacker" and
the card started trembling. I felt bad for him.

When my group loaded we saddled ourselves up with gear and
crouch-walked under the rotors before handing everything to a crew
member and climbing up into our seats. The helicopter lurched
upwards until I saw the giant gray-and-white fire column in the distance. Many of the mountain peaks were topped with boulders. Some

still had remnants of winter snow. I closed my eyes, surrendering to the shuddering of the helicopter. In the buggies I was always overcome with a nervous, hesitant energy when we neared fires, but that was never the case with helicopters. Flying out into the backcountry calmed me. No cell service. No contact with the outside world at all. I loved it.

Finally the helicopter hovered and with increased shuddering lowered into a marshy meadow ringed by forest. We unloaded, then stood with our supplies as Owen scouted out a good camping spot. There was one more load coming—arriving by helicopter was a slow process. We got to set up our tents, and I crawled inside mine, pulled off my pants, and lay on my sleeping bag. No one could see me. The day was more than halfway over, and I knew we wouldn't do any work in the few hours before dark, so I briefly reveled in my solitude, grateful to be back out in the field.

Someone must have been sick at the party because by our second day back on the fire everyone was plagued with stuffy sinuses and sore throats, all of us coughing all over each other. Owen's "wakey wakey" was punctuated with coughing and moaning. Daniel started counting down the days, starting with "Twenty-one and a wake-up," until we could go home again. This was the only thing differentiating one day from another. It was August. The thought of the season's end kept us going like a distant, bright beacon.

Howard wasn't worn down by the fire season like we were. He was fresh and full of energy. But I quickly realized that he didn't respect me. He spoke to me in a singsongy voice, as if I were a child. Everything I did, he corrected. I carried my tool wrong—I should wrap my thumb around the handle rather than grasp it with my whole hand. He adjusted the straps on my line pack, so it was less comfortable, and then got upset when I readjusted them. For Jason, Daniel, Max, and Gunnar, Howard had no feedback, no matter what they did. I never pointed out this incongruence, but it grated at me. I stopped respecting Howard as an authority. He constantly deferred to Jason but got angry with us when we began treating Jason like the de facto squad boss. When Howard was off scouting, the guys would rant about how untrustworthy he was, how incompetent. I kept my mouth shut. No one on my squad felt trustworthy anymore now that Jonah was gone.

Howard hiked fast, as if he were trying to prove himself. He liked making little switchbacks as we trudged uphill. Daniel and Jason soon started breaking off from him and hiking straight up, like we had always done. It was more taxing, but faster. Max and Gunnar followed, but I stayed behind Howard until one day I finally broke off to make my own path. When everyone crested the ridge Howard told me the crew would be better off without me. "You're not strong enough," he said, in front of everyone. I stayed silent. So did everyone else. On our next hike he hiked so fast that Max and I both fell out. Even Jason slowed, hindered by the weight of his chainsaw. But I knew it didn't matter what the guys did. Howard wanted to see me fail.

About a week into our second roll, A-Mod came together to conduct a burn, led by Howard. This was a test of his competence. Howard was terrible at reading maps and often got lost, but usually Jason was there to reorient him. On this day Howard hiked ahead with his torch, ignorant of the larger shape of the burn. He got separated from our group. Jason took charge and found Nickolas and a squad from B-Mod. Howard's tinny voice crackled over the radios, high-pitched and fearful. "There's fire all around me," he said. Everyone was making fun of him; even Phillip's voice, when it came over the radio, sounded on the edge of laughter. I knew how the fire had been burning—there wasn't enough accumulated fuel, wind, or extreme topography for things to get too hairy—but Howard didn't know the terrain like we did. When we finally found him he was wide-eyed like a child, his face blackened with soot. He became the butt of every joke. Howard had broken the cardinal rule of hotshotting: Don't show fear. He stopped picking on me. As precarious as my position felt on the crew, Howard was now on the bottom. I knew how it felt, so I tried to be nice to him when I could.

Whenever the sawyers got tired I always volunteered to run a chainsaw, donning a pair of Kevlar chaps. Daniel gave me pointers and I learned to hold the saw with straight arms, leveraging its weight to conserve my energy. It vibrated so hard my fingers went numb. I sunk the saw into logs, pressing the bar down into the wood as sawdust scattered around my feet. I'd watched the sawyers fell many trees; it was satisfying when they let me take down the smallest ones. Working with the sawyers fostered a much-needed sense of camaraderie. Things were easier when I was a pupil, looking to them for guidance. Soon enough I started looking at every tree and assessing its lean, branch weight, and surrounding obstacles. At night I'd wake up, my forearms cramping until I massaged the muscles. I started wanting to be a sawyer, but sawyers had to hike with their saw. Whenever I did this it slowed me down too much.

Phillip had decided I should have a radio, and Nickolas showed me how to program all the channels using the tip of a pen. I'd resisted. I didn't want the responsibility, and I didn't trust most of the guys I worked with to listen to me, but Nickolas promised I wouldn't have to tell anyone what to do. It was the only way I'd take the radio. A few days after that, Owen recruited me for a two-person burning operation. The radio came in handy because we sometimes separated and laid down fire adjacent to one another, both following the red lines drawn on photocopied topographic maps. I liked talking to him on our own personal channel, where no one else could hear us, and I cherished the days I got to burn. We hiked with full Dolmars of fuel, sometimes burning for a solid ten to twelve hours. With the torch in my hand, I navigated fallen trees, branches, and brush, climbing over and through them leaving trails of fire. Spiderwebs clung to my face and clothes. I tried to spare flowers and berries, but knew they'd burn, too. On those days, my mind was completely clear.

The Sequoia National Forest, southwest of the Inyo, curls around the western side of Sequoia and Kings Canyon National Parks. The land we hiked was steep in some areas, and meanderingly hilly in others, with some plateaus. There were giant sequoias, sugar pines, and ponderosas, and the pine needles had spread themselves on the forest floor like a carpet. They draped bushes and shrubs. Sugar pines have especially long needles, five to a bunch and all held together tightly so they catch on branches of other plants, where they cure in the sun. Pine trees, along with sequoias, are fire-adapted, and this is one of many adaptations that encourages undergrowth fire, which in turn allows the serotinous cones of the trees to release their seeds.

There was a clear demarcation between lands that had burned consistently at a low severity, usually near ridges where lightning-ignited fires frequently backed slowly downhill, and those that had gone too long without fire. The former's widely spaced trees allowed sunlight to shine through the canopy, warming the forest floor, as opposed to the overcrowded forests with dense, shadowy understories. There, our boots crushed layers of dry sticks, leaves, and needles, and the trees were skinny and colorless. There was too much competition for them to grow tall and healthy. We meandered through designated wilderness areas belonging to the Forest Service and Park Service. In wilderness areas we only used chainsaws if it was absolutely necessary—anything powered by fuel was either discouraged or disallowed. On Park Service land, the method of firefighting was completely different. National Parks function differently than lands owned by the Forest Service, due to a quiet revolution within the National Park system that occurred about forty years before.

In 1962, A. Starker Leopold became chairman of the Special Advisory Board on Wildlife Management. Several national parks were being overgrazed by elk. In what's now referred to simply as "The Leopold Report," the 1963 advisory board demanded a rethinking of Park policy, which had previously prioritized the public's enjoyment rather than environmental sustainability and health. One of the most important aspects of the report was its claim that fire must be reintroduced into National Parks in order to recreate "vignettes of primitive America." Native species also needed rehabilitating. The report was optimistic but firm, and significant for the NPS and USFS, although many of its recommendations have been ignored by the latter (and in some cases, the former).

By then, fire suppression had been the norm for well over fifty years. Entire generations had lived without the presence of wildfire or prescribed fire. In the early 1900s, there was ample science indicating that fire was ecologically necessary for western ecosystems to thrive. Along with scientists, some ranchers and foresters advocated for what they called "light burning" to increase forest health and replenish grasses for grazing animals. Much of this science was suppressed by both the Forest Service and the timber industry, as detailed by Stephen Pyne and other fire historians. The Forest Service built its platform on fire suppression, leveraging public fear. Without fire suppression, they argued, there would be a "timber famine." During World War II, when Japanese submarines fired incendiary shells close to the Los Padres National Forest, fear was stoked about forests being more vulnerable to fire, especially because the draft had created a shortage of firefighters. This ignited a fearful media narrative. In response to the attack, Japanese Americans were villainized and targeted. Many were sent to internment camps. In 1943 the United States Forest Service created a racist fire prevention campaign, leveraging fear to further the full-suppression narrative. Slogans like "Forest Defense Is National Defense" and "Our Carelessness, Their Secret Weapon" were imprinted on posters with images of men in overalls digging fireline in a burning forest, or, in the case of the latter, a grotesque illustration of Hideki Tojo and Hitler leering above a burning forest.

Soon after, Disney loaned Bambi to the USFS for their fire prevention campaign. The film *Bambi* had included a forest fire, and these images were a good match for the campaign, but the rights belonged to Disney. The agency needed something more permanent. Much of the workforce was fighting the war overseas, and the USDA was more worried about fires on its public lands and the lack of resources to fight them. If they educated the public on the dangers of wildfires, wouldn't that do some of the job for them? Another plush forest animal would surely convince people that fire suppression was necessary.

The first ad featuring Smokey Bear was designed by Albert Staehle, a well-known illustrator at the time. Smokey appears as a burly bear with shiny brown fur, wearing a wide-brimmed forest ranger hat and long rolled-hem jeans held up by a thin leather belt. He pours a bucket of water on a small campfire. The caption reads: "Smokey says—care will prevent 9 out of 10 forest fires!"

In the 1950s the ads became more sophisticated and included radio spots with "Smokey" having conversations with Bing Crosby and Roy Rogers. They preached keeping wildlands pristine, and keeping the lands "like old times" when buffalo roamed. At the beginning of the decade the "real Smokey'" had been found—a bear cub rescued by the Taos Pueblo Snowball Crew on the Capitan Gap Fire in New Mexico (by then the Bureau of Indian Affairs was managing its own fire crews, and there were several crews composed of Native Americans, particularly in the Southwest United States). The bear's paws and rear were singed by the fire. This cub further solidified the archetype of Smokey, cementing the public's idea of forest fires as a solely destructive force.

In 1968 Rod Serling, still at the height of his fame after creating and appearing in the uncanny series *The Twilight Zone*, starred in a television ad, where he was depicted driving in a station wagon with his family. He's smoking a cigarette, and when he tosses it out his window the motion in the ad is paused for dramatic effect. The cigarette lands in a pile of dry grass and the scene cuts to several trees engulfed in flame. Rod, now back at home, picks up a newspaper whose front page reads: "Forest Fire Still Out of Control." He shakes his head in consternation. Then he shifts from actor to spokesperson, now standing in front of the camera to educate his audience about the dangers of wildfires. "Anyone who handles fire, in any form, is a potential killer," he says ominously. The camera pans to a poster of Smokey stapled to a tree. "Only you can prevent forest fires," he says, echoing the words written on the poster. An icon was born.

A new television ad follows a year later. Called "Bomb in the Forest," the ad depicts a repeating image of the atom bomb exploding. The explosion repeats seven times, and the voiceover claims that "We destroyed ten-thousand-square miles of America last year. That's more land than ninety hydrogen bombs would destroy." With each explosion, a bell tolls. In each ad, wildfire was depicted only as a destructive force—as destructive as the most destructive bomb on earth.

A. Starker Leopold knew that this kind of all-or-nothing messaging did more harm than good, and the reintroduction of fire he sought included both natural (lightning-started) and man-made. After the Leopold Report, fire was reintroduced on Park Service land. But the anti-fire campaigns continued into the 1980s.

In October 2022, a Forest Service burn boss in Oregon was arrested after his approved prescribed burn in the Malheur National Forest escaped its bounds and encroached on private lands. The landowners called 911, and the sheriff concluded that the burn was inappropriate given the weather conditions. The escaped fire didn't damage any property, but the landowners expressed dismay that any of their land had burned at all. The burn boss was criminally charged with reckless burning, but the charges were dropped in June 2024.

Neither the Park nor Forest Service has learned how to gracefully navigate the inevitable escaped burn without retreating into full suppression, though the Park Service is improving. Nor is there consensus about fire suppression at the agency or governmental level. National Park officials continue to advocate for prescribed burning, including those at Sequoia National Park. Sequoias are fire-adapted: As mentioned earlier, they lack lower branches, which prevents fire from climbing their trunks, and their thick bark protects them from flames and heat. Over the past decade, fire suppression has weakened these trees and their habitats; now, with climate change, normally fire-resistant sequoias and redwoods are more vulnerable to fire. Excess undergrowth, which accumulates in the absence of regular, low-severity fire, diverts essential water and nutrients from the trees while also acting as ladder fuels, carrying fire into the canopy. Sequoias are adapted to release moisture through their leaves in the presence of fire, but that defense mechanism fails without adequate water. Since 2015, up to 20 percent of remaining giant sequoias have died in fires. These deaths are directly correlated with high-severity fires. Recently firefighters have begun wrapping trees in the same material used for fire shelters to protect them, but this isn't a sustainable practice.

Although Sequoia National Park is one of the leading advocates for prescribed burning, the risks, regulations, and constant lack of funding inhibit the practice. Funds are continually funneled into fire suppression rather than prescribed fire. Because Sequoia National Forest burns less often, fires that do develop can amass greater strength and slop over onto Park Service land. And once a fire is big enough, there's not much anyone can do to stop it.

Eventually the McNally Fire burned more than 150,000 acres, requiring over fifty-three million dollars in suppression efforts. Months after the burn, in November 2002, heavy rains flooded the area. Charred soils, decimated by high-severity fire, had turned hydrophobic, nearly incapable of absorbing water. Landslides damaged local watersheds whose restoration consumed an additional three million. It was the largest California fire of the 2002 season, and at the time was one of California's twenty largest wildfires in history. As I write this, the impact of climate change and lack of advancement in fire suppression policy have come home in the form of ever-more-extreme fire seasons. Half of California's twenty largest historical wildfires have occurred since 2020.

Chapter Twelve

Yosemite

In the last week of our season we were called to a small fire in Yosemite, an iconic national park. When John Muir beheld Yosemite's grandeur, he saw a miracle of nature. He called California the "Pacific land of flowers," and said Yosemite was "the absolute manifestation of the divine." But its lasting aura of wilderness now belied an increasingly stagnant ecosystem. The whole European concept of wilderness was counter to what formed the land Muir first encountered—they understood wilderness as separate from human civilization. What Muir saw as divine was, as M. Kat Anderson writes, "really the fertile seed, bulb, and greens gathering ground of the Miwok and Yokuts Indians, kept open and productive by centuries of carefully planned Indigenous burning, harvesting, and seed scattering." The Ahwanechee, too, tended Muir's Eden. The "inviting openness" that Muir remarked upon has long been destroyed by logging and subsequent fire suppression, resulting in a crowded canopy.

Yosemite, unlike many national forests, encourages fire, letting it burn if the weather conditions are mild. We flew by helicopter into the heart of the park, where a passing lightning storm had ignited several small and slow-burning lightning fires. After landing Owen led us through a section of wilderness commonly off-limits to most park visitors. The dogwoods, clad in their autumn foliage, danced beneath the forest canopy. Martin, always clumsy, dropped a red plastic Dolmar of gasoline into a stream, and a petroleum rainbow bloomed into a serrated circle. A replacement hire, Ray, and I watched the rainbow lengthen downstream like multicolored threads unspooling. Ray rolled his eyes. "No big deal," he said. "Not like this is a precious and protected ecosystem."

The undergrowth was thick, layers of leaves and needles all in differing stages of decay. Some of the leaves were skeletal, their formerly sturdy bodies now worn and transparent; their veins, which had once carried water, dry and stiff. I carefully placed one in the crease of my small pocket notebook. Everything surrounding us was hushed and cool, and we worked quietly in a haphazard grid formation slowly extinguishing disparate patches of fire.

I felt lucky to be in Yosemite, on an untrailed path, where people never walked anymore. I couldn't stop myself from gazing upwards and marveling at the canopy, a mix of lodgepole pine, hemlock, and canyon live oak. At the beginning of the season they'd all been unfamiliar, but now I looked at each of them and imagined the way I'd cut them as a sawyer. I imagined them toppling. The way I inhabited the space of forests and landscapes had changed from when I was on the contract crew—back then I had imagined how the land would burn. Now I saw the ways in which I could transform the landscape. Which trees needed falling, which bushes were overcrowding the forest floor. This was partially destructive but mostly intuitive—not all landscapes need a spaced-apart canopy to remain healthy, but without realizing it, I could now spot the ways some landscapes needed help.

John Muir thought wilderness needed to be protected from humans. This instinct makes sense in historical context: Lands east of the Mississippi had once been an almost unbroken expanse of forest, containing four-fifths of the estimated 850 million acres of forest that once covered the entire contiguous United States, before logging and colonization more than halved that number. But Muir's focus was on protecting lands to be enjoyed separately from civilized life. This further displaced the land's caretakers.

One of the first white settlers to set eyes on the Yosemite Valley, Lafayette Bunnell, described its "light as gossamer" haze, which "increased the awe with which I beheld it . . . a peculiar exalted sensation seemed to fill my whole being, and I found my eyes in tears with emotion." But he was not there to admire the scenery. Bunnell came to Yosemite with the Mariposa Battalion, to battle the Ahwanechee, who were forcefully removed from their homelands after a fierce battle.

In 1864, Lincoln signed a bill declaring the protection of Mariposa Grove and Yosemite Valley. From then on, these lands were only to be enjoyed by the public. The bill moderated damage inflicted by miners, loggers, and settlers, but it also categorically prohibited inhabitation by anyone, including the tribes who had lived there for thousands of years. Thus began the ecological decline.

Twenty-six years later, in 1890, Muir took Theodore Roosevelt on a backpacking trip through the Sierras. Muir and Roosevelt, along with Gifford Pinchot, had an enormous impact on land policy in the United States. Roosevelt would later assign Pinchot, the son of a timber baron and graduate of the Yale School of Forestry, as the first chief of the U.S. Forest Service. The three were friends. Muir and Pinchot both commodified forests: While Muir's focus was conservation for touristic enjoyment, Pinchot's conception of conservation was linked to the monetary value of trees in board feet. Both Pinchot and Muir exerted great influence on Roosevelt, who established 230 million acres of public lands while he was president. Shortly after Muir and Roosevelt visited the Sierras, Congress named Sequoia and Yosemite the second and third National Parks, after Yellowstone. Although the West contained less forested land than the East, this decision was one of many that ultimately resulted in unnatural encroachment of trees and forests. By this time Indigenous Californians were in the later stages of separation from their lands. The Ahwanechee and Miwok, like so many other groups of Indigenous Californians, couldn't make clothes, basketry, weapons, or tools for hunting and fishing. They were dependent on the rare generosity of whites for their survival and basic needs.

After being declared a national park, Yosemite suffered. Pests flourished. Brush, grasses, and tubers grew unchecked. The park began calling meadows and small lakes "transitional" as they shrunk in size and sometimes disappeared into forested land. Dead litter accumulated, year after year. Without fire, white firs took root on the forest floor, creating ladders for fires to climb. Now, over 130 years later, you can compare pictures of the famous Yosemite Valley. One hundred years ago, there were only hints of future tree overcrowding, with ample open space. Since then, the valley's tree population has increased substantially while grasslands and meadows have continually decreased. Dense canopies allow less sunlight to foster native grass and shrub growth. While thinning the forest could help, it cannot replace the regular presence of fire. Thinning increases sunlight on the forest floor, encouraging the growth of small trees and brush. If these don't burn, they will carry fire up into the canopy. In this particular ecosystem, the two must be implemented in tandem for the best results.

Currently several tribal groups, including the Ahwanechee, Miwok, Nüümü (Paiute), and North Fork Rancheria of Mono Indians, have been advocating for a return to cultural burning in Yosemite and its surrounding forests. The American Indian Council of Mariposa County (AICMC) and Yosemite National Park are collaborating to restore Mariposa Grove by reintroducing cultural burning practices. Yosemite is also working with tribes to develop a Traditional Ecological Knowledge (TEK) program, which incorporates land-tending practices, including fire. But these projects face barriers like fear of liability, lack of funding, and, ironically, the Clean Air Act, which imposes strict regulations on human-set fires that do not apply to wild-fire, despite no real difference in the fires themselves. These groups need federal funding and policy workarounds, but they also deserve respect and autonomy. Funding should not come with strings attached, specifically when it comes to tribal projects.

About 110 years after John Muir and Teddy Roosevelt transformed Yosemite, the soil was carpeted in dense layers of dead leaves and needles exhaling tendrils of white smoke, signaling the presence of orange heat smoldering its way through the duff. Some of us removed our gloves so we could discern the burn's edges, where we separated the burned from unburned. With my bare fingers, I sifted through layers of dead matter accumulated through years of fire suppression. There was no emergency here, only tiny flames cleansing the forest floor, consuming dead matter, regulating harmful pests, and facilitating new growth.

This place hadn't burned for a long time.

PART II

SECOND SEASON
(2003)

Chapter One

Winter

Colin and I had spent part of the winter together, meeting each other's families and traveling to Central America with his brother. The trip was a disaster. After discovering that his brother didn't want me there, I came home early, seeking refuge in my teenage bedroom.

My mom and Vern still fought, but their thriving project management business kept them occupied. Still, there were remnants of our past conflicts: my bedroom door's missing doorknob; the lock on the bedroom window to keep me from climbing out. Huddled in my old bedroom, made cavelike by the dark winter, I watched *Twin Peaks* for the first time. (Those beautiful women, the men who dominated them.) Colin and I were still together. It was impossible for me to admit that our relationship wasn't working. Breaking up with him, I thought, would only prove that I wasn't worthy of a long-term relationship. And my mother treated him like a prize I had won. I agonized over these things, wandering into the kitchen several times each day to gather food, which I ate and threw up silently in my old bathroom, same as when I was a teenager. It was like no time had passed.

Many dark afternoons I walked down the main road all the way to Logan's house, where I was raped during a party my sophomore year, only a month or so after we moved to Olympia. I'd had way too much to drink, and Logan had helped me to his bedroom, where he said I'd be safe. He'd left a bucket nearby after I threw up. I remember the ceiling spinning hypnotically. The door was slightly ajar. A sliver of gold light from his hallway expanded each time someone entered, and each time someone entered they approached the bed, first whispering to me, asking me things, then crawling, assuring me it was okay when I protested. The light expanded. Compressed. One after another they entered, until the light was obscured by my classmates, watching.

Here is Laura Palmer pleading with James Hurley to leave her at the stop light. There is my naked body, foreign hands touching it, voices saying *it's okay it's okay.* My limbs someone else's limbs. My disembodied voice pleading, please, it hurts, stop. Here is Dale Cooper at the diner, enjoying his pie. The fan spins above Laura Palmer's bed. Her torn journal. A white horse.

I became a myth. A pariah. Whispers trailing me down the hallways. *Slut. Whore.* The girls were the worst: glaring, laughing, and pointing. Yelling from their car windows as I walked home. I blamed myself. I didn't call it rape. I gave my body more freely, no longer my body.

After several weeks in my cocoon, my mom came and sat on my bed. "Are you okay?" she asked. I held the covers to my chin like a child. Dishes were stacked messily on the nightstand, topped with crumpled food wrappers. I wanted to tell her that I was not okay. I wanted her to wrap me in her arms, to send me away for a cure. But I nodded my head. Long ago we shared everything. I comforted her and, in her softer moments, she comforted me. But she had sharpened my secrets like weapons. *That's why you don't have any friends,* she'd say, if I did something wrong, or *You're the worst kid in the world. If you stopped eating so much you wouldn't get so fat. If you weren't so selfish maybe things wouldn't be so hard for you.*

I wanted to share myself with my mother, but it was her or me, and I had to choose myself.

Chapter Two

Slow Start

C olin and I had both accepted permanent positions with the crew; he was promoted to lead firefighter and switched to B-Mod, while I was still on A-Mod. A permanent position came with status, but also health insurance and a federal retirement plan. Adam, Max, Kieran, and Nickolas were all gone—I still saw Nickolas often because his wife Helen and I had become friends. Kieran was now working on a different hotshot crew, not far from us. Hank was gone, too. He had died of alcohol poisoning in mid-winter. We were all still reeling from the loss, but especially Kieran and Eric, who had found him in the morning after a house party.

Half of A-Mod was new, but I liked almost everyone, including my squad boss, a veteran who'd transferred over from another hotshot crew up north. Now I was one of the youngest. Almost everyone else was twenty-three or older. Gunnar was still on A-Mod, unfortunately, but I was excited that Martin had been moved into our module. Juan had replaced Nickolas as B-Mod captain. And there was a new woman: Chloe, a former USC lacrosse player from San Francisco. She was one of the fastest hikers on the crew, stronger than most of the guys, silencing any talk of women being weaker than men. I was much stronger than the year before, always in the middle on PT hikes and happy to do push-ups and pull-ups.

My permanent position on the crew didn't lend me authority, as I had thought it might have; it only put me under a more exacting microscope. Phillip enrolled me in a bunch of pre-season classes, including advanced chainsaw operation, fireline leadership, and incident commander training. He gave me a squad boss training booklet. That was the direction I was headed. I knew I could be a good leader, but once I started wearing a radio some of the guys treated me differently. Juan and Owen were fierce advocates for my training. Owen gave me a talk about how to lead a squad, but I mistrusted his rigid leadership style.

During the beginning of the season, when there were no fire calls, our crew spent a couple weeks in the foothills, thinning out dense oak and manzanita. I ran a chainsaw like everyone else but also began directing A-Mod, carrying down orders from Owen. It wasn't complicated stuff: What to cut and where to cut it. Half the guys on my Mod resisted my authority, especially Gunnar, but also Eric, and Corey: A big guy who never spoke to me unless it was absolutely necessary. They rolled their eyes and snickered. At one point Gunnar puffed out his chest and asked me what would happen if he didn't listen. I froze and gave up. Owen told me to assert myself, that it didn't matter what they thought of me, but their hostility was like a brick wall. It scared me.

Martin was no help, either. Our conversations had become critical workshops where he deconstructed my habits, work ethic, physical appearance, fitness, and demeanor. He compared me to Chloe, who was more reserved than I was, and more athletic. I was receptive to criticism in the name of self-improvement, but he also pronounced me a heathen and said I was going to hell because I wasn't Christian. I asked him how he could say that when he knew me so well, and he shrugged. "You just are," he said. "You can't go to heaven if you haven't accepted Jesus into your heart." I tried not to take it personally. I needed him as an ally. But I couldn't help but notice that his sudden vigilance about my conduct and worth coincided with me getting a radio.

This time on base wore away any remaining adhesive bonding Colin and me together. I had gotten two DUIs in New York and the state of California suspended my license, so now I had to rely on him for rides. Colin wanted to camp all summer to save money, but I insisted on a little studio apartment in a larger town about an hour's drive away—we couldn't afford to live closer. He blamed me for forcing him to endure what he called "city life." We spent our long drives to and from base not speaking, listening to his reggae music. I couldn't PT after work anymore. Some evenings I lounged at the small pool in our complex, sitting in my swimsuit, occasionally swimming and reading. I was lonelier than I'd ever been on my own. On our long drives I watched for hawks perched atop telephone poles, scanning the tall yellow grass for prey. I glimpsed our neighbors; a man with his adult child, who had Down syndrome, brushing her hair in their darkened doorway; a woman my age doing a home workout. Everything seethed with loneliness.

When I rejected sex Colin pouted, criticized me, and gave me the silent treatment. I always relented and blamed myself for lacking desire. His silence, suffused with tension, was more painful than just letting him have my body, although sleeping with him only gave me a couple days of peace. At least I knew where I stood with him, I thought, and told myself I was lucky he didn't hit me or yell at me. I was the one who was too emotional, melting down at the relentless criticism. This made it easy for both of us to see me as the problem.

I knew that staying with him meant marriage and kids, fulfilling my purpose according to the mainstream cultural narrative. But the closer I came to that life, the less I wanted it. I started to dream of my own plot of land surrounded by a garden and bleating animals. Writing in my journal whenever I wanted, beholden to no one.

Chapter Three

Hoteled Up

It must have been late June when we were "hoteled up" in Southern California and given per diem so we could buy our own dinners. Most of us ate at chain restaurants like Outback and Applebee's. Martin saved his per diem and bought the cheapest food at the grocery store. When I asked him about this we began talking about my own finances, which were a mess. Poverty was my baseline and anything extra was, well, extra.

"You need to save money," Martin told me. We were hooched up on a mountainside near San Bernardino. He smelled of sour sweat and I wondered when he had last showered. Martin said my money should go into my new USFS IRA. My mistake, he said, was putting too much of my paycheck into savings, not leaving myself enough to spend. I was used to dipping into my savings regularly. It was good advice, but I didn't listen. My mother had always maxed out her credit cards. To me money was mysterious, a finite resource over which I had limited control.

During the previous year I'd learned to cut down straightforward small trees and spent time cutting brush, but I was only a level A sawyer. There are three levels: A, B, and C. Squad bosses need their saw level B certification. Chainsaw work on hotshot crews can get complicated—often it involves cutting down midsized or large trees in various stages of burning. Fire can completely hollow out a tree, creating what the guys called a cat face. Cat-faced trees lack a center and can fall unpredictably, so it's better to take them down than risk someone being crushed.

Before a sawyer fells a tree, they must assess branch weight, which direction the tree leans, and which portions of the remaining trunk to cut so the tree falls predictably. This must be learned through practice, and cutting down a burned or smoldering tree is much more complicated than a healthy one, especially because the burned ground surrounding the tree lacks stability and is sometimes hot.

On a slow day of gridding Juan found the perfect practice tree: a giant, unburned oak whose width was way beyond my expertise. Several of the guys gathered to watch. I strapped on some chaps and started the saw, positioning the bar diagonally along the trunk before revving the engine, cutting downwards and sawing my top cut. I paused to reassess the direction. The guys were all gathered around and staring at me. I felt an intense amount of pressure to fall the tree perfectly. I checked with Juan, who nodded, his face impassive.

I cut straight through until I could push the giant crescent of wood out. "Good job," Juan told me. I knew it was good, but my nervousness was like an internal earthquake as I circled to the back of the tree for my back cut. The tree could fall at any moment. Once I started cutting I could see the cut opening as the tree leaned more and more, until my cut widened and the tree's center cracked. I ran diagonally away as it crashed, landing exactly as predicted. Juan and I looked at the cuts. I was proud of myself. He patted me on the back, smiling. In that moment, I imagined being a squad boss, or a captain. I felt like a real hotshot. It all felt possible.

*   *   *

I shared a room with Chloe but I rarely saw her because her friends lived nearby. Sometimes she came out with me. Despite not having much in common I liked hanging out with her. She was proudly gay. I knew I was bisexual and had many queer friends, but none like her. Her language was littered with big words and theoretical concepts. It was intimidating. It felt like she thought I was stupid, or uneducated. She talked about trans rights and the queer community, naming people like Adrienne Rich, bell hooks, and Foucault. I didn't understand back then how someone with access to education can take it for granted, assuming a shared language.

Chloe's features could read masculine; I envied her flat chest. Her first time in public wearing her hotshot uniform, she was delighted when a male gas station attendant called her "sir." Although I'd experienced the exhilaration of the hotshot uniform's power to alter my status the year before, my body marked me as feminine; there was no escaping it. Men looked at me and I was impaled by their gazes. The weight of their assessment. Their gazes constructed my value, just as they had constructed my mother's.

During my first year on the crew we spent almost all season in the field; rarely in hotels. On our rare days off I was usually with Colin, aside from a few crew parties. Now, most nights I went to Margaritaville, which was next door to our hotel, and drank. The bar was another dimension, far from the hot, burned ground we traversed all day. I disappeared in its dark corners, distorted by its neon pink and green strobe lights. I loved the way alcohol felt but hated myself when I drank too much, which was often. At the bar I let the moist condensation melt into my hands and savored the sharp taste of alcohol; the soft, loose feeling trailing through my body, easing my anxiety. I wore no makeup and often arrived with wet hair from the shower. The guys were always talking shit about girls and their makeup. I didn't want them to think I was trying to look good for anyone, especially them. I still sought their approval, tracking the bar and clocking who noticed me and for how long. The attention was more valuable to me without makeup. I looked down on those girls, too, and saw myself in opposition to them.

Nights usually devolved into shots. Colin and I were still together but he rarely showed. Without our secret hotel rooms and time alone I was adrift, stumbling back to the hotel, trying not to wake Chloe. One night Juan and I stopped near some bushes bordering a parking lot and kissed. I barely remember it. Sometimes I drunk-texted Colin: *I miss you.* I always regretted it the next morning. Training as a squad boss left me feeling unsure of my place in the world. I knew some of the guys were waiting for me to fail, but instead of spurring me forward, as it had the year before, I awaited my failure, too. It didn't help that Gunnar and Corey both refused to listen to me, constantly snickering behind my back, sometimes boldly glaring as I gave orders. There was no winning: I was either a bitch or a pushover, with no in-between.

Many of those nights are blank in my memory—I would black out after just a few drinks, a sign of progressive alcoholism. The previous season had kept us out of civilization, sheltering me from this part of myself, but now I was exposed, and lost.

Chapter Four

Slopover

Watch out situation number 8:
constructing line without a safe anchor point

One morning we were shuttled by helicopter to a ridgetop. The main fire was roaring up a canyon, spitting flaming debris into the little eddies of air curling upwards in puffs and tendrils of smoke and heat, threatening to slop over a previously constructed fireline. We needed to catch it before any firebrands floated over the ridge. If the fire twinned itself in the canyon bottom, it would sprint up the next ridge and we would lose it for good. The midday weather was scorching and dry. I questioned why we were going in at all, with no structures or people in immediate danger.

I was in the second load out. Owen shouted for us to unload fast onto a flat, narrow ridgetop less than a hundred feet wide. The fire was devouring oak and chaparral like a last meal. We tumbled out of the helicopter, crouching down and then running towards the other side of the fireline, squeezing our eyes tight against the dust and crispy flaming oak leaves swirling up with the thundering rotor wash and landing across the line in the green. We rushed downhill and began digging a deep trench in an arc down the hill to catch any falling debris. We dug frantically, all of us alternating between the trench and stepping away to extinguish the smaller fires popping up around us. For the first time my fear overtook me, my adrenaline surging until the world looked like I was viewing it through a pinhole.

When the helicopter returned with its third load I glanced up to see more embers and burning leaves levitate with the rotor wash before blowing outwards, some of them landing below our trench and sparking more little fires. I knew we'd be fucked if a fire ignited below us. This was one of the "watch out" situations. A voice blared in my head: *why are we out here?* Owen and a couple of the squad bosses screamed, "Catch the hot spots!" They sounded scared, too. Without water we had to tag-team: one person digging in the dirt and the other dragging the materials into the hole and tossing more dirt in to suffocate the flames. My Pulaski was almost useless when it came to extinguishing embers.

With each successive load the rotor wash fed the flames like bellows until the fire was too big for the last load to land. The helicopter hovered about a foot from the ground. Everyone except Phillip jumped out. For a millisecond I saw Phillip's face peering through the flimsy window. His amplified voice screeched through our radios. I attacked the spots with a partner, quickly digging holes so he could shovel in the embers. The next time I glanced up I saw the main fire cresting the ridge. If we could get all these little spots out, we would be okay. Unless the main fire caught something like a tree branch and leapt over the fireline through the canopy. I prayed that the main fireline would hold. If the fire jumped the line, or if we missed something and it established itself below us, we could die. A hill is one of the worst places to deploy a fire shelter.

After a lot of screaming and yelling, both via Phillip and the other overhead, the fire stopped at the fireline and we managed to catch and extinguish all the small spot fires. Relief was stark on everyone's faces, including Owen's. No one acknowledged we had been flown into a potentially deadly situation. No one mentioned that we had risked our lives to stop a fire burning into more chaparral, a fire headed into the hills and threatening no structures or lives. No one had briefed us on safety zones or escape routes, because there were none.

Maybe, I thought, the overhead knew something we didn't. In my head I skimmed through the relevant watch out situations, which I'd memorized verbatim: *fire not scouted and sized up; no escape route or safety zone; uninformed on strategy, tactics, and hazards; on a hillside where rolling material can ignite fire below; attempting frontal assault on fire; getting frequent spot fires across the fireline; constructing fireline without a safe anchor point, wind increases and/or changes direction.* How had we come so close to disaster? I couldn't dwell on it—not if I wanted to stay sane. I told myself it was fine.

After reinforcing the fireline we hiked down and out, our faces marred with dirt, soot, and sweat. My soaked Nomex turned the hot wind frigid. For the rest of the day everyone was quiet. When we eventually tied back in with Phillip he gave us an unusually short After Action Review. No questions were allowed, not that we would have asked them. He talked in circles, insisting that everything was safe without explaining how. I wanted him to acknowledge any possible mistakes, or reassure us that we'd been safe despite all appearances—the panicked shouts and expressions of our most stoic superiors, the contagion of fear and rush of adrenaline. We all stood there, physically unscathed but holding the experience in our bodies, with nowhere to release its energy. Incidents like this are accepted as part of the job. Keeping silent is less risky than speaking candidly about potential close calls: Any such admission might summon mountains of paperwork, or damage a crew's reputation. As Owen always said, perception is reality. It was vital to keep the crew's image squeaky clean. What was the use of an AAR if mistakes were interpreted as personal failures, rather than an inevitable part of the job?

* * *

According to a survey conducted by Grassroots Wildland Firefighters, 76.8 percent of wildland firefighters have experienced close calls like this. Without injuries, vehicle damage, or shelter deployments these incidents can go unreported, but they aren't without impact. Fifty-seven percent of wildland firefighters reported binge drinking in the past month, compared to a national average under 30 percent. And 22.3 percent of surveyed wildland firefighters screened positive for PTSD, compared to 6 percent of the general public. In the same survey, past-year suicidal ideation was double that of the general public. There are few resources for wildland firefighters. Crew overhead, like supervisors and captains, are under immense pressure to project an aura of safety, making it harder for crew members to properly process these situations. As much as we focused on "lessons learned," these lessons came from death or injury—not when there was a near miss. And I experienced many near misses. Our survival was more dependent on luck and chance than we wanted to admit.

Chapter Five

Distortions

Kieran's mandatory days off on his new crew coincided with ours and we had a party at Eric's house. It was out of control—almost everyone there had been drinking since the afternoon and most were blacked out. At some point Colin grabbed my arm and jerked me into the spare bedroom, closing the door. The dark, humid room pulsated with blasting music from the living room. I wasn't as drunk as everyone else and asked Colin if we could get a cab to a hotel, because our apartment wasn't in town. "No," Colin said as he pulled me into the bed. "I already asked if we could sleep here." The sheets smelled sour. "Can I?" he asked, pulling off my pants and underwear. He wouldn't let up until I said yes. He lay his body behind mine, tightened his arms around me. Something crashed against the door, and Kieran yelled my name. "Where's Ana?" He slammed his fist against the door. Something in me snapped and I jumped up from the bed, frantically feeling around for my clothes. "I need to leave," I said, hyperventilating. Colin restrained me and yanked me back into the bed. I struggled in his arms. "Let me go," I said, standing again. He wouldn't. Not until I started sobbing. Then he started kissing me and telling me he loved me, pulling me down to the bed again. I let him do whatever he wanted.

The next morning, he said I'd gone crazy, as if I couldn't remember what happened. "Why would you act like that with me?" I didn't understand why he felt entitled to my body, and I knew he'd restrained me, but I was as baffled as he was by the strength of my reaction. I thought I trusted him. I apologized to him. "I don't know what's wrong with me," I said. He told me he forgave me.

I met Niels for a drink when Colin went home for a weekend. Niels was a veteran in his early thirties, a squad boss on A-Mod. He reminded me of the soft-spoken regulars at the strip club, or the contract crew guys. He talked about strip clubs and porn but many of his friends were women. Colin was comparatively straight edge, much more masculine. Niels's teeth were crooked, his stature slight. He smoked cigarettes. We were both wounded in different ways. Niels knew what it was like to be addicted to something, to fall apart. He could see me in a way Colin never would.

When he walked me to my car we kissed, languid summer air breathing all around us. My body slackened. I'd been holding it rigid for a long time. His kiss was soft and free from expectations. I knew we wouldn't end up together, but I also knew I needed to break up with Colin. When he returned from the weekend I sat him on our bed and told him it was over. We both cried.

Nickolas's wife Helen worked on our base. She and Nickolas had two kids, and she worked as a forest patrol, handing out tickets or warnings to people breaking the rules. I had started spending more time with her, out on the plot of land she and Nickolas shared. Maybe this is why I kept thinking of my own little plot of land. Nickolas was usually gone on dozer boss assignments. I told her about the radio, and Martin's constant criticism.

"If it gets bad," she said, "just tell him you'll go to human resources and file a report unless he leaves you alone." I reared back and shook my head, but she told me it would get him off my back. "It's not like you'd actually go to HR."

An unspoken rule on our crew was that conflicts got solved internally. Stories of nameless women filing complaints with HR circulated like urban myths, all with similar endings. A woman files. She gets punished. A woman files, and nothing comes of it but her own misery. A woman files, and she quits. Didn't women understand what came with this job? This man's job? Men decide who stays here. Threatening to file was like pinning a target on your own back.

The namelessness of the women in these stories made them sound like rumors, or myths. They weren't. Women have named themselves, and testified to their experiences. Whether they share their names or not isn't of consequence—they never escape unscathed, unlike most perpetrators. I'd heard the story of a female crew member being thrown in the water by her male peers, but didn't know the details, which were recounted during a hearing in 2016. Those men who threw her in the water wanted her to participate in "a wet T-shirt contest," and also told her she was hired because of the Barnardi "cuntsent" Decree. They shot her with BB guns. She reported them and was quickly reprimanded for spreading rumors. Soon after, she quit.

At the same 2016 hearing, Denise Rice, a Region 5 firefighter, described her experiences both before and after reporting ongoing sexual harassment perpetrated by a superior. Rice had been a firefighter for over twenty years. In 2011, directly after reporting, she was forced to repeatedly recount her traumatic experiences, which included sexual assault. A district ranger described Rice's sexual assault to Rice's peers, while she was in the room. "The moment you speak up," she said, "you are committing career suicide." Rice was demoted after reporting, while the offender got a promotion. Soon after, he retired, with benefits, and was later hired to give motivational speeches.

"I know what happens to me happens to women all over the region and [the] Forest Service. I don't know of any women who have been able to recover and lead successful careers after filing sexual harassment claims."

Rice's home base was less than 200 miles away from my hotshot base. I had met the man who would later be named as her perpetrator. I only heard stories. Soon I would be one.

Martin followed me everywhere, always stepping in to correct me as if I were a naughty pet in need of training. The more I resisted the worse it got. I tucked Helen's advice away like a smooth rock, worrying it with my fingers.

Colin told me that Martin had seen me at the bar with Niels. He accused me of having slept with Niels in our shared bed, which was untrue. He thought I was lying. This flipped a switch inside me. He was so much more judgmental than I first assumed, though he had a right to be angry about my kissing Niels. We had changed in each other's eyes. We were seeing each other more clearly. I had kissed Niels, and Juan, both before we broke up. I reached for Colin and he stepped away. "He's not a good guy," he said of Niels. "He's not a good person." Maybe no one is, I thought. Martin had been following me. I had seen him at Trader Joe's, outside my gym, and several times on his bicycle. He didn't drink, which meant he had followed me to the bar, too.

Chapter Six

Idaho

In July we were briefly in the Idaho panhandle, near Wallace. The tiny town, tucked in a narrow canyon and surrounded by mountains, showed no evidence of its complete obliteration in the Great Fire of 1910, which is often referenced as the first catastrophic forest fire in the United States, and led to the Forest Service as we know it today. The Great Fire was part of a progression of large fires following logging from east to west beginning in 1825, with the Miramichi Fire in New Brunswick and Maine, which killed around 160 people and decimated 2.9 million acres. Dried brush and discarded trees deemed worthless because of their small diameter—debris from logging operations, called "slash"—as well as a recent infestation of Spruce Budworm, contributed to its force. Then, in 1871, forty years before the establishment of the United States Forest Service, there was a cluster of large fires in the Midwest, where logging had increased with westward expansion. The Peshtigo Fire, which burned 1.2 million acres in Wisconsin (and killed thousands), ignited on the same day as the Great Chicago Fire and several large fires in Michigan. An October cold front stoked them with erratic winds. It was typical for landowners to burn their land around this time, making way for new growth, but this season had been particularly dry, making this ill-advised. Landowners burned anyway. Peshtigo was a logging hub. Lots of slash. These fires may have been part of a natural drought cycle, but the presence of dried and cured timber slash certainly exacerbated them. As with the Miramichi Fire, logging itself had fed these fires, but timber companies had already moved west with settlers, who increased demand for timber as they claimed occupied land.

Unchecked logging directly led to the Great Fire of 1910. After a parched spring, train sparks ignited midsummer fires across Montana and Idaho. On August 20, lightning storms rolled through the Northern Rockies and the fires exploded. They killed eighty-seven people and burned three million acres. Congress tried to pin the blame on the rangers, many of whom had been paying their workers from their own savings accounts and who, during the fires, dug deeper into their own pockets to add manpower by paying day laborers. Ed Pulaski, one of the few rangers without a forestry degree (and the namesake of my line tool), had forced his forty-three-person crew into a small mine shaft and guarded the doors from the inside, threatening to shoot one man when he tried to leave. When the doors began burning, he doused them with a bucket of water. Pulaski's hands and lungs were badly burned, and he was never properly compensated for his injuries. Five of his crew members died, but thirty-eight survived the fire that would otherwise have killed them.

The Forest Service would leverage the Great Fire of 1910 for increased influence and funding. To understand how, it's necessary to examine how the agency was established. The U.S. Forest Service was inaugurated in 1905 by Theodore Roosevelt. After Roosevelt hired Gifford Pinchot as its chief, Pinchot installed fire rangers throughout the West, hiring fellow Yale graduates who could easily pass his newly implemented civil and field exams rather than choose men who had more direct knowledge of the landscape but lacked college degrees.

His men were charged with punishing trespassers on federal land, including Indigenous Americans.

The Division of Forestry was the predecessor of the Forest Service, having been established in 1881 under the care of Franklin B. Hough, who had ties to the American Forestry Association (AFA). The Division became deeply entwined with the AFA, which claimed to be focused on conservation. Internally the organization was less interested in forest preservation than it was in creating a sustainable logging industry, what Mark Hudson calls "extractive capital." This was not sustainability in the modern sense. The AFA wanted to suppress fires and increase logging. Many settlers throughout the United States had previously accepted fire as part of their landscape, some of them utilizing fire in ways that mimicked Indigenous burning, or to create pasture for their herds of grazing animals.

In 1886 Bernhard Fernow, Hough's replacement, reshaped the Division of Forestry, further steering its purpose away from conservation and towards forest management, with a focus on logging. Fernow wanted to extinguish fire completely; to eliminate what he called the "fire problem." Many scientists and conservationists were against this and argued for fire's importance. During Fernow's tenure at the Division of Forestry, the AFA began strictly regulating fire, which they deemed "the most destructive enemy of the forest." At this time, all forests were still public, but by 1892 thirteen million acres of land were purchased (for much less than they were worth, often from Native Americans) to create fifteen forest reserves. These would eventually land under the U.S. Forest Service's jurisdiction.

By the time Pinchot took over in 1905 and established the U.S. Forest Service, the agency had the support of railroads, livestock associations, and timber companies. Pinchot promoted Hough's European model of forest management, prioritizing mining and grazing and contradicting his own conservationist ideals by commodifying trees into timber. Without the support of extractive industries it is unlikely the Forest Service would exist today. Organizations and companies like the National Lumber Manufacturing Association and various livestock organizations were integral to the agency's transformation from conservation to extractive fire suppression apparatus.

Shortly before the Great Fire of 1910, President Taft had fired Pinchot, but his influence remained strong. In the wake of the public response to the fire, Pinchot seized an opportunity for increased funding, capitalizing on the public's increased fear of fire. Complex debates regarding suppression were quickly distilled into two opposing arguments—light burning and full suppression—allowing the U.S. Forest Service to manipulate public opinion and influence government funding by painting fire as a manageable menace. Wildfire became a stand-in, used to exploit forests. Pinchot coined the sensationalized term "timber famine." Instead of understanding forests in ecological terms, as interconnected systems, this narrative reduced nature to chaos requiring government control. It was an extension of the visions of explorers and colonizers, many of whom conformed to exploitative modes of agriculture rather than the kin-centric agricultural practices of Indigenous Americans. As Mark Hudson details in his book *Fire Management in the American West*, this resulted in the prioritization of fire suppression, rather than more proactive and ecologically sound methods of forest management or land stewardship. The simplistic binary neglected to address an important truth: that some ecosystems produce, and depend on, uncontrollable wildfires, and benefit from high-severity burns. Local action was impeded by federal policies. Congress authorized unlimited emergency funds for fire suppression. Despite this windfall, the USFS neglected to pay many of its rangers and firefighters for their efforts fighting the fires of 1910. Many of the firefighters were impoverished immigrants. The families of those who died fighting the fires were never compensated for their losses.

Before the passage of the Weeks Act in 1911, the Forest Service had limited power to convert private land into national forests, but the Weeks Act allowed the USFS to purchase land near stream and river headwaters specifically for the protection of watersheds, greatly expanding its reach. In 1924 the Clarke-McNary Act granted the USFS decisive power to build "an adequate system of forest protection and fire prevention over several states." The USFS could now buy land freely for the production of timber. The Clarke-McNary Act also included funding for states to create their own fire suppression organizations, and included a section ensuring funding for private organizations and individuals so they could "continue growing and renewing useful timber crops," effectively establishing state and private forestry in the United States.

By 1935, Pinchot's ideal of absolute suppression was realized. The ten a.m. policy was enacted, mandating that all fires be extinguished by ten a.m. the morning following their discovery. This policy decisively snuffed out the ecological harmony that settlers, conservationists, and explorers had admired when they first arrived in the West. No longer were humans burning the land to make way for new growth or control pests. No longer were lightning fires allowed to burn. With each passing year of suppression, green, vibrant meadows were swallowed by trees. Healthy forests became tangled with unmitigated new growth tendriling towards the sky, creating ladder fuels ready to carry fire into the canopy. The ten a.m. policy was abandoned in 1978, but the belief that all fires must be immediately suppressed persists.

Martin had worked as a hotshot in Idaho and spent much of our time there reminiscing about his old crew. According to him, the women on that crew were superior to me in all respects. He now shadowed me constantly, recounting my failures to measure up to his standards. I had rationalized this behavior, telling myself his brain injury was the root of this hypercriticism. Nothing else justified the deterioration of our relationship—my sudden turn from friend to unwilling pupil. He was unrelenting, no matter how many times I asked him to quit following me. It was exhausting.

The Idaho terrain was so steep that we sometimes needed to pull ourselves up with a slackline. Many of us had fallen behind on hikes; at least a quarter of the crew, including Niels and Juan. I fell out once. Martin mentioned this every day thereafter. "You fell out on the hike," he'd say, and I'd counter with, "a bunch of people fell out!" This didn't matter. "Look at Chloe," he repeated, like a mantra. Chloe was an athletic badass. She never fell out on hikes and maintained a stoic persona throughout the whole season, not once revealing a crack in her exterior. I was not stoic. I was emotional, Martin said. Too emotional. I laughed too loudly, too often. I talked too much. I was too expressive, my facial expressions too transparent. He never mentioned my work ethic, which was unflagging. It was my hiking, my demeanor, and my conduct.

Whenever my distress was obvious Martin patted me on the shoulder, my friend once again. "I'm telling you this because I care about you," he'd say. "I want you to be successful." He said I was stronger the year before, but now I was getting lazy. Last year, I told him, I was new. "Why should I have to keep proving myself?" I asked, and he replied that women always needed to prove themselves. I shook my head. "That's bullshit," I said. "I don't have to do more than everyone else." I had made an internal decision not to destroy my body to prove that I deserved my place on the crew. Perfection was unattainable. The bar was always moving.

What confused me the most was that I was stronger than the year before, which he admitted. I was a stronger hiker, with more upper body strength and endurance. Many of the guys struggled during our long days digging fireline, but I thrived, dipping into my seemingly infinite reserve of endurance. The Idaho soil was deep and interwoven with roots; the firefighting methods almost opposite to Southern

California. More trees and much less brush. The sawyers felled trees
and sliced branches as everyone else dug fireline with hand tools,
using the "swipe and go" technique. Each individual swung their
tool, stepped forward, and swung again, one person after the other
improving the line until we left a trench of inflammable dirt and rocks
in our wake. The work was akin to ditch-digging. I sharpened my
Pulaski during every break, spinning its honed edges deftly, chopping
roots with the axe end and extracting tangled roots and chunks of soil
with the adze. Many roots were several inches thick, requiring the full
swings one would use to split firewood. My Pulaski kept time like a
metronome, comforting me with its rhythm. The work itself was a
refuge in which I knew I could fulfill my purpose.

It never occurred to me that my performance may have amplified
Martin's self-doubt. He wanted me to stay the same: at the bottom,
where he could dominate me.

Chapter Seven

Montana

We drove to Montana, taking a detour through Glacier for some brief sightseeing. The buggies snaked along the Going-to-the-Sun Road. I thought of my trip to Montana in 2000, my first year on the contract crew. I missed the anonymity. No one I worked with then had cared what I looked like; no one chastised me for smiling or laughing too loudly. They didn't require me to wear a hat or a belt or tell me I was too loud or too emotional. I was a good worker as long as I worked hard. I missed joking with the guys and feeling like part of the crew, rather than outside of it.

On the drive, Gunnar took out a *Hustler* magazine, rustling the pages loudly. I saw him side-eyeing me. It was obvious he wanted me to look. This was another battle. When he first bought the magazine at an Idaho gas station and opened it in the buggy, he held it out towards the aisle, making it impossible for me to ignore the pictures from my vantage point directly behind his seat. He was waiting for me to say something, but I stayed silent, not wanting to give him a reaction. I gazed out the window, feeling the suffocating sensation of my throat tightening. I willed myself to hold everything in. I willed the tightening grip of fear to loosen. I willed the vibrating rage buried deep in my chest to calm.

*   *   *

Fires were burning all over Montana, and it was now August, nearly my twenty-third birthday. We were north of Missoula, south of Flathead Lake and far from any city, but the area was still considered the WUI (Wildland–urban Interface) because of the cluster of mountain homes. This is increasingly the case in many rural areas, and presents complicated problems, especially if residents haven't cleared defensible space around their homes or properties, or if the homes themselves have large, unprotected gaps in their insulation, or wood shake roofs or paneling. Wood decks can ignite, embers and firebrands can enter houses through small openings, and roofs constructed of flammable materials are especially vulnerable.

Each mod was assigned a different structure. I was with Corey and Eric. At our assigned property, one of the residents' sons, my age, stood shirtless, holding a bright green garden hose, spraying down the main house and shrubbery. We didn't tell him this, but garden hoses lack both the water pressure and volume to make them useful protection against fire. Even fire hoses can be insufficient in the face of an established wildfire.

It was time to build our hose lay. We snaked lengths of large white hose around the house, connecting each length with gated Y nozzles. When the hose was all connected, we installed smaller, narrower lengths of hose on to the Y connections, threading them throughout the property in various directions and topping them off with metal sprinklers. This hose lay would protect the houses if the fire came too close. I carried a MARK-3 water pump to a nearby stream. The MARK-3 is a two-stroke engine, same as a scooter engine. I set up the priming/sucking hose, submerging it in the stream before weighing it down with rocks to anchor it in place. One of my preseason classes was about using pumps and I liked putting the knowledge to practice. Eric helped me attach a fuel can and we primed the pump before finally attaching the end of the hose lay. I pulled the cord and ignited the engine. Our sprinklers switched on.

This sprinkler system would surely give the homeowners some much needed peace of mind, but they had done the work of keeping their house, propane tank, and toolshed cleared of fuel, including trees, save for a couple large, healthy pines. In many of the places where we had been called to protect houses, especially in California, where there was more brush, homeowners neglected the areas around their houses, allowing brush, grass, and leaf litter to accumulate. That is a point of frustration for many firefighters; homeowners greeted us with homemade snacks, drinks, and thank-you signs when we came in to "save" them, but we resented their ignorance, which sometimes seemed willful and fostered dangerous situations for firefighters. But, of course, clearing defensible space requires money, time, and education. Many communities vote down measures and initiatives funding local firefighters, WUI protection, and education.

It's becoming common practice for the wealthy to hire private firefighters while voting down tax increases for public fire mitigation. In some regions limited small grants exist for disabled and low-income residents. Many cities and towns have more recently implemented initiatives and requirements intended to protect residents and their property from wildfire, but this only happens with community buy-in and usually only in reaction to destructive fires rather than preventatively. Couple this with uneducated home buyers and shady real estate developers building in high-risk areas, and the results have proven disastrous. In October 1991, the Oakland Hills Firestorm destroyed 3,354 homes and 437 apartments, causing $1.5 billion in damage. Because of lack of funding, low-income residents were the most affected; they couldn't afford to clear defensible space, and there was no evacuation plan in place. Residents living in wealthier neighborhoods failed to implement supportive fire safety protocols and voted down taxation that would have bolstered fire departments in low-income communities. Many low-income residents were unable to rebuild after the fire. This is a common theme in WUI situations. More affluent residents have the resources to keep themselves safe and are therefore less willing to contribute to inclusive community funding and safety.

Low-income residents and communities often lack the time, education, and resources to apply for protective state and federal grants, and individuals living in poverty face the most dire consequences. Because poverty is poorly understood by those with privilege, these communities and residents are often retrospectively blamed for circumstances beyond their control. The 2021 Marshall Fire, which occurred in Boulder County, Colorado, is the costliest in Colorado's history as of this writing. Despite the county's median income of ninety-nine thousand dollars per year, local governments failed to resource low-income communities and residents, many of whom lived in older wood houses and mobile homes. Boulder County's prohibitive cost of living contributed to a massive displacement of impoverished residents. The temporary housing and rental assistance programs provided in response were limited and insufficient. Some low-income residents mounted GoFundMe campaigns, but the University of Colorado in Boulder conducted a study proving that wealthy residents not only were more likely to seek help via crowdfunding, but benefitted more when they did. Those with household incomes above $150,000 received nearly 30 percent more support than low-income households. They also had more donors overall. The researchers were also surprised to find that the campaigns belonging to lower-income residents received smaller amounts from donors who contributed to more than one campaign. Often these multiple campaign donors gave more money to high-income campaigns. This baffled researchers, but I think it's self-explanatory; access to higher education enables wealthier residents to create rhetorically persuasive campaigns, which could have translated to higher donation amounts.

Boulder County has taken several measures to improve future outcomes for low-income residents living in the Wildland–urban

Interface, including the expansion of its Wildfire Partners program, stricter building codes, increased community outreach and education, and increased funding for wildfire mitigation in high-risk communities. I hope this is enough to protect low-income residents in the future. It is vital that those with means act to fund and advocate for wildfire disaster prevention and protection for everyone in their communities, and essential that states receive federal funding to implement protective changes.

Eric and I high-fived each other after setting up the sprinkler system, a rare show of camaraderie. He snapped a picture of me standing in the dirt driveway, holding my hand up in a wave. My hair is in two braids. My smile is genuine. I loved interacting with the public, and I was proud to be a woman on a hotshot crew. People were almost always kind and grateful. Their praise was a soothing balm. When the guy from earlier emerged holding a pet raccoon I immediately took it in my arms. Eric, still holding my camera, took another photo. It's the last photo of me on the crew.

A few days later when Martin was helping me assemble a hose lay I asked him why he'd told Colin about seeing me with Niels. He wouldn't answer me. Wouldn't speak to me, now that I wanted something from him. Helen's advice had been playing on a loop in my head, getting louder and louder with each of Martin's corrections. I turned around one day to see him following me through the woods as I worked, shadowing me. He wasn't doing his job anymore. I had become his job. He turned to leave, but I called him over. "You need to stop following me," I said. "It's not okay. I'm just trying to do my job." His face flushed. This was the third or fourth time I had said these words to him. Nothing had changed. I lowered my voice. "If you keep doing this, I'll file." I didn't have to say what I'd file. When his face blushed crimson I resisted the urge to reassure him, to let him know it was an empty threat. He stomped away. I exhaled. *Thank fucking god. Please, just leave me alone now. Let me do my fucking job. Live my fucking life.*

The next day I was sitting in the buggy, two seats in front of Niels. It was lunch. Eric and Corey stomped up the stairs and stopped in the aisle. Both of them were over six feet tall. Corey blocked me in my seat and Eric kneeled on the seat in front of me. His head and shoulders hovered above me. "What the fuck do you think you're doing?" Eric hissed, his face contorted.

I didn't know what they meant, but this wasn't the first time in my life I had been asked what the fuck I thought I was doing, and never did these conversations end well, or without physical violence. Vertigo overcame me. I felt as if I were free-falling into an abyss. I reminded myself that Niels was in the back seat and looked out the window where some of the crew was gathered, oblivious. "What are you talking about?"

His words are forever imprinted into my memory. "You think you're gonna get Martin kicked off the crew?" They asked me where Martin would go, what he would do. I tried to explain myself, but they wouldn't let me speak. "You're a fucking bitch," Eric spat. Corey chimed in, pressing himself against my seat. "You better not file a fucking report." I squeezed my legs together as they yelled down at me, so I wouldn't piss my pants. If I pissed my pants, I thought, everyone would know I was a coward. They asked me who I thought I was. I stopped trying to speak over their shouts. Finally, they both yelled "FUCK YOU," in unison. Eric's saliva left a fine layer on my skin. They stalked out of the buggy, stomping their feet so hard on the metal steps on their way down that I shook in my seat.

I dropped my forehead onto the back of the seat Eric had kneeled on, trying to catch my breath, then leaned back and laid my trembling hand on my forehead. My whole body was shuddering. Someone laughed outside. The sound had a hallucinogenic quality, as if I were deep inside a cave and they were far away. My body was numb.

Paranoia kicked in. Was everyone in on this? Did everyone want me gone? I turned around, hoping to see Niels. He was gone. Had he left before it happened? Or had he snuck out while the guys yelled at me? Either way, I was on my own. That much was clear.

At our AAR that evening Phillip told the crew that we needed to treat each other with respect; to preserve our crew's image. I figured Niels must have told him what happened, but he didn't mention anything specific. Instead, he repeated the line I'd heard since starting on the crew: perception is reality. We were at a fire camp, and during dinner he pulled me aside to express his concern, but I knew he didn't care about me. He spoke in platitudes, avoiding saying anything specific about the incident. I didn't know how much he knew, and he didn't ask me for my version. He seemed more concerned about the crew and encouraged me to be the bigger person. Perhaps he wanted to keep me there for the sake of appearances, or was worried about Colin following me if I quit. It never occurred to me that he may have wanted to prevent me from filing. That was my only move, even if it came with consequences. I felt powerless and reflexively blamed myself. My life, thus far, had taught me what to expect. I accepted what now felt inevitable. Phillip didn't try to convince me otherwise. A supervisor sets the tone of their crew. Everything comes from the top down.

Colin asked me the next day why I'd said anything when the season would be over soon. I was causing drama. I reminded him that I'd have to work with Martin again next year.

"It would be different," he said. We were surrounded by trees, away from the buggies but still visible. I rolled my eyes.

"It's not okay for him to follow me around. Not just here, at work, but when I'm at home, too. How did he know what I was doing all the time? Who is he to say I don't belong here?" I glanced at the buggies, where the rest of our crew milled around. We were done with our day, sharpening, filling waters and fuel, and getting ready to head back to camp. "How can I be a squad boss on a fucking crew like this?"

"Maybe if you were more like Chloe—"

I threw my hands up, my voice going high-pitched. "I work so hard on this crew," I said. "I've worked circles around some of these motherfuckers. Lazy-ass motherfuckers. They get out of work as often as they can, but I'm the one people notice? I'm supposed to be volunteering for everything, just like a first year would? I should be more like Chloe? Chloe is a different person. I'll never be like her. Half of these guys aren't even as good as her!"

"I'm sorry," Colin said, shaking his head.

Colin and Gunnar were friends now. I never asked myself how things might have unfolded if Colin had supported me, or how I felt about this betrayal. I had betrayed him, too. Instead, I turned my emotions off as much as I could. Even though Gunnar and I were on the same squad, he always looked past me. After the blowup he pulled out his *Hustler* every day. We were on our way to our division, traversing a dirt road, and he was holding the pages open to the centerfold: a naked woman with her legs spread. I finally asked him to put it away. He ignored me, so I asked again. "No," he said, holding the pages open wider. I started to argue. "I'm not putting it away, you fucking bitch. Leave me alone."

I scanned the buggy. Everyone avoided my gaze. The vertigo returned. Gunnar was so overcome with hatred he looked like he wanted to destroy me. For almost two years I had naively excused his anger. Now that there was no one defending me his rage was laid bare. I sat completely still, my seat like an invisible silo, only turning my head to look out the window. The landscape blurred. I was scared. Not just of him. Of all of them.

None of the guys on A-Mod spoke to me now unless it was work-related. No one looked at me. Not even Colin. Not even Chloe or Niels.

Phillip switched me and Chloe, so I was on B-Mod. This brought some relief. The guys there were nicer to me, but there was no coming back from what had happened. Not in my mind.

I had been here before. My mom and I had fought violently when I was a teenager. Once, she pushed me on the ground and pinned my arms, her face a mask of rage. *Who the fuck do you think you are?* Even when I was smaller, she would chase me and tickle me until I couldn't breathe, her fingers digging too sharply into my ribs. She wouldn't stop, despite my pleading. Not until I cried.

Many of the men I worked with dismissed me categorically because I didn't conform to their standards. I was the wrong kind of woman. I resisted their macho posturing. This entire time I'd been trying to discern their expectations, tracing and retracing some imagined outline of who they needed or wanted me to be and trying to inhabit that. This was second nature, a survival mechanism perfected with each new school, with each parental outburst. *If only I can figure out who they want me to be, they will love me.* Abandoning myself was an unconscious reflex. When I finally felt safe enough on the crew to assert myself, it had proven itself unsafe. I kept combing over the past few months, picking out where I went wrong. But what happened was inevitable, and it wasn't my fault.

When we returned to base in early September I talked to human resources. They warned me: People who file are often harassed even more. They usually end up leaving. It was like they didn't want me to act. So I left the crew, and the life I had made for myself. It was that simple, like a knife straight through everything I'd worked for, irrevocably slicing it apart, and me with it. I lost my health insurance and retirement package. As a permanent employee I would have worked well into November. I packed up the apartment I shared with Colin and left without a goodbye to anyone but him and Niels, surrendering my permanent position. I told myself I was leaving fire forever, but I'd be back.

PART III
SoCal (2005)

Chapter One

The Inland Empire

In April of 2005 I drove down to San Bernardino, visiting Niels on the way there. No one else on the crew was on my radar. After leaving Solar Hotshots I worked briefly as a live-in nanny in Bakersfield, a barren town in California's Central Valley. Colin offered to take me with him to Costa Rica, but I declined. My mom convinced me to move to Olympia, where I took classes at the community college and worked odd jobs to finance my drinking. After a summer away from fire I accepted a job on another hotshot crew, telling myself I'd save money and go back to school when the season ended.

Niels told me Owen had left the crew. Phillip would soon retire. There were rumors of claims against him from former crew members, including Helen. I later support a statement of harassment from her, but she may have never ended up filing. I left my finger off the crew's pulse. It was too painful. Martin was gone, too. He'd called me a few months before, to apologize for what happened. I told him he had ruined my life, knowing the phrase was hyperbolic, but the sentiment felt true. He kept repeating that he was sorry. "I don't know what came over me," he said. He used the word "scapegoat" in reference to my role on the crew. I told Niels all of this. We sat in his living room.

"I'm scared," I said. "That it's all going to happen again but on a different crew. Is there something wrong with me? I feel like I just end up being a target. I don't know why. It was like this growing up, too. There must be something wrong with me."

"There's nothing wrong with you," Niels said. "You're sensitive. You pay attention to things." He hesitated, thinking. "I think some of the guys were threatened by you. I know some of them regret the way things went down."

"That's nice," I said.

"No, really. They do. No one wanted things to end up that way. Everyone was just caught up in this storm, and we were all tired, and Phillip didn't take the reins. I regret the way I acted," he said. "I should have stood up for you."

"Yeah," I said, agreeing. "I don't understand why no one stood up for me."

"Don't be scared, though," Niels said, reaching out and playfully tapping my knee. "Everyone will love you. Everyone always loves you."

Clearly this was untrue.

What Martin said about my being a scapegoat stayed with me. According to Jung a scapegoat is someone who absorbs the negative projections of those who are unable to accept personal responsibility. It fit. I had spent my childhood absorbing my mom's negative emotions and grew up into someone who blamed myself for the faults of others. I unconsciously took on the role of scapegoat on the crew. And I'd do it again.

If there were a place in near-complete opposition to Olympia, both culturally and ecologically, it was the Inland Empire, an amalgamation of city and country, with pale brown hills sprawling southwards and scrubby foothills rising gently into broad, snow-painted mountains often obscured by smog. The San Bernardino Valley was miles of sun-bleached concrete lined with palm trees; sprawling housing tracts and warehouses; five-lane freeways packed with fast-moving traffic; fast-food signs perched on tall metal poles; and lifted trucks adorned with Tapout stickers, some with stainless steel scrotums hanging from their hitches. The Tapout stickers were familiar, although I didn't know at the time that Tapout was an MMA brand; the scrotums baffled me. Inland Empire culture straddles Arizona's conservative politics and Los Angeles's penchant for debauchery and excess.

The town of San Bernardino is nestled against its namesake national forest. Just north is the Angeles National Forest. The San Bernardino Mountains are southwest. To the west is the valley, then the Santa Ana Mountains and then Los Angeles, Orange County, and the Pacific Ocean. The entire area is Wildland–urban Interface, highly populated and prone to fires because of its chaparral landscape. Fires burn year-round in Southern California, usually ignited by engine sparks, tossed cigarettes, or some other human activity. The region is a collision of fire-adapted ecosystems. Fuel breaks and dirt roads snake through hills and mountains. Most of the fuel breaks, which are swaths of cleared land, were constructed during the Civil Conservation Corps (CCC) era, in the 1930s, throughout the western United States. They slice through ecosystems and theoretically reduce the rate of spread and intensity of fires. The effectiveness of fuel breaks has been debated for nearly a century.

In California, what's now called Cal Fire (we knew it as CDF back then) was founded in 1885. It was one of the first state forestry boards in the nation, but it dissolved in conflict in 1893. It wasn't until a logging company and other landholders began advocating for fire protection to secure their timber assets that a position of state forester was created in 1905. After they filled the position land wardens were appointed, replicating the National Forest ranger system. The wardens were funded by counties, not states. When the Weeks Act passed in 1911, one year after the Great Fire of 1910, everything changed. The state was one of many that were granted funding for local wildfire defense. During the Great Depression men flocked to California, where CCC labor camps had been formed, many of them on military bases. The camps were run by Army Reserve officers.

The CCC gave the Forest Service control over nearly 3 million men and around $40 million dollars, an amount equivalent to $96 billion dollars today. With the financial windfall and an increased workforce the Forest Service modernized fire control, but its structure was unstable and dependent on emergency funds. As Stephen Pyne outlines in his deeply researched book *Fire in America*, the CCC's partnership with the USFS was not a thoughtful development of policy, and the agency's accelerated growth during that time resulted in what he calls a "fatal separation of means and end." Ongoing and nuanced debates were sidelined in the face of new money and cheap labor. When the ten a.m. policy was implemented in 1935, CCC laborers were the ones fighting fires.

The Forest Service leveraged its control over CCC camps and resources to further establish itself as the primary fire suppression agency. By this time scientific evidence clearly indicated that fire was ecologically necessary for western ecosystems to thrive. Many scientists, and even ranchers and foresters, advocated for "light burning." Not only was it perceived by some as healthy and necessary for forests, but it also helped grow new grasses for grazing. This science and its advocates were suppressed by both the Forest Service and the timber industry. Several prominent environmentalists, including the nature writer and activist Aldo Leopold, protested both fire suppression and the accelerated expansion of roads and fuel breaks into wilderness areas, citing fragmentation and the risk of ecological decline, but the trajectory proved unstoppable.

My San Bernardino hotshot crew was one of the first hotshot crews in the United States. During the CCC era the nation's first cohesive fire crews loosely formed from the thousands of men hired as laborers. After the great depression, the CCC was disbanded (many men were recruited into the military), but the establishment of fire crews was taken up in Southern California and the Southwest, with two hotshot crews forming in the former and several Native American fire crews forming in the Southwest (the CCC had an "Indian division," and the crews grew from that). It's no coincidence that the first organized crews were in two of the most fire-prone regions of the U.S. The elements of a catastrophic fire season align more often in Southern California than anywhere else in the states. This is because of the chaparral and the Santa Ana winds, which originate in the Great Basin and rush westward, dehumidifying as they rise into the San Gabriel Mountains before heating and descending at speeds up to ninety miles per hour. These winds can dehydrate plants, particularly brush and grass, in as little as twenty-four hours. Recently PG&E, the large electrical company in California, started shutting off their electrical lines in red flag fire weather, which often occurs during Santa Anas, to prevent fires ignited by sparks from ill-maintained power grid infrastructures.

I met Hernandez, a crew member, at the bottom of a hill and followed him into a small parking lot ringed with several Forest Service buildings: the hotshot headquarters and a large facility for various personnel offices and training rooms. Two rectangular manufactured homes tucked near the steep foothills served as barracks. A fire had incinerated the old barracks a few years before. I pulled up behind Hernandez. No naked lady stickers for him, or any of the trucks in the parking lot. No steel scrotums, I noted with relief, cutting the engine of my car. This was one of the oldest hotshot crews in the United States, and its forest, once part of the Angeles National Forest, was the first National Forest in California and one of the first forest reserves in the country, established in 1892.

Hernandez led me into the barracks, showing me my room before inviting me to hike with him that afternoon. I accepted, and he left me in the tiny bedroom. Frigid air poured from a vent near the ceiling. A toiletries bag sat on one of the two twin beds, beneath a small window. I unloaded my clothes into an empty dresser and arranged my books on a shelf, plucking one out before plopping onto the bare mattress. Its pages were worn, edges creased, passages underlined. My therapist had given me the book, called *Sensing the Self*, as a parting gift. I was on my second pass. The author, a doctor specializing in bulimia treatment, collected case studies of her patients. In each of them I saw parts of me reflected. They stole. Lied. Hid themselves away. Although I had first shoplifted when I was eight or nine, I'd never connected it to my bulimia, but it was an accompanying symptom, an antisocial behavior, arising in the absence of a normal childhood. A normal childhood: when someone loved you consistently, without reservation or qualifications. I lay back on the bed, setting the book on my chest, and thought of my mother. We'd fought only a few days ago, right before I left Olympia. "I don't understand why you're leaving," she kept saying. "You could work for us." She wanted me to become a project manager. I'd tried it for a week but the office was claustrophobic. They paid me less than my housecleaning jobs.

She hated that I was going to Southern California, where she'd met my father in the Church of Scientology. As I stood at the open sliding glass door, my feet on the loose patio stones, she tried to convince me to stay. "I've already taken the job, Mom. I'm leaving," I said.

"Take this back," she said, grabbing a book from the office and throwing it at me, her lips tight. It was another book from my therapist, about borderline personality disorder. "It almost convinced me I have BPD. That's why I hate psychology." I caught the book and turned without saying goodbye. It was just another fight, one of so many. I cried for a while on the freeway.

I knew from reading *Girl, Interrupted*, that BPD was sometimes hereditary. Despite my therapist assuring me I didn't have it, I feared I did. I would learn later that complex post-traumatic stress disorder can mimic BPD.

I lay on my new bed listening to my familiar internal dialogue, the voice telling me I was a failure, too needy. Selfish. Saying that disaster was inevitable, happiness impossible. It whispered and roared.

A couple hours later Hernandez led me to the bottom of a steep hill extending farther than I could see. Nausea edged up my throat. He was genuinely friendly, but I suspected he was testing me. I followed him down a narrow hard-packed trail and we traced the bottoms of the foothills before veering left and straight up. Dark green oak trees, their leaves spattered with dust, dotted the yellow-grassed hillsides. I was struggling despite not wearing a pack, cursing myself as a gap widened between us. I didn't call out, but I kept going. There was the burning in my calves and quads and lungs; here I was again. Mini Hill had been nothing compared to this. Hernandez waited briefly for me but continued before I caught up. When I reached another crest he was waiting there, his breath even. I was at least a full minute or two behind him. When we got to the top my lungs were burning. The hike took nearly an hour. I caught my breath and asked if I should quit. He laughed, patting me on the shoulder. "You'll be fine," he said, flashing me a good-natured smile. I welcomed the kindness. If he'd said yes, I'm not sure what I would have done.

The crew was transitioning superintendents, and Jerry, who usually worked as a captain, was acting as interim superintendent while they searched for someone permanent. He led our PT hikes. Nothing could have been more different than the atmosphere on Phillip's crew. No one was singled out. No one scrutinized me more than anyone else. Falling out on a hike wasn't a big production if you kept hiking and didn't give up. Our daily hikes were three times the length of Mini Hill. We supplemented them with two weekly trail runs into the foothills and afternoons lifting weights. I still felt nauseous before PT, but no longer feared being ostracized. PT hikes were for training,

Jerry said. Everyone had bad days. As long as we kept up on fires, we were fine.

Only a few people on the crew were under twenty-five years old, and the crew's composition was racially diverse. I was on A-Mod, once again in the back seat near the trash. Two guys on my mod were formerly incarcerated firefighters; Suarez, a Hispanic man in his thirties with gang tattoos, was on my squad. He was laid-back and easy to get along with. Al was also on A-Mod, but on the other squad. He sat across from me. He had a round, shiny white bald head, giant biceps, and was usually smiling. They were both nonviolent offenders, a requirement for working on CDC crews. There was also Bobby, a curly-haired lead firefighter on Saw One; Gary, a pale ex-Ranger obsessed with the band Tool; and Stephanie, the only woman on the crew other than me, who worked as a lead firefighter on B-Mod. She was thirty-one, as strong as most of the guys and very feminine. The guys drooled over her washboard abs. They hated that she was dating one of the crew's captains. I was envious but not jealous. Her strength and confidence were aspirational. She preferred working out in only a sports bra.

Then there was Vincent, a friend of Colin's I'd met years ago. They'd grown up together, and he told me he was bitter that Colin hadn't invited him to the wedding. I did a cartoon-worthy double take. Shortly after I moved to Olympia Colin had told me not to contact him anymore because his new girlfriend told him not to talk to me. Now he was married? That could have been my life. Why, I asked myself, had I rejected that life? Vincent said Colin had bought land in Costa Rica, but not long ago had been home. Home was close to the hotshot base: Jerry, our stand-in superintendent, lived in the same town. Vincent commuted back and forth.

During our first week Jerry led us on a brutal midday hike through the sun-drenched foothills. Suarez fell out. I passed him but was struggling to close the gap in our line. When I paused for a breath my squad boss, Yusuf, stopped behind me. "Do you feel like you're gonna die?" he asked. I nodded. My lungs were burning; my entire body cramping. I expected him to respond sympathetically but instead he said, "You're not dead yet. Keep going." I resumed hiking. That phrase became my mantra: *You're not dead yet, keep going. You're not dead yet, keep going.* It embedded itself into my psyche. Eventually I'd realize that not being dead wasn't a good measure of well-being, but it was effective at the time, like an override switch allowing me to push my body further than I thought it could go.

Chapter Two

Desert Fires

The effects of climate change have lengthened fire seasons in Southern California—its peak has moved from August to July and large fires burn throughout winter, though this is becoming common throughout the United States, too. Reduced humidity has increased fire occurrences and sizes. In 2023 State Farm announced the elimination of home insurance in California counties with high fire risk. Other insurers followed suit. Winter brings less snow and rain overall, and earlier spring warmth lowers soil moisture, making plants more vulnerable to fire and fires severer as a result. Several studies have predicted the continuation of these trends, with fire season starting earlier and lingering longer into autumn and winter. This is directly correlated with greenhouse gas emissions, which have been rising since 1950. In 2005, when I was in San Bernardino, fire season was reliably milder in spring and summer, but as the effects of climate change take hold it's become almost impossible to rely on past templates.

The first fires of our season were desert fires in southeastern California, western Nevada, and southwestern Arizona. Our buggies looped from the Chiricahua Mountains to Tonto National Forest to Joshua Tree; from the Mojave Desert to Death Valley and throughout

Nevada, often arriving after the fires had done their worst. We gridded over hills and flatlands, poking our tools in the ground listlessly as the days plodded along. The sun breathed down our necks, unrelenting. Midday temperatures were as high as 114 degrees. In the shade. Our boots loosed heat-blackened rocks and we side-hilled parched ridges made chalky with soot and ash. Our noses bled in the dry heat; our sweat evaporated into thin air, leaving the edges of our lips lined with salt. There was no ice; there were no fire camps. We drank hot water from our packs and warm water from the coolers. I began to envy the helislackers and, as Yusuf called them, engine slugs; both stayed close to their vehicles, taking refuge from the heat.

Sometimes someone wondered aloud what we were doing out there when there was nothing to "protect"; it was empty country with no structures or towns. Most of the wind-driven fires had puttered out once the wind stopped. None of us could answer the question. I thought that monitoring the fires rather than suppressing them was more ecologically sound, but I didn't understand the legal complexities of that: How the federal and state agencies were held accountable if a monitored fire destroys public property or takes lives. I knew some domino had been toppled by phone calls from the public, concerned about that far-off smoke, and the only response was immediate suppression. The public demanded it, and that's where the funding was—agencies on average spend over three billion dollars a year on wildfires. These funds are otherwise locked away and unavailable for fire management practices capable of reducing the size and severity of summer fires. The apparatus reacts, because it must.

Western deserts have been adversely affected by warming temperatures, resulting in fewer freezes and longer seasons without frost. In the past these freezes kept many cold-intolerant invasive grasses at bay; now they thrive, especially as desert winters with heavy rains rather than snow support their establishment. More frequent and larger fires can create a vicious cycle beneficial to invasive grasses.

Cheatgrass and buffelgrass, both invasive species, carried fire for miles. Before grazing animals compacted the soil and more flammable plants took root, fires would burn patchily, leaving swaths of ground untouched. Now fires burn hotter, thoroughly incinerating vegetation more frequently.

There are several tactics for controlling the growth of invasive grasses. These include burning in the cold season, when native plants have higher fuel moisture and can withstand more fire. Some species of invasive grasses retain their seeds well into fire season, so carefully timed burns can kill the current population before the seeds mature and disperse. For other perennial invasives, prescribed burning is less effective, but can be useful when integrated with herbicide. Burning can clear out vegetation, allowing herbicides to be more effectively applied to newly resprouting, tender growth. Burning in the early spring, before warm-season native perennials emerge, can also give them a competitive advantage over cool-season invasive perennials.

All of these strategies will be most effective when proactive, rather than reactive, implemented as part of a long-term management plan. They require proper funding. The involvement and education of local communities, ranchers, and fire personnel is vital, especially because fire has long been framed as destructive rather than regenerative. Agencies, both local and federal, must cooperate rather than compete.

As warm weather increases, our window for action shrinks. We can't rely solely on federal agencies, whose local knowledge is limited. The Nature Conservancy has long been employing these methods not only in deserts but throughout the United States. More local organizations, like the California Native Plant Society, the Great Basin Institute, and the Malpai Borderlands Group, are conducting research and native species conservation. The Malpai Borderlands Group was founded in the early 1990s by a group of ranchers in the borderlands region of southern Arizona and New Mexico. Their work supports environmental and community needs while also helping ranchers.

They practice what they call "grassbanking," which allows ranchers to rest overused ranches so the environment can recover. Their methods of prescribed burning and research-based land management are especially successful because of community involvement and education, which involves workshops, field tours, and other educational opportunities for landowners, managers, and the general public.

In the face of behemoth federal organizations whose bureaucratic processes often impede immediate action (except when it comes to emergency fire suppression), these nonprofits are essential. Federal Agencies like the Forest Service have historically proven ill-suited and insufficiently funded to implement proactive fire management on a smaller, local scale in nuanced and diverse ecosystems. In 2022, President Biden launched a ten-year strategy called "Confronting the Wildfire Crisis: A Strategy for Protecting Communities and Improving Resilience in America's Forests." The strategy acknowledges some of the damage caused by extreme fire suppression and posits collaborative approaches to forest health and wildfire mitigation. It's a detailed plan, but it left me wondering if the federal government, especially the Forest Service, can rework their approach without overhauling the entire agency. Despite its recommendations, lawmakers implemented full suppression once again during the 2022 fire season. The negative effects were colossal. Throughout most of the United States many regions had perfect burn windows, with high fuel moisture and cooler weather, but federal employees were unable to burn because of the federal pause on prescribed burns.

The same strategies that have created the wildfire feedback loop will never fully suppress fires once and for all. We are under the false impression that wildfires, natural phenomena akin to hurricanes and floods, can be fully suppressed. It should be common knowledge that these most destructive fires can be muted both by monitoring smaller wildfires burning in cooler seasons and prescribed and cultural burning with timing and implementation managed by those knowledgeable and able to ensure safety. While these ideas are becoming more main-stream, there's still a lack of balance between suppression and management. The federal government (and many state governments) continue to prioritize the funding of full suppression, because suppression is, in many cases, a response to an emergency, and therefore essential. But so is intentional fire.

There are several ways to monitor weather on wildfires. Spot weather forecasts are produced by the National Weather Service (NWS) Weather Forecast Offices. These forecasts cover the current acreage area of any given wildfire and are broadcasted hourly over the fire's designated weather radio channel. The zone forecast is less specific, akin to a forecast one would see on any weather app (which we didn't have back then). Type I and Type II fires, which are the largest, employ an on-site meteorologist who updates the incident weather forecast every twelve hours. Incident weather forecasts are incident-specific, used to strategize and implement fire suppression tactics.

We, like all hotshot crews, also monitored weather regularly, especially to assess the relative humidity, which determines fuel moisture. I learned how to spin weather on the contract crew, but Phillip's crew used Kestrels: little devices capable of calculating wind speed, relative humidity, and temperature, along with other factors. Because the San Bernardino crew used manual weather kits, I asked Bobby to refresh my knowledge. He unrolled the red canvas kit, revealing a small plastic bottle of water, two thermometers affixed to a thin, rectangular metal backing, called a sling psychrometer, a small ruler, a Dwyer wind meter, and a compass. After extracting the thermometers, he handed me the water, which I uncapped so he could dip one of the thermometers in, wetting the little piece of cotton cloth attached to it. Once the cotton was soaked he held a metal rod at the end of the chain, affixed to the backing, and spun the thermometers around. This is called "slinging" or "spinning" weather. The cloth-covered thermometer measured wet bulb temperature. Bobby spun the thermometers. The moisture evaporated from the cloth.

Bobby gestured to the kit. "Take the chart out." I picked the kit up and found the paper chart, writing down the dry bulb and wet bulb temperatures and connecting the numbers on the chart. We were standing beneath the only shade we could find: a scrawny creosote bush. The temperature was 117, the relative humidity low, which meant fuels would ignite easily. This wasn't surprising. Everywhere we went was scorching hot, and we were currently in Arizona, where the air was always parched. We wilted in the sun like unwatered flowers and sipped our steaming water like tea. I sweated like crazy and received the occasional cooling breezes gratefully.

Sometimes I had to conserve my water supply and went half days without peeing. When I did pee, it was a dark yellow trickle. The resources for Arizona fires—if they weren't threatening communities—were minimal, and cubees of water and food were slow to arrive. There was no ice for our cooler, but the lukewarm drinks felt cold compared to our water bottles. We subsisted on MREs. I memorized the contents of every pouch. Three times a day we tore apart the thick matte brown plastic packaging and traded Jalapeño cheddar for peanut butter or plain cheddar for M&Ms and ate the meals without heating them because they were already warm. As we ate, we talked about what we wished we were eating. Our conversations always circled back to the first meal we'd have when we got home, or our favorite meals. I dreamed about air-conditioned restaurants, steak, sushi, or milkshakes. An ice bath. Ice.

My nickname from Phillip's crew, Pee Spot, followed me, because I hated peeing near the guys. Even if they turned around they could still hear me. Whenever I spotted a good place to pee semi-privately, I took it. Although a couple of my crewmates were kind enough to point out prime locations, there were never any accommodations. Instead of resenting this, I considered my fear of exposure irrational.

* * *

On one particularly long day we hiked back to our buggies through a wash, which is a dry sandy riverbed. It was the only flat pathway through two large hills. I was thirsty and almost out of water. The sun sucked moisture from our breath and pores. My squad boss, Yusuf, led the hike at a slow pace, but every step felt like a mile. Suarez fell out, collapsing to his knees. Then Luke, a blonde surfer dude, stepped aside. I was surprised—he was one of the strongest guys on the crew. His face was scarlet. We hiked past them; Bobby and Stephanie stayed behind.

I kept hearing Yusuf's voice from one of our first hikes: *Do you feel like you're gonna die?* My vision blurred, turning hazy and gray. I could pass out at any moment. My heart could stop. *You're not dead yet, keep going. You're not dead yet. Keep going.* I kept going. When we spotted the Forest Service green of our buggies one of the guys whooped, and I whooped too with a sudden burst of energy. Limbs heavy, we clambered inside and closed the doors and windows, blasting the air conditioner until the buggy filled with frigid, smoke-scented air. My sweat cooled; my drenched shirt clung to me. We gasped when we opened the cooler. Jerry had bought ice for us. Bobby tossed me a red Gatorade. It was my first cold drink in over a week. I parsed out the salty from the sweet, holding each icy gulp against the roof of my mouth until it warmed. Melting into my seat, I stuck a frosty bottle of water inside my sports bra. Heaven.

Chapter Three

Project Work

When we weren't on fires we hiked and ran, huffing up miles of dirt trails into the mountains, through invasive eucalyptus groves and brush. We jogged through sandy washes, lifting our feet high. We also conducted project work, taking a bunch of chainsaws into the hills and thinning out the thick brush accumulated after decades of fire suppression, or reinforcing fuel breaks implemented by the CCC. After two years as a hotshot I had become accustomed to running the chainsaw, but by June I was so proficient in cutting brush that the saw was like an extension of my arms. We regularly PT'd on various trails located near project work sites. On one hike, when I was falling behind, Bobby told me to grab a strap hanging off his line pack. He took off and I followed closely, more focused on making sure I wasn't dead weight than the pain in my limbs or lungs. "You didn't even hold me back," he said when we got to the top. He was pouring sweat but grinning. We high-fived before starting our saw work. We were working along a ridge in full sun, trading off sawing and swamping tank for tank. When I was running the saw I forgot my body completely, focusing on cutting the brush efficiently. Each piece was like a puzzle: I'd cut a section of outside branches before finding my way to the center, where all the branches were tightly woven, then I'd work my way outside again until there was nothing left but a small stump cut close to the ground.

Despite how hard we were working, I was still suffering from bulimia. Some of the guys must have known I was sick because I always snuck off to the bathroom after meals. That day we stopped at the crew's favorite burrito place, and Bobby was waiting for me when I came out.

"You've lost weight fast," he said. "I don't understand how you can eat the way you do and lose weight so fast." I knew exactly what he was implying.

"I work out a lot," I said, which wasn't untrue. I went to the gym every day, even on workdays. I fidgeted, terrified he'd question me further, but he didn't.

I was embracing the Southern California aesthetic, dyeing my hair platinum and straightening my curls. The scent of Pink Sugar perfume followed me everywhere. For the first time, I vomited regularly on fires. My body had changed drastically but I only wanted it smaller.

We got called to a fire near Palm Springs, then another one only a few miles from base, then another. Because the fires were brand-new starts, time was of the essence. We worked in tandem with federal and state engines and California Department of Corrections crews. We would have lost all those fires without the help of the CDC crews, who cut line almost as fast as we did, faster than some hotshot crews. Most western states have some sort of wildland fire program for incarcerated people, but California's is the largest and most established, officially dating back to the early 1940s. CDC crews are composed of nonviolent offenders and led by specially trained wardens. Each firefighter can be paid up to five dollars a day (as of 2024), but many are paid as little as two dollars a day. Working as a wildland firefighter is a point of pride for many incarcerated people, as well as an opportunity for reduced sentences and expunged records. But there are major downsides (other than the astronomically low wages), including the risk of death and injury all firefighters face. Formerly incarcerated wildland firefighters weren't allowed to serve as municipal firefighters until 2020, when California enacted a bill allowing courts to clear the criminal records of formerly incarcerated firefighters. In many states they're still not eligible for municipal jobs. The subject of incarcerated firefighters is complicated and should not be separated from overall conversations regarding prison labor and the prison industrial complex.

On Solar Hotshots we usually arrived after the fire was established and had to sit around while the Incident Commander figured out where to put us, but there was little sitting and waiting with these fires. Jerry had stepped back into his role as captain after being replaced by a much grumpier guy who we addressed only by his last name, Gardinelli. Sometimes he or a captain would step into the role of incident commander, dictating actions not only to us but other arriving resources. The adrenaline surges were intense, cresting as we drove and when we arrived, as we hiked and cut line. The four squads would split, leapfrogging each other to quickly establish fireline. By now it was all second nature to me. Load up, gear up, hike up, start swamping or digging. Rest, repeat. Dig fireline parallel to flames? Not a big deal. Reverse tool order back up the line because things got hairy? No problem. Swamp bundles of poison oak? Drink steaming water? Eat MREs for weeks on end? Done.

We hiked miles every day. Frequent high-intensity fire has damaged soil systems in Southern California, and this resulted in rocks loosening as we climbed; voices yelling "rock!" as they tumbled down; those below scrambling to avoid being injured or killed. Falling rocks are one of the most dangerous elements for wildland firefighters, along with falling trees. The sound of someone yelling "rock" is like a klaxon blaring in an emergency.

Black ash and dirt coated our teeth, our faces, our saliva and throats and bodies. We hiked and cut and dug alongside bright orange tendrils of fire billowing into pillowy puffs of choking smoke. Fire tore through brush, swelling to twice or three or four times the size of the bushes it consumed, expanding and shrinking, flame-points transforming into curlicues of black smoke reaching towards the sky, towards the fireline, towards the black, searching for a point of continuation. The bulbous flame-bellies glowed yellow and white like the sun. In the darkness of night coursing waves of embers shot upwards from conjoined flames as if the sky were reclaiming its lost stars. Flares hissed from our guns like arcing firecrackers.

The bigger the fire got, the more the leadership changed. When we waited for the "window of safety" to open for a chance to burn or cut line I reveled in the pause. I liked this waiting just as I liked the long drives along dirt roads, because I could listen to music and relax. Some of the guys hated the way I popped in and out of conversations, yanking an earbud out to ask a question or contribute. Once I heard Stephanie's name and muted my music. The guys were talking about how much they wanted to fuck her, how hot she was, her *dipshit boyfriend* and why they needed to break up. Although everyone was more friendly, the language was the same as my last crew's, peppered with homophobic insults and sexist tropes. They mused about the women they wanted to fuck or were fucking, who had the best and worst bodies, and who was the most and least annoying, ranking them using absurd hierarchies primarily based on appearance. Not everyone participated in these conversations, but they were loud enough no one could escape hearing them. After a while I stopped engaging.

I wouldn't have called anyone on the crew my friend, except for Jerry, who I adored, but most of the guys were friendly and none of them were outright hostile. Suarez and Al were convivial, always up for good-natured banter. Both were in their thirties and more mature, kind. To them I may have seemed guarded. I carried the weight of what had happened on Phillip's crew everywhere, always fearing this crew would turn against me, constantly policing myself, riddled with shame over the smallest missteps. Any hint of aggression shut me down, and in a high-stress job it's inevitable that people occasionally snap. When that happened I couldn't let it go, even if it was an unintentional slip.

At the same time, my concerns weren't all in my head. When the guys left litter behind after field lunches I quietly picked it up, until Smith, the ex-Marine, got mad at me about it. I didn't speak to him for several days, until he finally apologized. They called me sensitive, and I was, but I tried to hide it. Many of them were sensitive, too. Expressing any sort of emotional woundedness wasn't acceptable and would get you called "butthurt." Someone made fun of me for the way I only swung one arm when I walked. It was playful, but I must have looked upset. "Don't get butthurt," was the response, followed by a comforting tap on my shoulder. I wanted things to be different. They were different in many ways. No one was intentionally trying to hurt me. But I was different, too. More wary than only a few years before. Hypervigilant.

On the crew I faded into the background. In public it was the opposite. People stared. I got used to it, and sometimes enjoyed it, especially when women and girls remarked on my being a firefighter. At a taco shop we frequented, a young girl and her mother stared, wide-eyed. I smiled and the mother whispered in her daughter's ear.

"Are you a firefighter?" the girl asked. She must have been eight or nine. I said yes, and she turned to her mom. "She's a firefighter!" Her mom nodded. "See," she said, "you can be whatever you want." Moments like that carried me through. I was unaccustomed to being a role model.

I came to appreciate Stephanie's habit of wearing her sports bras everywhere, even at fire camp, because it shifted the focus to her. I learned to seek a different kind of attention. In fire camp I always carried two cases of water, one propped on each shoulder. People stared, not ogling but impressed. It was easy to differentiate the two.

* * *

If I could construct a graph of drinking and exercising for the summer of 2005, both would spike together. Because we were based in a high-fire forest, we were home more than out of state. Initial attack lasted a day or two. At home I had myself to contend with. I began overexercising—working out with the crew on base days before our project work and chugging a pre-workout drink packed with caffeine after work, hyping myself up for the gym. I'd lift heavy weights, run, and take spinning classes. By mid-season I could do ten pull-ups and tons of push-ups, a result of my workouts and time spent running the saw, but also my lighter body weight. Eventually I could squat and bench press as much weight as some of the guys. I'd have been stronger without my eating disorder; I knew that then, but couldn't stop. After the gym I drove to meet the guys for drinks, listening to Lhasa de Sela, Juana Molina, and Jolie Holland, rolling my windows down and wailing along.

One evening in my spinning class I got a fire call and sped to the barracks, donning my Nomex and mixing more pre-workout because I went all out at the gym. We raced up Cajon Pass, sirens blaring as we parked on the shoulder. Traffic whizzed past us while we geared up to cut line uphill. I started swamping—grabbing giant masses of brush and stuffing them into holes made by the sawyers, throwing my body against the bundles to shove them into the tight spaces. As I did this, a large piece of whitethorn embedded itself deep into my forearm. I barely noticed. Adrenaline muted all sensation. We were making quick headway. I ignored the cramping sensations in my muscles, focusing on the present moment, my heart roaring with the oceanic sound of traffic below us, radios belching commands and chainsaws screaming. The smoke-scented night crackled around us. I didn't know exactly where the fire was; didn't need to. I was a worker. A drone. A grunt. I loved it.

Chapter Four

Chaparral

Whitethorn is one of many types of chaparrals, the most dominant ecosystem in California, its territory extending from
Southern Oregon into Mexico. Deceptively beige landscapes con-
ceal complex and diverse plant and animal communities with equally
diverse seasons. While plants throughout the U.S. bloom during
spring and summer, Southern California chaparral enters dormancy,
conserving water and slowing growth. In late November and early
December, the landscape blooms, welcoming the dew and humidity.
Single hillsides can host various plant communities depending on slope
aspect, moisture, and elevation. More drought-hardy species thrive on
south-facing slopes parched by sunlight and heat. North-facing slopes
are shadier and therefore more verdant. This differentiation occurs
because of long-term drought adaptations.

Each plant living in a chaparral ecosystem has evolved to thrive
under specific conditions. Coastal mountains in Southern California
act as a rain shadow; moist air rises into the mountains and releases
its moisture so that trees dominate mountains rather than lower
elevations. Wherever their location, chaparral plants have various
methods of drought survival, like increased photosynthetic abilities

(transforming sunlight into food), extensive underground root systems, and oily or waxy leaves that reduce water loss.

There are six unique chaparral ecosystems in Southern California—chamise, manzanita, Ceanothus, scrub oak, montane (mountain), and red shanks. There's also mixed chaparral, which often occurs in the borderlands where differing ecosystems meet and has no dominant species. Ceanothus, also known as California lilac, is nitrogen-fixing, converting atmospheric nitrogen into a form that other plants can use, enriching the soil.

All these chaparral subtypes are fire-adapted, meaning that they have specific characteristics allowing them to survive the infrequent, mid-to-high-severity fire regimes. Typical fire regimes for chaparral occur every 30–150 years and are stand-replacing, which means entire stands of brush and trees are killed, making way for a new generation. Unlike ponderosa pines, which thrive with low-severity fire regimes, chaparral composition encourages crown fires. Leaves are coated in volatile oils; thick, weblike canopies capture and hold fallen leaves and branches which act as tinder. The presence of smoke can cue internal seed germination in some plants; heat breaks down otherwise impermeable seed pods in others. Many chaparral species require fire for germination. Some species regenerate from underground root bulbs. Shortly after fires burn, plants like yucca and laurel sumac emerge from underground, their primary roots protected from even the most severe flames.

Because of higher mortality rates, chaparral habitats need at least ten years to reach healthy maturation after high-severity fires. Increasingly short intervals of low-severity fire have negatively affected the chaparral in California because they require high temperatures for regermination. Hotter fires will kill most weedy and invasive species, but frequent low-severity fires prevent chaparral regeneration and help invasive species flourish, resulting in type conversion. If several low-severity fires recur in a single area in quick succession, chaparral can be completely converted to more flammable invasive grasses and shrubs, transforming the entire landscape in only a year or two.

Fire suppression in Southern California directly contributes to chaparral degeneration. Heavy machinery like dozers, vehicles, and even foot traffic through burned areas interrupts natural processes of reseeding and germination. Retardant composed of water and ammonium phosphate pours from tanker bellies and helicopter buckets, fertilizing hillsides already overrun with non-native species. In such a highly populated region conservation strategies and fire management methods must be nuanced and strategic. It's also important to consider where and how housing is built in and around these habitats. When fires burn and reburn, growing larger with each burn, is it worthwhile to rebuild in their footprints?

Protecting chaparral is complicated because it requires land managers to reestablish and maintain the natural fire regime. It's a complex and diverse ecosystem, requiring knowledgeable caretaking. Fire suppression is vital to the ecosystem because of the prevalence of human-caused fires, but so is well-timed prescribed burning, which may sound counterintuitive. Burning during cooler months and mimicking the mosaic patterns of high-severity fire regimes can help decrease the impact of more light and flammable invasive plants. Protecting and stewarding contiguous areas of chaparral heightens their resilience and encourages species restoration. The Kumeyaay Diegueño Land Conservancy, California Chaparral Institute, and the Nature Conservancy are all proactively engaging with chaparral conservation in Southern California.

Chapter Five

Hollywood

In mid-June I drove out to Hollywood during R & R to escape the Inland Empire. My birth certificate said Los Angeles, but I barely knew the city. My mom arrived there at sixteen or seventeen, after leaving home and working as a dancer in Ketchikan, Alaska. In her journals she expresses ambivalence about accepting gifts from the men she danced for—it felt immoral to accept a fur coat but displeasing to see it handed to another dancer. By the time she arrived in Los Angeles she had been raped more than once. But she was only nineteen and filled with hope.

The city unfolded in front of her like a cardboard cutout, movies come to life, everything resplendent with potential. She had long blonde hair, blue eyes, a petite frame with large breasts, and a smile made crooked by a tooth she'd bonked as a child. Beautiful but naïve, an easy mark for my father: a handsome man twice her age, with salt-and-pepper hair, already thrice divorced. He bought a pretzel from the stand where she worked. In a photograph she stands in front of the pretzel cart, her tight blue T-shirt tucked into tiny red cotton shorts cut high on her smooth legs, her head tilted, long straight blonde hair obscuring half her face. My father was tall, well-dressed, older, and authoritative—none of these traits rang alarm bells. He was also someone important in Scientology, according to her, and commonly wore the Sea Org uniform, which resembles naval uniforms. His lapel was decorated with medals and patches symbolizing his clearance levels and status as an auditor.

My mom often told me about Scientology, especially after her characteristic outbursts of anger and abuse, often while crying. Her time in Los Angeles was harrowing. She said Scientology brainwashed her. Their audits, which took place in a locked room, consisted of repeated questions about her most traumatic secrets: her father wielding the wooden spoon or belt; her mother passed out from too much dope, laying in a pool of vomit; her boyfriend's suicide. The rapes. The questions came and she answered them until she felt herself disintegrating. She said the audit lasted several days. Afterwards she joined my dad at Sea Org, the Scientology center in the desert. The one that wasn't for movie stars. She said they worked all day, seven days a week, with no pay. In return they got housing and classes. She became pregnant and had an abortion. I was her second pregnancy. The birthing details changed with each telling. I was born in a hospital. No, a doctor's office on Hollywood Boulevard, in a tub of water. My father took the car and made her ride the bus. He wasn't there, or he was.

I once asked her why my small face is so often bandaged in childhood pictures from that time. It was a fall from a bookshelf; a broken glass table. There are photos from apartments we may have lived in when I was very young, yet my mom said they didn't let her see me at Sea Org. It was that and my father's lying that led to her leaving. She called him a sociopath. The bottles of expensive cologne; the other women. The lies. I have physical mementos of this time, like my mother's Sea Org bracelet, a polaroid of my father in his Sea Org suit with its medals and sailor's cap, and the blanket his mother crocheted for me just before I was born, a patchwork of pastels and little owls. She died shortly after I was born.

My mom's escape story never changed. She called her parents and said the church was holding her there illegally. Her parents called the church and threatened to call the FBI. My mom drove us back to Washington, my face marked with three scars I still bear today, the worst on my forehead and chin. She kept having to pull over and change my diapers because I had diarrhea. Where did she get the diapers? The gas money? I never asked those questions.

Now I parked and walked past the Hollywood Scientology Center, where they were offering free audits. I wanted to see what it was like, but was too scared to go inside. I walked and watched how others watched me. I wanted to be watched and also didn't want it. Was I pretty? Was I beautiful? Were my shorts giving me a wedgie? Was I ugly? Was I disgusting? Would someone discover me and put me in a movie? I took refuge in a Sephora, where I bought lip-plumping gloss, foundation, and eyeliner. I wanted to go to a bar. I wanted to meet people. But I was too shy. Too scared. After only an hour or two I drove back to the barracks, feeling empty.

Chapter Six

Arrowhead

In early August we drove up into the mountains; lightning had ignited a small patch of land near Lake Arrowhead. We parked and hiked to the snag where lightning had struck and dug line around the fire, containing it quickly. The forest was uniform and full of dead trees. It had once been inhabited by the Yuhaaviatam, or "People of the Pines," a clan of Maara'yam, part of the San Manuel Band of Mission Indians. Back then, before colonization, these mountains and valleys were a diverse mix of conifer forests, chaparral, and black oak woodlands, and the Yuhaaviatam encouraged biodiversity with frequent patchwork burning, creating a mosaic of meadows, shrublands, and forests in varying stages of growth. Their late autumn burns stimulated the growth of deer grass, used for basketry materials, and black oak, whose acorns provided sustenance. Fire stimulated the germination of medicinal wild tobacco, yerba santa, mugwort, and basketweed and kept pests at bay.

In the 1850s Mormon settlers started harvesting trees, using horses and buggies to transport timber to the lowlands. In 1899 Brookings Lumber Company installed a narrow gauge railroad to support clearcutting. Loggers took the largest, healthiest trees, leading to an overall decline in forest health and resiliency. Disturbed soils and increased sunlight led to invasive species and disrupted the equilibrium maintained by the Yuhaaviatam, whom the settlers violently displaced. Fire's natural cycles were suppressed, knocking everything out of balance.

Our drive up to Lake Arrowhead snaked through miles of browned, dying trees, ravaged by bark beetles. Dull orange pine needles layered the ground, creating a monochromatic landscape. The apocalyptic scenery was a direct result of fire suppression, in combination with climate change and increased drought. Following logging in the late nineteenth and early twentieth centuries, the CCC planted thousands of ponderosa and Jeffrey pines in an effort to restore forests. This had the opposite effect, overcrowding forests with homogenous species. Before logging, the Jeffrey and ponderosas had grown alongside sugar pines, incense cedar, black oak, and white fir. Frequent fire maintained a relatively open canopy. Streams and meadows thrived, supporting cottonwoods, willows, and other riparian species. Most pine forests thrive with low tree density and diverse mosaics. Abundant pine trees were planted post-logging but were never able to reach maturity due to overcrowding. The trees siphoned moisture from the soil, dehydrating riparian habitats and draining the landscape. Then came drought, and again, and again.

Healthy trees have an arsenal of defenses against beetles: moist, honey-like resin protects their inner bark, where beetles lay their eggs, and toxic compounds, like monoterpenes and phenolics present in resin and bark, deter or kill the beetles. Some trees develop genetic adaptations, like drought tolerance, thickened bark, larger resin ducts, and increasingly toxic resin. The regular presence of fire also lessens beetle populations. In the absence of frequent fire and regular winter freezes, beetle populations have surged. Weakened trees are less defended and succumb more easily to the pests.

Scientist Diana Six argues that the bark beetles mimic fire by culling the weakest trees, killing saplings, and regulating overall tree health. There's evidence that beetles are attracted to trees from weaker gene pools, which means that trees surviving beetle outbreaks are naturally hardier and drought tolerant. I had thought this landscape was apocalyptic, but it was adaptive.

In 1962 carbon dioxide measurements taken at Mauna Loa proved that levels were rising in the earth's atmosphere. Since then, scientists have, with increasing frequency, urged public, corporate, and government sectors to reduce global carbon emissions. They've made little headway. In 1997, President Bill Clinton signed on to the Kyoto Protocol, a worldwide effort to lower rates of greenhouse emissions, but this was vetoed by the U.S. Senate, citing economic harm. President George W. Bush exited the Kyoto process altogether in 2001. In the years since, climate change has been increasingly politicized, with many arguing that the earth's natural temperature varies throughout history. While this is true, there's clearly a direct link to rising temperatures and rising greenhouse emissions. In 2005 when I was working in Southern California, the dominant phrase was "global warming." We never talked about it on the crew, just as we avoided any political conversations. Global warming was a political debate rather than a scientific fact.

With the acceleration of climate change high-severity fires are now more frequent than when I was working in Southern California. Since the mid-1980s fires have tripled in acreage burned, averaging three million acres per year. The average temperature in California rose two degrees between 2005 and 2020, exacerbating the effects of California's natural drought cycle. Scientists estimate that temperatures will rise another four degrees by mid-century. I thought I had seen drought in California, but the worst came after I stopped working as a firefighter, from 2012 to 2016, when California experienced its worst drought in 1,200 years. Because of invasive species encroachment and overdevelopment, much of the soil in California has difficulty absorbing snow in wet seasons, and because of the temperature increase, less moisture comes as snow; instead, it rains, and rain is more ephemeral, disappearing in runoff instead of slowly melting into soils. When snow does come it melts faster, reducing absorption.

After the 2002 fire season, George W. Bush passed the Healthy Forests Restoration Act (HFRA), which called for increased logging in protected areas under the premise of controlling fire danger, a win for timber lobbyists. Federal land purchasing power was once again expanded, allowing the establishment of forest reserves on previously private land. The HFRA removed due process permitting, so timber companies could thin otherwise protected areas, like wildlife refuges and designated wilderness, through a simplified environmental review process, restricting public input. Timber companies repeated past mistakes, logging the largest and most valuable trees while leaving smaller trees and brush behind. They worked without the input of scientists and often left highly flammable slash in their wake. The HFRA was essentially a free pass for logging companies to reinforce negative feedback loops under the guise of "restoration." Instead of protecting vulnerable WUI communities, the HFRA focused on rural areas. And of course, since its inception, the Forest Service has profited from selling timber to logging companies, although these profits have diminished greatly in recent years.

Thinning and logging operations conducted by timber companies and without scientific guidance are unequivocally detrimental to local ecosystems. Soil impaction from machinery washes runoff into local waterways, choking local marine life with sediment, pesticides, and other pollutants. Algae blooms, dies, and decomposes, absorbing the water's oxygen and leading to mass die-offs of aquatic species, the impacts of which ripple outwards. Habitats fracture. Disturbed soils hang their welcome signs for invasive species. Greenhouse gases belch from dozers and excavators. We are also in the age of climate change, with its lengthened summers and warmer winters. Snow melts faster in warmer, vigorously thinned forests because of increased sun exposure. Dry soil means parched and dying plants. Logging destroys the soil's fungal networks and decreases forest resiliency.

The HFRA included provisions for prescribed fire, but allocated significantly less funding for its implementation. Most funded projects failed. Tens of millions of acres of land in the United States currently suffer from the effects of fire exclusion and suppression. Because of proximity to communities and high fuel buildup, not all areas are prime candidates for immediate burning.

In 2024, the pace of prescribed fire application accelerated, likely a result of the Biden Administration's support. By June 2024 over sixty thousand acres had been burned on prescription in California alone. Thinning has its drawbacks, but it's an essential component to this process, because overgrown forests burn at temperatures too high for even the most fire-adapted trees to withstand. In some cases, this can be remedied by clearing fuels from the bases of trees, but this isn't always enough. When it's done correctly, thinning removes the less valuable smaller trees while leaving the larger, healthier ones in place. The process is slower and more methodical than traditional logging, and is undertaken with the guidance of ecologists. It's also less economically profitable. But small diameter trees and brush can be repurposed as mulch and compost, biomass fuel, artisanal lumber, and biocomposite products (think IKEA). Government subsidies and community initiatives can provide employment while also promoting forest health. Defunct logging mills can also be repurposed and redesigned. Studies have shown that mechanical thinning has a negligible effect on wildfire mitigation when it's not paired with some sort of prescribed burning. Restoration thinning is not a standalone solution—thinning works best in tandem with prescribed fire.

Many scientists claim that restoration thinning is harmful, no matter how carefully it's conducted. Post-fire salvage logging compounds harm. This is a hotly debated topic. Some of the research is conducted by the Forest Service and is therefore not necessarily reliable. Just as tobacco companies suppressed internal studies proving that smoking was safe, any research funded by an agency or company where profit is involved is inherently questionable.

President Biden's ten-year strategy acknowledges some of the damage caused by extreme fire suppression and posits collaborative approaches to forest health and wildfire mitigation. It's a detailed plan, but as long as the Forest Service is enmeshed with extractive industries, its success may be limited. In the scientific journal *Ecosphere*, one study proved that forests protected from logging are more fire resilient—this plainly suggests that logging, and even thinning, can exacerbate fire behavior and damage forests. Ideally thinning is a temporary measure. Once fire is fully reintroduced on a regular schedule, forests won't need mechanical thinning.

One strategy of Biden's plan is aimed at managing what the document calls "high-risk firesheds." Firesheds are fire-adapted (or fire-prone) areas most likely to impact WUI communities. While it seems logical to prioritize the treatment of landscapes where humans and their homes will be the most "directly" impacted, this doesn't take into account the long-range impacts of large fires burning in more remote areas—their choking smoke and negative impacts on watersheds and vital water sources—as well as the ecological impacts of large high-severity fires on flora, fauna, watersheds, and water sources. We also need to account for effects on the electrical grid and communications infrastructure, on tribal lands, as well as the danger of ember wash, which can sometimes float miles ahead of the fire and, upon landing, ignite new fires. While Bush's plan focused on more remote areas, Biden's does the opposite. This is the habit of federal land management, always swinging from one pole to the other and rarely lingering in the middle. Still, Biden's plan is swinging in a more optimistic direction. A 2021 memorandum proclaimed that Indigenous Traditional Ecological Knowledge (ITEK) "can and should inform federal decision making along with scientific inquiry." Three years later, in 2024, the Biden-Harris administration invested $120 million towards tribal climate resilience.

Emphasizing high population areas, accounting for impacts on disenfranchised populations, and uplifting ITEK are all avenues that have rarely been explored on a federal level. The key is bipartisanship, which isn't as impossible as many assume. Many ranchers, farmers, and citizens across the political spectrum share the same goal of fostering ecological health in the United States. Biden's plan prioritizes prescribed fire, but bipartisan commitment is essential to success over time, as is cooperation with environmental nonprofits, fire advocacy groups, and Indigenous tribes. Implementing prescribed burns, which often need to be repeated every 2–20 years (depending on the natural fire return interval of any given landscape), continues to be a maze of bureaucratic red tape for government agencies and nonprofits. Many tribes have been advocating for cultural burning rights, but Indigenous burners and nonprofits alike report that some local, state, and federal agencies are reluctant to relinquish power. Each agency's level of cooperation differs depending on personal and/or departmental preference, because there aren't any overarching guidelines regarding the allowance of cultural burning.

There is also an urgent need for certified burn bosses (who can lead prescribed burns) and reducing the risk of personal liability in the case of escaped fires, which are rare but inevitable. Federal fuel management plans are allotted under one hundred million dollars each year, whereas the federal government spends billions each year on wildfire suppression, and wildfires blazing through lands hungry for fire can cause upwards of thirty billion in damages in a single fire season. More fire-prone states need additional federal funding specifically designated for local agencies and advocacy groups—not only for fire management, but also public education, emergency response, and community safety updates.

Biden's strategy, like those that came before, focuses on acreage and fuel treatment, but Lenya Quinn-Davidson, director of the Northern California Prescribed Fire Council, says that one of the primary issues with these acts is language-based. Rather than acreage and treatment, agencies should focus on stewardship. The idea of land stewardship rather than land management requires an entire paradigm shift on the part of government agencies across the political spectrum. Letting cultural burners guide our way forward, rather than simply including them in federal documents and plans, would be a productive way to begin shifting the fire paradigm from management to stewardship. Supporting federal land management agencies and their employees is also an integral piece of the puzzle.

Chapter Seven

Lewis

I met Lewis, a white guy in his mid-thirties, when we were out at a bar. He was only a little taller than me, balding, with a sexy gravelly voice and a soft, quiet demeanor. The guys were always looking to hook me up with someone—a few of them had surmised my preferences by watching who I turned away at the bars. I wasn't attracted to masculine posturing or overtly feminine women; nor did I care much about physical appearance. It was an energy. The guys called me picky; alternative. Maybe "alternative" was a catch-all term for something outside of the binary paradigm of straight or gay, masculine or feminine. When Bobby saw Lewis watching me he covertly pointed him out. "Go stand at the bar," he said. "No guy is gonna come up to you when you're with all of us."

Lewis and I shut down the bar. He was a former hotshot in school for pharmacology. We ended up at his house; in his bedroom the streetlights glowed a dull, diaphanous orange as he removed my shirt, kissed my chest, and unclasped my bra before kneeling to pull off my pants, wrapping his arms around my legs before making me come. I realized I'd never orgasmed with a man before, only with women. He put on a condom without my having to ask, which was sexy. After he came I held his shuddering body and he slept. I never slept well after one-night stands. A couple times I woke him with my tossing and turning, and he asked me if I was okay, gently rubbing my back as if I were a child that needed comforting. I did need comforting. I hadn't been touched with affection in many months. Or years.

He drove me back to the barracks in the morning, after bringing me coffee in bed. Without alcohol I was self-conscious, both of myself and him. I didn't know him. I was so starved for intimacy and so scared of being seen. He kissed me when he dropped me off. In the cool, sparse barracks a sadness bloomed inside me; a longing. I wanted to go back home with him, live with him, marry him. Intellectually I knew these feelings weren't about him in particular, but my body thought they were.

Chapter Eight

Pinyon-Juniper

N ear the season's end we were called to Utah, chinking fireline in the overwhelming desert heat. Throughout the season there had been periodic turnover—this is common on hotshot crews; people quit, injure themselves, or stay behind for personal reasons. Krista, my barracks roommate, had come with us as a replacement for an injured crew member. She usually worked on an engine. On base she struggled during hikes and runs but no one faulted her. Instead, we encouraged her, and she quickly improved. We'd been extended after a twenty-four-hour shift. All of us were exhausted, waiting for the rest of the crew to fly in via helicopter. Clayton, one of the younger guys, aimlessly spun his shovel in the dirt while the rest of us sorted through our brown bag lunches. Krista and I were sitting on the ground, using our packs as makeshift camp chairs.

"I thought hotshotting would be so cool," Clayton said, gazing dead-eyed at the dirt formations traced by his shovel like they were tea leaves bearing future fortunes. "I thought I'd do it forever. But this shit sucks."

I snorted. It did suck. We were all exhausted and burned out. Mornings and evenings were filled with the sounds of our hacking coughs. Every day brought another sweltering desert hike through sharp rocks and trailless wilderness. My entire body ached. I'd gone through several bottles of ibuprofen and countless packets of Emergen-C. Our yellow shirts were stained pink with retardant from the previous day, when we were cutting direct fireline along the fire's flank, right in the path of a tanker drop. All of us got soaked.

The fire in Utah was in what Phillip had called "PJ": pinyon pine and juniper woodlands and savannah, a prevalent fire-adapted ecosystem throughout the Great Basin, which spans Nevada, a sliver of northeastern California and southwest Oregon, and the western half of Utah. The arid Great Basin resides in a rain shadow created by several mountain ranges. When it rains, the water sinks underground, evaporates, or settles into saline lakes, which are remnants of the water that filled the entire basin thousands of years ago. The word "basin" is deceiving; really there are many basins interspliced by mountain ranges. This topography creates many ecologically diverse microclimates. The Great Basin contains both the lowest and highest points in the U.S.: Death Valley's salt flats, called Badwater Basin, and Mount Whitney, both in California. Its lower elevations are often four thousand feet above sea level, mostly consisting of sagebrush and mixed-shrub woodlands. In higher elevations, there are bristlecone pines and alpine and subalpine forests. The foothills are predominantly pinyon-juniper woodlands.

Much as Indigenous Californians depended (and depend) on acorns, Indigenous people living in the Great Basin depended (and depend) on the pinyon pine nuts, eating them whole and grinding them into flour. Their high fat content is perfect for pine nut butter. They used pinyon pitch for medicinal salves, glue, and waterproofing. Buildings and boats were once built from pinyon pines and juniper wood, along with hairbrushes and weapons. Juniper seeds adorned their jewelry; juniper berries were eaten, made into medicine, and transformed into dye. Tribes living in the Great Basin also burned the land frequently, lighting ground fires to renew grass and shrubs and lure grazing animals for hunting. For over ten thousand years Indigenous tribes like the Ute, Shoshone, Navajo, and Paiute coexisted with the ecology of the Great Basin. They maintained permanent winter dwellings in the valleys and spent the warmer months searching for sustenance. Although I am using the past tense, many of these practices are still in place today.

Pinyon pine and juniper are both small scraggly trees, adapted to arid climates. Some junipers are over 1,500 years old, but never look like what most people consider old-growth. Their wood grain is so rough that it quickly dulls chainsaws; their tree rings are minuscule and close together because lack of moisture slows their growth. Pinyon pines can live for hundreds of years. These two species grow together and separately. PJ ecosystems contain over four hundred types of plants and are home to over one hundred species of vertebrates.

Domesticated grazing animals were first introduced during European settlement and have transformed the Great Basin. The Bureau of Land Management manages thousands of miles of grazing land throughout the Great Basin and the Southwest, and leases this land to ranchers. The presence of grazing animals has altered fire regimes in the region. Habitats are now threatened by increasingly short fire intervals because of cheatgrass and other highly flammable invasive species. Cheatgrass carries fire faster and hotter than other plants because it sheds its stalks more often, creating dry fine fuels, and, unlike many native species, continues growing rapidly throughout the winter. Like most of the United States, this ecosystem has also been adversely affected by fire suppression. Pinyon jays, a keystone species, will disappear without pinyon pines. Their beaks are especially adapted to extract the oily pine nuts from their cones, and without the jays spreading their seeds the trees themselves will disappear. Clark's nutcrackers also depend on pine nuts and spread seeds. All are integral to each other's survival. In the early 2000s, when I was working in this fuel type, pinyon pines and junipers were already facing the effects of long-term drought—one study predicted that pinyon pines could be extinct by 2100. These ecosystems have limited ability to adapt to climate change, with low resistance to warming temperatures.

Both the USFS and BLM claim pinyon pine and juniper habitats are "threatening" sagebrush woodlands, the home of the endangered sage grouse, but in fact PJ ecosystems exist in concert with native sagebrush woodlands, blending along their edges. Over 250 million acres of land are currently leased by federal agencies (primarily the BLM) to livestock and grazing interests. PJ habitats are being decimated throughout the Great Basin. The BLM has stated outright that they do not have a cohesive plan for properly managing these habitats, nor are they willing to engage with conservation or tribal groups in a significant way.

The trees themselves are also being clear-cut and sold. Nevada governor Joe Lombardo signed an agreement with Denmark in 2024 to convert 1.6 million acres of pinyon-juniper into green methanol. Ironically, removing the trees will lower land resiliency and carbon storage. Many scientists and advocacy groups have spoken out against this, expressing concern that newfound profitability could result in increased deforestation. The BLM continues to insist that PJ habitats should be destroyed for environmental reasons; they use machines with names like "Bull Hog" and "Ely Chain." A Bull Hog is a bulldozer equipped with a giant mulcher. The Ely Chain uses two bulldozers, attaching two ends of a giant chain to their hooks and then raking the chain over the habitat. Neither method has been proven successful for increasing habitat for the sage grouse, but these methods have increased receptiveness to invasive flammable grasses. To make matters worse, the BLM reseeds with non-native seeds rather than native seeds, claiming that there aren't enough native seeds available. Critics believe that they are simply clearing lands so they can lease them for grazing, prioritizing profit over the environment.

These so-called restoration projects also implement selective thinning. Scientists claim that lack of oversight inhibits these projects from being truly helpful. Prescribed fire is much more useful. Pinyon pine and juniper ecosystems don't benefit from wide tree spacing, unlike some other pine ecosystems, like ponderosa. While fires in ponderosa ecosystems are most often low severity, with short fire return intervals of 5–30 years, fire intervals for Great Basin PJ, determined by tree-ring data, are much longer, about 150–500 years, and burn hot. Like chaparral, PJ habitats thrive with stand-replacing fires.

I loved the stunted little trees sprouting on plateaus and in valley crevices and in rocky outcroppings. The tall, stalky cheatgrass shot up in prolific spikes, but I also noticed native grasses, like bluebunch wheatgrass. The fire we were called to was wind-driven. When wind pushes a fire, flames can skip over certain portions, leaving them unburned. Fire personnel often call this a "dirty" burn because fires can be reignited and reburn, or start a new fire by throwing firebrands. A clean burn means the fire has a clear edge, and within that edge it burns the fuels consistently, but with PJ dirty burns are more commonplace, and healthier from an ecological standpoint. A jagged, spotty edge and portions of green within the burn made it imperative that we gridded thoroughly to make sure everything was out.

The language of "dirty" and "clean" was ours and not nature's. We saw dirty burns as a bad thing, but they are part of the natural fire mosaic, essential to its overall health. Dirty burns are, in an ecological sense, an ideal outcome of wildfire.

Chapter Nine

Dream Self

When we got home, ineligible for mandatory days off, I called in sick, sure that my raw, scratchy throat was the beginning of strep. I never connected it to my bulimia or smoke inhalation. The next day Gardinelli, our new superintendent, called me into his office to confront me about my absence while Mike, the other captain, sat silently. Bobby's girlfriend had seen me at the local shopping plaza and Gardinelli thought I was shirking work. I wondered how Bobby's girlfriend could have recognized me because we had never met.

"I was getting a Jamba Juice," I said. "My throat hurt, so I thought it would help me get better faster." This was true. Gardinelli reluctantly accepted my answer. I could tell he didn't believe me and was stunned that they really thought I was trying to skip work. For what? Mike followed me out of the office and tapped me on my shoulder, an earnest expression on his freckled face. "I had nothing to do with that," he said.

We had been washing the buggies, and when I rejoined the crew I was near tears. Not from sadness, but anger. Several of the guys had taken time off throughout the year. Why was it me who got questioned? As I scrubbed the side of the buggy questions roiled through

my mind. I always worked hard. I always volunteered and did everything that was asked of me. Secretly I suspected I'd never be fully
accepted on any hotshot crew—was it my fault, I thought, for letting
down my guard? Suppose I had called out of work without being
sick. Why would that matter? I imagined conversations behind closed
doors; imagined that no one wanted me on the crew at all, that even
Jerry thought I shouldn't be there. My body flooded with adrenaline,
reliving what had happened on Solar Hotshots.

I pulled the hose inside the buggy and started washing the floor.
When I was finished I slipped off the edge of the last buggy step,
careening backwards and slamming the back of my head on its hard
metal edge. Everyone gathered around me. My vision blackened
momentarily. When the black receded Jerry was there, tracing his
fingers in front of my eyes. "I'm fine," I said, not wanting to call more
attention to myself. But I wasn't fine. An hour or two later Jerry sent
me to urgent care, where I was diagnosed with a concussion.

I told Lewis about the meeting and my concussion. He always
answered if I called and responded to my texts, but never initiated
contact. We'd only spent a handful of nights together, sometimes
watching football or going straight to his room to have sex. Afterwards we'd lay in bed, talking. He was smart. He thought I was
smart. I told him how much I liked him. Both of us were naked in
bed. "If you don't like me, tell me now," I said, propping myself up
on an elbow. "If you're scared of things getting serious." He put his
hand over mine, resting on his chest. We kissed. I surrendered myself
to him, relishing the freedom of physical intimacy, the only kind of
intimacy I was comfortable with. We shivered when we touched.
When he came his teeth chattered. As he slept I listened to his soft
snoring and wondered who he wanted me to be. I imagined myself
wearing a USC baseball cap, baking green bean casserole, my hair
dyed light brown, his favorite color.

I sought out people like Lewis. People who'd never answer a question directly but always responded to my messages. People who didn't see me. For them I could be totally vulnerable, kept safe by the distance between us. I thought I wanted him. That I wanted to be loved. But I was terrified of love.

Near the end of the season crew leadership threw us a celebratory dinner at an Italian restaurant. I invited Lewis and he said he'd meet me there. The lighting was dim and everyone surrounded the table: all the guys, many with their girlfriends and wives. I kept glancing at the entrance, hoping to see Lewis. When I got up to go outside some of the guys gave me concerned glances. They knew about Lewis, that I liked him.

Outside the spindly palm fronds rasped and quivered in the wind. I texted Lewis three times. The blank square of my Nokia screen glared at me. I called. Direct to voicemail. My heart sunk to the bottom of my stomach. I pictured him at home, looking at his phone, not answering, spiking my tongue with metallic desperation. Fuck him, I thought, hardening. I lit a cigarette, leaning against the restaurant's façade, trying to look cool. I pictured Juliette Lewis in *Natural Born Killers*, smoking and driving through a desert town. This was what I pictured when I needed strength, an image of a woman running away from herself, looking for another man to satisfy her when the one she loved had let her down. I finished the cigarette and went inside. Al asked me if everything was okay. His concern scalded me with my own reflected vulnerability. We had a shared experience of being alone, both of us for our own reasons.

The younger guys announced an exodus to the Roundup, a hybrid country hip-hop club that never failed to entertain me. I chain-smoked on the way there, too buzzed for driving. That night I went home with a woman I'd line-danced with and woke up encased in her black sheets, smelling of her cologne. We'd had good sex; sex with women was almost always better than the sex I had with men, but too intimate. It exposed me in a way I couldn't tolerate. She bought me a Frappuccino on the way back to my car, then gave me her number, on a business card. I found it in the cracks of my car's console months later. I never called her.

I took a few trips to L.A. for OkCupid and MySpace dates, to distract myself from being stood up. I liked the city and the people I met. One date brought me to a small gathering in Silver Lake, where several people played instruments and sang a Gillian Welch song. I clanged a triangle, singing along. Someone said I had a good voice. I rarely hung out with such charismatic and intelligent people who also happened to be supporting themselves financially. These were my people. I look at myself in those moments and ask, *Why didn't you stay there?* The prospect of a welcoming community was almost painful. It was easier to reject them before they could, as I figured they would, reject me. I didn't go back to L.A. again after that, despite several texts from my date and a few from his friends, with whom I'd exchanged numbers.

Instead, I stayed in the Inland Empire, in the town where Lewis lived, renting a room in a house I shared with two guys. I had called Lewis crying after he hadn't shown at the restaurant. It was too much, he'd said. What was too much? I asked. Having dinner at a restaurant? He didn't answer. I told him it was okay. His wanting me felt essential. When he went days without texting or calling, I holed up in my room, the blinds closed and ceiling fan whirring as I hid under my covers, refusing to speak to anyone.

I withered away that winter, subsisting on microwave frozen veggies stirred with a dollop of Vegenaise, hard ciders and Smirnoff malt liquor and cheap beer. Going to the gym halfheartedly. Some evenings I drank with my roommates in the garage, staring out at the blank suburban street and pretending my own life wasn't the exact thing I'd wanted to avoid. I saw him at a bar. We ended up in his bed again. He told me how much he liked me, how he wished he was more available. I told him it was okay, hungry for scraps of his affection. I'd acquired a taste for scraps.

One evening I drove to his house to give him a letter I'd written, telling him how much I liked him. He read it in his lounge chair and said we were finished. "This is over," he said. Then we slept together.

Greta, my best friend from summer camp, visited San Diego. I put on my cutest, sluttiest dress and drove out there, drinking from a bottle of Bombay Sapphire. Years later I asked Greta what she had thought of me, arriving to the restaurant with stick straight blonde hair and gin breath. She said that it was like I wasn't even there, like I was someone she didn't know anymore.

In January Gardinelli offered me a permanent position on the crew. I accepted a seasonal position on a hotshot crew in Colorado instead. I wanted to live somewhere totally new. Away from this spiraling version of myself. Leaving was my answer to everything. My mom and I never stayed anywhere long enough for me to know what home felt like. Life with her was like a roiling ocean; tranquil one moment, deadly the next. I strained to hold back the tide. If only I could transform myself into someone useful the waters would calm. I can conjure myself as a young girl: my fragile, undeveloped sense of self like the tender bell of a jellyfish, impotent tendrils tangling in my mother's waters, attempting to pacify the sea. I drifted along with her into the new lives she sought, always looking for something better, from school to school and apartment to apartment, each new place layering me with armor until my softest parts were hidden, even from myself. As I got older the world became my ocean, just as unpredictable. I soothed myself with fantasies of new lives. Better lives. Just as she had done.

PART IV
Colorado (2006)

Chapter One

Home

I had turned twenty-five in San Bernardino. I visited my mother and Vern over Christmas, in Olympia. She was newly obsessed with a book called *The Law of Attraction*. When we were out to lunch she confessed to renting an apartment in Seattle, so she could see her younger boyfriend. By April, when I visited her on my way to Colorado, she had left Vern and rented a house. I drove down the steep hill gridded with miniature speed bumps. The sun was setting over Lake Washington, painting the low heavy clouds deep amethyst. When I arrived my mom met me outside, followed by Sandy, the dog I'd gotten from a shelter before leaving home at eighteen, who was whining her happy greeting. My mom's watery eyes told me she'd been drinking for a while, and a knot tightened in my chest. It had been a long time since I'd seen her without Vern there as a buffer.

Her house was filled to the brim with knickknacks: mid-century ceramics; garish lamps with carved hula girls and tropical designs; strings of multicolored glass lights. There were random mounds of paper scattered about. She was nervous, asking me what I thought of the place, bragging about her job. "I'm making six figures," she said. The house was small, permeated with the scent of mildew and ancient, long-gone occupants. When she opened a closet, I was surprised to see at least ten suits hanging inside. "Those are Vern's," she said. But they looked too small for him.

Todd, her younger boyfriend, was on a trip to South Africa. She failed to mention buying his ticket; I found out later that she spent thousands of dollars on him. Her blank eyes avoided mine as she offered me wine and suggested we go out for a night on the town. Her treat. She knew I'd been living on unemployment all winter, waiting for the next fire season. She didn't know how much I'd been drinking or throwing up.

We had dinner and ended up at a tiki bar downtown. Her cackle caught the attention of two men sitting nearby, both of them a little older than me and much younger than her. She was only forty-six years old, three years older than I am now, pretty and charismatic. Nudging me conspiratorially, she asked them to join us. I was buzzed from dinner and wine. We'd dug a tunnel through my adolescence back to my childhood, back to when I was her little best friend and confidant, as if the thirteen years between then and now had never happened. The men scooted in; her demeanor changed and I saw myself reflected in the way she shapeshifted in the presence of men. The sharp focus of her gaze told me she was calculating their attention, noticing their attraction to me. This was dangerous.

Three women my age came and squished themselves into the booth with us, chattering about a house party. "Let's go," my mom said, surprising all of us. We made our way to the door, my mom leaning on one of the guys.

Outside I noticed the Mexican place where I'd devoured tortilla chips and water after running away when I was twelve. This sobered me up. My mom stumbled into the front seat of the men's car. I took the back seat, sitting next to the other guy. His beard glowed copper. He put his hand on my leg and I knew I'd go home with him.

At the party, the girls wanted to know all about firefighting. I mentioned wanting to live in Seattle. "But I can't live here," I said. "It's too close to my mom." Sympathetic nods. The one with a black bob and round brown eyes said it must be hard. "It's like she's not even an adult." I nodded, my sternum unraveling into a wave of nausea. She wasn't in the living room. Someone said they'd seen her on the front stoop.

I opened the front door and my mom was sitting on the stoop, making out with someone. I felt as if I were in someone else's body. Their mouths parted. She slurred a hello. The man left and I sat down; she slumped into me, her hair scented with Annick Goutal's tuberose perfume. "I just wanted to be kissed," she said. Of course she did. I stroked her head.

"You can leave me here," I said.

"Okay," she said. "I'll pick you up in the morning. Just call me." Once she left I snuggled into Copper Beard. The girls crowded around us as if I were a foreign treasure rescued from the ocean floor.

The whole visit she was manic—glued to the *Law of Attraction* CD set playing in her car on repeat, evasive when I inquired about her life. We visited an old Scientology friend at his record store. She kept talking about a possible divorce settlement; opening a bookstore and traveling the world with Todd. We ate at her favorite lunch spot but she wanted wine, not food. Her eyes cast about the room. "That guy is checking me out," she said, whispering. "I think the waiter has a crush on you." Glasses of chardonnay disappeared in three gulps. "Can I have a double?" she asked the waiter. "A double?" he asked, confused. I told him to fill her glasses to the top. There was no stopping her. By the time we got home she was drunk, chain-smoking on the porch. We sat out there staring at the lake's reflective waves, the lines of headlights and taillights on the floating bridge. "I hope this fire season is good," I said. "I need to make money."

She stiffened. "You're too negative," she said. "Negative thoughts attract bad things. That's why you're so unhappy. You need to be positive, like me. Now that I have the *Law of Attraction* everything is so much better."

So much better echoed into the darkness. Things were not so much better, clearly, but I said nothing. Who was I to talk? And what good would it have done?

Chapter Two

Yellowstone

I drove east, through Washington and Idaho, then southeast into Montana before taking 191 south into Yellowstone National Park, which is situated in the northwest corner of Wyoming. The land is ancient, pockmarked with calderas and interlaced with jewel-colored geothermal springs. Meadows bloom with wildflowers in springtime, painting the land with rainbow hues. Autumn turns aspen and cottonwood leaves gold. Many Indigenous tribes created vast trail systems through the landscape, including the Crow, Nez Perce, Shoshone, Blackfeet, and Flathead. Tribes hunted and gathered throughout the area in summer, collecting wild carrot, camas, willow, chokecherry, and bitterroot. They corralled bison and elk on horseback, stalked bighorn sheep, and hunted pronghorn in the open grasslands. All of the tribes cultivated vegetation with fire, luring game to fresh growth.

Fur trappers arrived in the early 1800s, followed by prospectors and then the U.S. Army. In 1872 Yellowstone became the nation's first national park, established to "preserve" the "wild" land from extractive interests like logging and mining, but it also served to officially break the Fort Laramie treaties. The first park rangers were plucked from the military. The Nez Perce warred with whites in 1877, until

the U.S. government forced tribes onto reservations and into hellish
Indian residential schools. One tribe, the Tukudika, remained in the
park for several years after its establishment, but they were nearly
decimated by smallpox and eventually joined the Eastern Shoshone
at Wind River Reservation. This was, of course, part of a pattern that
unfolded throughout the United States, and continues unfolding as
long as tribes are unable to access, protect, and occupy their ancestral
lands.

Yellowstone National Park is only a small section of a vast, diverse
landscape called the Greater Yellowstone Ecosystem, which hosts an
abundance of wildlife and remarkably biodiverse ecosystems. The park
is located just north of Grand Teton National Park, surrounded by
national forests not only in Wyoming but also throughout Montana
and Idaho. It's one of the most popular National Parks in the United
States, with over three million annual visitors. Yellowstone's history of
fire suppression and management is complicated. It was the first protected area to use military resources for fire defense. In 1886 the U.S.
Army took over administrative and protective duties and established
the first fire crews to battle large fires. The Army built campgrounds,
instigated patrols, and fought every fire they found. This established a
working model for firefighting in "wild" areas throughout the country.

When I drove through the park in 2006 I saw scars from the
infamous 1988 "Yellowstone Fires." Blackened lodgepole pines stood
like narrow sentinels, surrounded by tall green pines and green undergrowth. I was only eight years old when lightning ignited eighteen
fires inside Yellowstone National Park boundaries in June of 1988. The
Park Service had, for the past fifteen years, been letting fires burn if
they didn't threaten structures. Lightning strikes often sparked fires
which sputtered out when summer rains arrived, or stopped when they
reached younger, less flammable forests or green riparian waterways.
A healthy fire mosaic usually prevents giant fires. This works particularly well in lodgepole-populated Yellowstone. Lodgepole fire regimes

occur once every 150–400 years. Fires burn hot and kill most of the trees. Yellowstone's thin volcanic soil deprives shrubs and bushes of vital nutrients so they grow slowly. Instead of shrubs, the forest floor is populated by small spruce and fir trees, which can take decades or centuries to fuel a large, destructive fire.

July 1988 was atypical according to records, which are short in terms of geological time. In retrospect the year foreshadowed a future of shifting fire regimes with the coming of climate change. The summer rains didn't come. The park called in suppression resources but they couldn't contain the fires. By July 28th, the intensifying fires had burned a hundred thousand acres. The media portrayed the fires as catastrophic, working the public into a frenzy. They blamed the fire's voracity on the decades of fuel buildup and likened the "buildup" to gasoline, tacitly ignoring scientific evidence proving that the fires were, essentially, normal. Reporters politicized the fires, inventing the term "let it burn" and blaming environmentalists. Tourists and homeowners fled the park and surrounding areas. Erratic winds threw firebrands ahead of the flames, rendering fire crews useless. Air attack failed to extinguish the flames. Arriving National Guard soldiers geared up in Nomex, but nothing could stop the fires. On September 11, 1988, snow extinguished the fire, doing what firefighters couldn't. All that money and only snow could douse the fire. This happens more often than federal agencies want to admit.

In 1984 fire historian and former wildland firefighter Stephen Pyne had written a fire plan for the park, encouraging more prescribed burns to enhance protective fire mosaics. He warned officials that they were ill-prepared for large fires, but they were too preoccupied with debates about whether there should be fires in the park at all. They couldn't accept fire's integral role in the park's ecosystem; all of this despite the 1963 Leopold Report. The issue wasn't their "let it burn" policy, as outlined by the media, it was their failure to implement more prescribed fires.

Yellowstone's distinctive ecosystem wasn't part of the news cycle, just as its past fire suppression wasn't. Intense crown fires kill lodgepole pines while also releasing seeds locked away in their cones. Once the 1988 fires passed the seeds propagated in the ash-layered soil. Research into soil-fertilizing microbes shows that they increase only a few days after fire burns. News footage portrayed the park as destroyed, its natural splendor "gone forever." Clips of blackened land paraded across TV screens with words like "moonscape" and "decimated." The public was left unaware of Yellowstone's dynamic fire intervals: repeating cycles of disposal and renewal, burning the older trees and encouraging a flush of new, green growth. In the northern range of the park, where there are richer soils, the fire interval has been as short as twenty-five years, burning through grassland, aspen, spruce, fir, and riparian (riverside) vegetation, which replenishes more quickly than lodgepole pine. Media coverage of fires has improved in recent years. Most journalists include blurbs about the importance of prescribed fire and the enduring impacts of fire suppression. Though sensationalist fear-mongering still exists, it's no longer the norm.

As I drove through the Yellowstone almost two decades after the '88 fires, the tall gray snags surrounded by new growth represented something lost. I assumed a forest would never grow there again, that we should plant trees and aid the process. But Yellowstone has recovered from the fires. The blackened moonscape was part of a resilient patchwork of burned land and unburned islands. Satellite imagery proves that the land is regenerating. Burned areas first read as brown, then green. It will take a long time for the land to completely regenerate, if that's what it's meant to do. The premise of land "healing" falsely assumes that "healed" is an endpoint when in truth everything is cyclical. Nature has no endpoint.

As climate change progresses, the question is whether the new growth can thrive in warmer and drier conditions. Studies show accelerating fire frequency in Yellowstone's lodgepole pine, shrinking from hundreds of years to intervals of less than thirty years between fires. One study predicted that annual burn areas could exceed those of the 1988 fires by 2075, making life intolerable for many conifer species, including lodgepole pine and resulting in a transformation called type conversion, changing trees to brush. But there are other studies projecting tree persistence. The truth of the matter is that we cannot predict the future. Stephen Pyne continues to advocate for prescribed burning in Yellowstone.

Chapter Three

The Front Range

My new crew was in Fort Collins, a bright and sunny college town, walkable from the hotshot base and barracks, where I had my own room. I was one of two women, and Victoria was unloading her things into the barracks when I arrived. She was tall, with long straight blonde hair and a crooked welcoming smile. Instantly I liked her, the crew, and the town. I marveled at the fox family who lived under the barracks deck. Cottonwood fluff laced walkways and roads and the sweet smell of budding leaves floated through my open window at dusk. I attended the preseason class and trained with the crew, by now a pro at pull-ups and push-ups. With no mountains near the base, we ran. Every day. Running is one of my least favorite forms of exercise, but because I'd stayed consistent with winter training (despite my drinking), I was solidly in the middle of the pack. Ray, our superintendent, could do more pull-ups than any of us. His captain, Paul, had a face overrun by thick eyebrows, always fixed into a quizzical expression. He slicked his black hair back with pomade. It was interesting to me, to watch how they worked together. Paul respected Ray, but in class he interrupted Ray's teaching. He couldn't control his need to speak. His voice was loud and overpowering whereas Ray's voice, like his facial expression, were neutral, and his words came out clipped. There were no captains on this crew like I'd had on the California crews, just a superintendent, an assistant superintendent, and three squad bosses, with two GS-5 lead firefighters on each squad and three GS-4s. I was a GS-4 again. The lowest position on a hotshot crew is GS-2, always reserved for brand-new hotshots.

PT in the morning, class all day. The first two weeks of fire season were always predictable in this way. Almost half the crew lived in the barracks, double the number in San Bernardino—our barracks were bigger, too, luxurious in comparison. I joined the guys for beers in the living room most nights. They were curious about me. A lot of them enjoyed hiking and nature. Many read books. I'm not sure if it was the nature of our barracks that fostered a sense of camaraderie, but I thought my dreams of blending in were coming to fruition.

One of the lead firefighters, Raul, had a barbecue at his house after our last day of training. He lived outside of town, in a big house surrounded by farmland and cottonwoods. Raul's black lab greeted me when I arrived, along with the majority of the crew and their girlfriends. I loved meeting the girlfriends and wives, and always noted the guys who had them. Although having a girlfriend or wife didn't exempt some of the men from being assholes, they were usually more comfortable with me. We barbecued, drank beers, and then all headed out to the bars. The night was warm, golden, and I was drunk and happy. Raul looped his arm through mine and led me to a dark bar where they served Jell-O shots. I liked the college-town vibe, the familiar, unchangeable bar smell, the way the bartender leaned on the counter, the electricity between Raul and I as our eyes met.

Soon enough we ditched the other crew members and went to an underground bar for some whiskey. Raul drove me back to his house in his truck. He wasn't cute. His shoulders were perpetually hunched, his mouth sat naturally in a frown, and his chin was slight. I slept with him anyway. The sex was disappointing. It wasn't until I woke up the next morning in his sparsely furnished room, the window open to birdsong, his mouth wide open and snoring, that I realized I was looking for something I didn't need anymore. Not with this person, in this bed. Maybe not with any man. Raul drove me home and dropped me off. I tried to forget it ever happened, but on our first fire, in late May, Gabe told me Raul was bragging about sleeping with me.

"I thought you should know," he said, not asking me if the rumor was true. This was the first time a co-worker had really had my back. The next time I saw Ray, our superintendent, he listened intently as I told him about the rumor. "It doesn't matter if I slept with him or not," I said, looking Ray in the eyes. My feet were solidly planted on the blackened ground. I waited for Ray's response. If he blamed me, I would quit. But he didn't. "That's not right," he said. "I'll take care of it." He stuck by his word, and Raul and I steered clear of each other for the rest of the season.

Chapter Four

Wolves and Bears
in the Wind Rivers

I n mid-June we drove north, from the expansive Wyoming flatlands
into sharp-spined hills draped with mint green sage, the narrow
roads leading us higher and higher, yellow center lines like vertebrae.
The hills coalesced into mountains, bald and jagged above the tree line,
gleaming snow edging their serrated ridges. I was now accustomed to
these high elevations, the austere gray mountains and honeyed scent of
sage and willows, often tinged with smoke. We were heading into the
Wind River Range, a glacier-carved landscape located in the western
center of Wyoming. Its mountain crests configure a portion of the
Continental Divide. Waters draining eastward flow into Yellowstone
River and then the Missouri. Westward-flowing waters drain into
Green River and join the Colorado River before coursing all the way
to the Pacific Ocean.

The Wind Rivers are composed of myriad ecological habitats.
Stunted and gnarled subalpine fir grow along the timberline. The trees
cluster in groups on the snow-nourished leeward mountainsides or
stand alone on windward edges and in shaded crevices. Gooseberries
and Oregon grape creep beneath their low branches. Whitebark pine

and Engelmann spruce encircle the firs. Ponderosas appear after fires. Lodgepole pine flourish atop the Flathead Sandstone, glacier-formed structures that have existed for over five hundred million years. Bright russet buffaloberry, woods rose, and juniper blanket the forest floor. Lodgepoles dominate the Wind Rivers, but their understories differ depending on soil type.

This was one of the most beautiful places I'd ever fought fire. After parking the buggies near a sharp drop, we geared up and began hiking down into a lush viridian-green valley divided by cottonwoods bordering a serpentine stream, our boots slipping as we descended the steep cliff. We'd been hiking a while when I realized I'd forgotten my gloves. McCane, a freckled guy in his thirties with a tiny mouth and large, expressive brown eyes, gave me his spare pair. My spaciness, a new characteristic, was already an inside joke on this crew. With the realization of each forgotten object—gloves or safety glasses or earplugs—I experienced an internal tremor, like a minor earthquake, followed by minutes or hours of scalding shame, cresting and subsiding in waves. I thought I was a daydreamer, and so did the guys. Only in retrospect can I see I was dissociating. As we hiked I alternated between admiring the landscape and berating myself for forgetting my gloves.

We arrived in a valley bottom laced with a patchwork burn, its edges quietly smoldering. After breaking into squads all of us gridded, cold-trailing with our gloves off, tracing the lines of fire with our fingers. The ground was dense with several types of thick grasses, the soil dark with organic matter. When we found heat we separated the unburned edges away. The ground was soft, interwoven with tenuous roots easily chopped apart with our tools. The fire seemed calm enough to me for monitoring rather than extinguishing.

Despite intimately engaging with the valley, I couldn't discern its ecological imbalance. I think this is a common experience, especially for those of us from the west; the stream and valley bottom appeared to be teeming with life, but this was nothing compared to what it was two hundred years ago, when an abundance of beavers maintained a wetland habitat. Before whites came, the Wind Rivers, like much of the U.S., were home to both beavers and wolves—it was the beavers who created so many wetlands. It's estimated that there were up to four hundred million beavers before European conquest. Their numbers dropped below one hundred thousand in less than a century. Fur traders killed beavers by the millions, harvesting pelts for hat-making. The animals wolves preyed upon—buffalo, bison, elk, and deer—were also slaughtered for various uses, and for sport. With the population of prey rapidly depleting, wolves looked elsewhere for survival, killing sheep and other grazing animals, leading to more wolf slaughters.

In community college my environmental science professor encouraged me to attend a Defenders of Wildlife conference centered around wolf reintroduction in the United States. I learned that wolves are a keystone species that helps to keep ecosystems in balance. Like fire, wolves were feared by settlers and explorers due to entrenched European stigma. Everyone's familiar with the wolf in sheep's clothing, or the wolf dressed in his red cape, ready to kill some innocent fairy-tale character. When Europeans initially settled in the Northeast they offered bounties for wolf pelts, and during westward expansion fur traders and settlers slaughtered hundreds of thousands of wolves. In the early 1900s the U.S. Forest Service launched a wolf-killing campaign in the name of livestock protection. By the 1960s, there were less than five hundred wolves in the lower forty-eight states, all of them in Minnesota and Isle Royale, Michigan.

That conference was in 1997, two years after wolves were reintroduced at Yellowstone. At the time, both wolves and beavers remained endangered throughout the contiguous United States. Over the course of a decade wolves were reintroduced in several regions, including the Southwest and Southeast. Few people predicted that this would in turn help to restore beaver populations, because a clear connection hadn't yet been established between high elk populations and reduced beaver habitat. Before colonization, elk herds grazed in forested areas rather than meadows, traveling nomadically in small herds, always vigilant of wolves. Without these predators, herd populations multiplied and groups remained stationary, munching on sweet willow, aspen, and birch shoots—the food beavers need for survival.

Ecologists call beavers "ecological engineers." They're also a keystone species, but they don't shape the landscape through predation. Their webbed feet and flat tails make them highly adapted marine and terrestrial mammals; they construct their homes in rivers and streams, strengthening riparian habitats. Before colonization the U.S. was interlaced with massive networks of beaver lodges, which house dry dwellings where they raise their families. The lodges look like water-stopping dams to the naked eye, but they actually act as filtration systems, catching sediment and debris, preventing erosion, and cleansing waterways. Each lodge has multiple underwater entrances with outward-branching channel systems extending in all directions, effectively irrigating surrounding soils and creating habitat for riparian vegetation and wildlife. These habitats increase carbon sequestration and support fish, amphibians, and invertebrates, which in turn sustain important predators (like snakes), reduce pests (like mosquitoes), consume leaf litter, and cycle nutrients. Beavers are speedy little workers: one family group can transform a single river channel into a flourishing wetland in less than a year. Beaver habitats create fire resistant corridors where animals can seek refuge during wildfires. This is one of many reasons why beavers were rarely hunted in precolonial North America.

Wolf populations in the contiguous U.S. currently hover at around seven thousand wolves, compared to an estimated four hundred thousand before European contact, though their numbers are dynamic. Some elk groups have resumed their nomadic lifestyles, leaving more food for beavers, whose numbers are rising. Even bears have benefitted from wolf reintroduction, feasting on leftover wolf kills upon emerging from hibernation.

But their reintroduction isn't without controversy. Past stigmas linger. Ranchers trap and kill wolves. Wolves do sometimes kill livestock, inflicting tangible economic losses. In 2021 Idaho and Montana greenlit wolf bounties. In the same year, Montana governor Greg Gianforte received a written warning for trapping and shooting a Yellowstone wolf when it strayed outside park borders because he hadn't completed the required course for ethically hunting wolves. Gianforte calls wolf protections "an attack on our heritage." He's signed laws extending seasonal wolf hunts and legalized night hunting and neck snares, which are a brutal method of entrapment. One Idaho representative complained about high wolf populations, when there are only fifteen hundred wolves living in Idaho as of this writing; one for every fifty-five miles. Some ecologists are advocating for financial incentives, like yearly stipends for ranchers in danger of losing livestock to wolves. This could help heal the historical antipathy ranchers have built up towards wolves.

In 2022, gray wolves were again granted protection as an endangered species in the United States (excepting Alaska, where wolves are not endangered and can be hunted). Defenders of Wildlife is one of many wolf advocacy groups throughout the United States. Beavers, too, are protected, though not as endangered species. Several organizations, including state and federal groups, are working to increase beaver habitat by building beaver dam analogs (BDAs). These are essentially fake beaver dams placed in dry or degraded rivers and streams. BDAs can mimic the ecological effects of beaver dams in the absence of beavers, and provide habitat for reintroduced beavers.

This fire was managed by the Bureau of Indian Affairs, which manages fires in and around American Indian lands. The Arapaho and Shoshone people, who'd long ago been enemies, were forced onto the

Wind River Reservation near Lander, Wyoming, one of the many reservations formed for tribes dispossessed of their homelands in and surrounding Yellowstone. The reservation was a restricted space in many respects, and barren, though its stark beauty is improved by the efforts of tribal members, who've introduced bison and pronghorn antelope. The reservation hosted us for several nights until we relocated to a ranch in the flatlands, nearer to where we were mopping up. In the daytime we traipsed through thick green brush and onto hillsides, jagged with sharp rocks hidden in the tall grasses. There were many rolled ankles, but the high elevation weather was blessedly cool, with plentiful breezes tinged with smoke and the sweet scent of soil.

I traded my iPod with McCane, whose room was near mine in the barracks. He was in his thirties and had previously worked on a Type II Forest Service crew in the Pacific Northwest. This was the summer I was obsessed with the Yeah Yeah Yeahs, Joanna Newsom, and Neko Case. McCane asked me why I listened to so many women singers. We were sitting in a patch of grass near the buggies. The absurdity of his question didn't occur to me; I'd never have asked him why he listened to so many male singers.

We talked about where we wanted to travel in the winter. I wanted to go to Southeast Asia—Vietnam, Thailand, and Laos—and planned to buy a one-way ticket to Bangkok. "You're gonna go by yourself?" he asked.

"Yes," I said.

"Well, if you change your mind, let me know. Maybe we could go together."

No way would McCane come with me to Southeast Asia. Or anywhere, for that matter. I had pictured the trip many times, always solo. Me and my journal, sitting in some tea shop, meeting other travelers. After my trip with Colin I didn't want to travel with a man again, but even I didn't fully understand why McCane's offer upset me so much. It was like he punctured my fantasy of independence. I'd been single since my breakup with Colin, except for Lewis and a string of one-night stands. Terrence was the only guy on the crew I would have traveled with, and he was married.

McCane's question reorganized the structure of our relationship. Now I thought he might want something more than friendship. I can see now how the ways in which some of the men I worked with tried to control me, the pressure I felt to conform, had colored my perception of men as a whole. But I was right about McCane—he eventually asked me out.

At dusk a silver-haired woman appeared and offered me and Victoria the indoor shower. I was honored. After collecting my toiletries I walked to the house, flip-flops slapping the dirt, everything incandescent with silver moonlight. Five black cows, their giant heads poking out of their pen, followed me with watery brown eyes as they muttered and chewed. A congregation of rabbits scattered like golden-furred spirits. As I neared the porch a shadow stirred in my periphery. A young doe stood statue-still, ivory ears perked. We gazed at each other for a moment. When I opened the door a white cat slinked along my shins. The doe vanished into the shadows. Each animal imprinted itself onto me, reminding me that I was never alone.

The shower was mercifully hot—my first in at least a week. Black water spiraled down the drain. I washed my hair and body three times and scrubbed my hands and fingernails. Cracks marred my fingerprints, their ridges etched in black. The water stung my blistered feet. When the water ran clean I stepped out, wiping the mirror of steam, and stared at my body, so much smaller now. I pulled and pressed at my belly and breasts, wanting them to be different. I didn't ask myself why. The wanting was reflexive. When I emerged back into the night the moon hung full and ponderous in the sky, a luminescent bowl only

made more beautiful by its canyons and craters. I stared at it, forgetting
the cumbersome vessel of my body.

The sun doused us in light and heat as we burned in the low elevation
valleys, the fire's flames pulsing up towards the sky and then collapsed
sideways as shifting winds flung them across the dirt road and into the
green, where they bloomed like bright orange flowers. First there was
one spot, then five; then we lost our burn. Bennett, a newly minted
squad boss, was leading the burn. He panicked. His squad was on the
road, between the two fires, and the buggies were parked half a mile
away. No road will save you from a fire—we all knew that. It wasn't
his fault; no one can predict the wind from moment to moment. He
shouted over the crew frequency, "We lost the burn. The fire's established in the green." I heard this through Oscar's radio; our squad was
about three hundred feet behind theirs and saw everything. Oscar, my
squad boss, told me Bennett was "shitting the bed." Letting the fear
take over. Ray called in a tanker drop and the plane appeared overhead,
its engine so deafening that I crouched down and covered my ears. Its
belly released a cascade of pink retardant, extinguishing the slopover.
Fat drops of pink goo floated on the wind, landing on our hard hats
and Nomex. We had caught it. Everything was fine.

Chapter Five

Grasslands

After an R & R we were back on the books but didn't get a call. I perched on barstools, scribbling in my notebook and sipping whiskey. The bartender at my favorite place learned my name and my drink. About a week later the crew completed first aid training in the barracks living room. We were all lounging on the couches when Bennett popped his head in the door. "Someone try to guess where we're going next." I blurted what I thought was a ridiculous answer: Nebraska. "Yep!" he said.

I'd been sure Nebraska was just cornfields, but the large smoke column in the midst of Nebraska National Forest taught me otherwise, though I wasn't entirely wrong—Nebraska National Forest was seeded in 1902 as an experiment. Gifford Pinchot, the first head of the Forest Service, had convinced President Theodore Roosevelt to sign off on planting two forests in an expansive northwestern Nebraska grassland. This doesn't mean that the Nebraska National Forest is entirely man-made—in the 1950s the forest was redrawn to include native ponderosa pine forest as well as a tract of native grasslands. But most of it didn't exist before 1902.

Pinchot was obsessed with the timber famine, obsessed with planting trees. Although he was a self-described naturalist, his family wealth was derived from selling timber. He loved nature. And money. Thus the tree planting. The irony of planting these non-native forests, and of tree planting in general, is that healthy grasslands have a higher carbon sequestration rate than forests. Their root systems absorb and lock away greenhouse gases. Trees store their carbon in their biomass and leaves, releasing most of it back into the atmosphere when they burn at high severity. In comparison, native grasslands are wildfire- and drought-tolerant. Their root systems extend far beneath the earth's surface and remain intact while their stalks burn. When properly cultivated, grasslands become carbon storage powerhouses.

But grasslands aren't immune to damage. Many grasslands throughout the U.S. are managed, meaning they're plowed, reseeded, and grazed by livestock. Plowing and reseeding unearths stored carbon, while livestock grazing degrades soils and plants.

Before colonization Native Americans intentionally cultivated grasslands, meadows, legumes, and tubers—all of which store carbon. They didn't use chemical pesticides. As a culture, Americans continuously seek a magic bullet to "manage" and "fight" pests, just like we fight fire. Government-subsidized farms fertilize crops and apply pesticides in an effort to control nature, but these pesticides poison us, and the fertilizers pollute waterways, harm wildlife, and deplete soil. Cultivating healthy grasslands and reassessing agricultural practices is vital. It's also complicated. No singular solution will produce immediate results. We can't eliminate grazing and current agricultural practices. Easing away from control and towards stewardship is something we can learn from Indigenous land-tending practices. The knowledge is there, and the people are, too.

In Nebraska my squad looped hose line around a house and a yellowing field dotted with giant cylinders of hay. After that we burned for days.

Days and days. I recall yellow grass. Loose dirt. Homeowners bringing us cold drinks. Long dirt roads and the crickets, mice, and shrews who fled across them, towards safety. Another crew lost their burn and it snaked into mountainous terrain. We quickly tied in our burn, stopping where one dirt road met another, and jumped into the buggies so we could assist the other crew. On the way there we guzzled Powerade and tore into our bagged lunches. Oscar predicted a night shift and he was right. By this time I'd spent five and a half summers working wildland fires—three and a half as a hotshot. On my first fire in Oregon I quickly learned not to wear my glasses because my eyes watered so much in the smoke that I could barely see. My contacts provided a protective barrier.

When we finally made it to the fireline the smoke was blowing towards us rather than pulling away. We inhaled smoke all the time, but this was thick and unrelenting. I tied a bandana around my neck, pulling it up over my nose and mouth, tucking the bottom edges into my shirt collar before digging line with my squad. The terrain wasn't necessarily steep, but crested up and down as we dug parallel to the main fire. Phillip would've called the winds squirrelly. They kept switching direction, dousing us in smoke and heat one moment and clearing the air the next. With each dousing a chorus of coughs, throat clearings, and loogie hawkings started, lasting until the smoke cleared again. Once we connected our line with the other hotshot crew Ray started a new burn operation. We lit our fire slowly and methodically, watching the green closely and rushing in to extinguish spots every ten or fifteen minutes, digging and throwing dirt until a tanker or helicopter arrived with water or retardant.

Compared to our earlier burn in the hilly fields, this felt like chaos. It was useless to think about things going wrong, and there wasn't time to think either way. I was either burning, holding line, or running into the green, following some firebrand floating on the wind with my eyes so I could catch it right when it landed, before it established an actual spot fire.

Night came. I switched my headlamp on for burning but turned the light off when I was watching the green. It was easier to see errant firebrands that way. The smoke never stopped folding over us, like a choking fog.

Sometime around one a.m. Ray told us the burn was finished. We had connected with the other crew. Now we had to hike out, through the smoke. None of us had expected this. We hadn't conserved our energy earlier in the day, and the constant smoke had exhausted us. We descended into a narrow canyon so congested with smoke that our headlamps made seeing more difficult, like car headlights in a heavy fog. I can still recall the full body sense of claustrophobia I felt down there—and I'm not prone to fearing small spaces. I couldn't breathe. I inhaled and exhaled but my lungs asked for more until I thought I might suffocate, or hyperventilate. Someone, I'm not sure who, told us we'd be out of there soon, so I couldn't have been the only one feeling that way. The canyon's exit was as steep as its entrance. One by one we hiked up, all of us wheezing. When I got to the top I grabbed Terrence's hand and he pulled me out. Outside the canyon the air was completely clear. I quickly turned and offered my hand, hauling the next person out before moving out of the way so the rest of the crew could join us up there. Once they did we all paused for a few minutes, gasping and coughing and catching our breath as if we'd barely escaped drowning.

The night was beautiful. I'd tugged my bandana down to breathe and now wiped my face with it, all the snot and tears and ash and dirt. The main fire had ccoalesced with our burn. Its flames made shadows of themselves on the trees and I could see the silhouettes of some of the guys on the other crew a ways off. Terrence took out his camera and snapped some photos. "Isn't it something," he said. "Kinda makes this job worthwhile." Right after he put his camera away we started hiking out again, away from the smoke and the fire, so we could catch some sleep. We would be on shift the next day.

Chapter Six

Tatanka

The following day we drove to South Dakota. Ray gathered the crew at a ranch at the edge of a ravine incised with a river. We spent most of the day installing hoses and sprinklers around the ranch, whose log cabin was decorated with stained glass and chipped ceramic figurines; trolls and lumbermen and fairies all coexisting peacefully. The owner said the place had been there for generations, since his family arrived from Missouri. Gabe and I shuffled down a sharp bluff and started setting up a MARK-3 pump in the river, which would feed the sprinkler system. We talked about a joke two of the guys had played on me in the Wind Rivers. I was berating myself for being forgetful, and for the first time Gabe, who was usually soft-spoken, raised his voice, he was so upset about what had happened.

They'd hid my hard hat from me when we loaded into the buggies. Hard hats are arguably one of the most essential elements of protective gear—you simply can't work without one. Everyone's seat was equipped with a wire compartment; we slid our hard hats in there whenever we loaded up, but when Evan, the other squad boss on our mod, asked me where mine was, I realized the compartment was empty. We had just loaded up. I panicked. From the front of the buggy Oscar asked if we were ready to go and I said no, my voice high-pitched as I explained the situation. I jumped out of the buggy and ran to the spot where we'd been sharpening our tools. No hard hat. This flooded me with nausea. "Has anyone seen it?" I asked as I climbed back into the buggy. My mind raced; I was scared of getting fired, being punished or ostracized. Of looking stupid. Oscar looked back at us again. "We can't leave until you find it." The words paralyzed me.

"I know I had it when I was sharpening my tool, but it's not there," I said, and Evan chimed in to tell me I needed to keep track of my things, that this was some rookie shit. My mind couldn't process the situation. I was sure I'd left it there. I was about to start crying when Evan smirked and reached under his seat. There it was. I grabbed it from him. "What the fuck?" I said, flopping into my seat. A few of the guys in the buggy were rolling their eyes, looking as upset as I was.

"You left it on the ground, so I picked it up. I bet you'll never leave it behind again." I shoved my hard hat into its compartment without another word.

This behavior wasn't unusual for a hotshot crew. No one except Terrence and Gabe knew what had happened on Solar Hotshots. The guys had played a joke on me, but its essence was rooted in an old-school mentality, where shame is used as a teaching tool. If Evan had handed me my hard hat with a firm warning, that would have been more effective.

"They're assholes," Gabe said now, and I nodded, thrusting the pump's filter underwater. My trust was so tenuous. The joke had triggered my hypervigilance, and now everyone was under suspicion. I secretly questioned how many of the guys wanted to hurt or embarrass me. It was such a small event, but it degraded my relationship with the entire crew.

*   *   *

The South Dakota terrain was steep and rocky—too dangerous for a coherent burn operation. We dug fireline instead. In Southern California most fireline construction had consisted of saw work because of the thick brush and shallow root systems. Here the soil was deep and rocky, interlaced with dense root networks. We were almost vertical. Every few minutes someone would yell, "Rock!" The rocks whooshed past us, some as big as our heads.

As we dug fireline up a steep hill, I carefully extracted the rock layers, carefully setting each individual rock aside so it wouldn't tumble down the mountain and maul someone. Beneath the rock surface I chopped at the earth, chunking out clumps of thick duff until I reached mineral soil. Our line was about sixteen inches across, more of a ditch than a trail. If we left any flammable materials the fire could easily smolder across our line.

The sawyers cleared trees and branches, cutting down smaller trees and removing limbs from the bottoms of the larger ones so fire couldn't climb into the canopy. It was hot, brutal work. My intense concentration insulated me from physical pain, but whenever we paused for a moment I could feel my wrists and finger joints throbbing, my shoulders aching, and my lower back protesting from constantly bending over and relentlessly swinging my Pulaski. My hands and fingers blistered and bled, despite my gloves.

Six or seven hours later we tied in with the other hotshot crew, completing the fireline. Then we hiked down our trail to the river to watch for spot fires. I sat with Oscar, my squad boss. He was an experienced hotshot in his mid-thirties, recently divorced, easy to talk to, and mature. I told him how much I loved working with Victoria. She was training as a squad boss and I respected the way she handled herself. Victoria had worked with Ray on another Colorado hotshot crew—we both had equivalent experience.

"You should start training soon," Oscar said. I snorted and said no thanks, but didn't tell him what had happened on Phillip's crew.

Then Oscar mentioned Victoria's size. "She's so much bigger than you," he said. "But you eat more than her. How are you so much smaller?" The question surprised me. At first I took it as a compliment; I was so obsessed with being small. "She's taller than me," I said, not remembering Bobby asking me the year before how I had lost weight so quickly. Everything lived in little compartments in my mind, including my bulimia. I thought I hid it well. For weeks afterwards I ruminated on the conversation, until I concluded that it was invasive. Inappropriate. Why was Oscar evaluating our bodies? I categorized it with the joke Evan had played on me and thought that Oscar, too, was worthy of suspicion. And maybe he was. But in retrospect I imagine that my suffering was more visible than I thought at the time, and he might have been trying to open a line of communication.

Near dusk we hiked out of the ravine. Victoria sometimes struggled with asthma and fell out. Terrence, an EMT, stayed back with her. As we continued hiking I remembered the previous summer on the San Bernardino crew, when we were driving through a fire camp and one of the guys made a comment about a girl on another hotshot crew, who we could see through the window. Without thinking, I asked the guys if I was as big as her. The words *as big as her* were like rusty nails in my mouth. No one answered.

Victoria and I shared a dorm at a university while we were in South Dakota. She was the first woman I really connected with on a hotshot crew. The only one. I knew she was bisexual and sometimes thought of hooking up with her, but I was too scared. I liked her too much. She was endearingly self-effacing, but also confident and strong, both physically and mentally. I told myself I didn't want to risk her friendship, but the thought of deepening our connection frightened me. Guys were easier, I thought. Sex had become a weird power play for me. I felt no tender fluttering in my belly and mistook my numbness for power. On days off I often went home with people from the bar.

I'd always felt things so strongly, and everything had been so painful, but somehow I'd found a place within myself where I could turn all feelings OFF, like a switch. I flipped it and: nothing.

Victoria and I always chatted before falling asleep across from each other, half-illuminated by the campus lights from outside. She told me she was tired of smiling all the time. "I want to be in a bad mood. These guys expect me to be some kind of Pollyanna." I understood this. The guys were allowed to be angry, but we were expected to be nice and peppy, like a camp counselor putting on a show for the kids.

Her squad boss training was changing her relationships with some of the guys. Even our superintendent, who'd worked with her on the other hotshot crew, treated her differently. As she told me this I could see her doubting her own perceptions, like I often doubted mine. Were they really resisting ideas for tactics and strategy, or was she imagining it? Was she being too sensitive? I assured her that she wasn't, on both counts. At the time I listened and considered that it might be impossible for a woman to be qualified in the eyes of these men, because being qualified means being confident, and if you're too confident you're a bitch. If you're a bitch, no one likes you. But you can't be a pushover either, because then no one will respect you.

It didn't occur to me that my only leadership examples were men. There was one veteran woman hotshot superintendent and everyone said she was a hardcore badass who could out-hike any man, but I'd also heard she was a bitch. "Bitch" was a catchall term, leveraged against women who didn't conform to men's requirements. Someone said she never hired women on her crew (untrue); another said she worked her crew into the ground (like many male hotshot superintendents). My interpretation, both now and back then, was that she probably didn't smile enough, wasn't as cheerful or acquiescent as so many men in fire wanted her to be. She eventually worked her way up to become the Forest Service Director of Fire and Aviation. I later met her online and, unsurprisingly, found her to be the opposite of what I'd been told.

I know there are hotshot crews and fire departments that are inclusive and welcoming to women and other marginalized people, but I never found that level of inclusivity. Victoria and I were navigating territory only faintly tread by other women. Even on this crew, which felt more inclusive than the California crews, it was difficult to find our way.

Chapter Seven

Priest Lake

My memories of August are like an old film reel, obscured one moment, crystallized the next, all of them out of order. From South Dakota we drove home for R & R, then back north to a fire near Red Eagle Lake in Glacier National Park. Once we hit two weeks the Forest Service wanted to keep us in Montana; we stayed in a hotel in Missoula for two days before continuing work in Glacier, then swung west to a fire near Priest Lake, Idaho. All of us were exhausted. I hated it when we couldn't R & R at home, but keeping us in Montana saved the feds money. It also guaranteed we'd stay out on fires, which we all wanted.

There were several lightning fires burning in Northern Idaho. The Idaho fire is interspersed with memories from Montana. I most clearly recollect the long hikes we took each day; two hours both ways, first through old-growth forest and then up into the mountains, where we were constructing fireline. I can't recall why we didn't just fly in and out. Perhaps resources were overextended—the season was a bad one, with lightning storms igniting fires throughout the Northern Rockies. The National Guard was there, along with Canadian and Australian firefighters; but we didn't see them, or any other crews. Not in Idaho.

The first half of each hike was my thinking time—things had devolved with Oscar while we were in Montana, and I was trying to parse out how. He'd given me a combi—a small shovel with a pick attachment—and moved me from my spot in the middle of the line to the back, where I worked as a "driver," moving the line forward. I liked the combi better than the Pulaski, though I would never have admitted this to anyone. It was lightweight, with a long comfortable handle so I didn't have to bend down as much. Oscar was really on me about training as a squad boss. Maybe he wanted me to succeed as a hotshot, but the way he went about it raised my hackles back then, and still does.

Oscar constantly hovered behind me, assessing my work. I was flattered that he saw my potential, until he began nitpicking my appearance. One day he said that my painted nails were too flashy. I always painted them deep merlot; the polish hid the dirt accumulated beneath my fingernails. I told him as much but he didn't believe me. "You're trying to look pretty," he said. Then there were my bug-eyed sunglasses, which I'd bought at a gas station in South Dakota. They covered a larger surface area than the ones the guys wore. My eyes have always been light-sensitive. He told me they were too girly. "Why do you need to single yourself out?" he asked, rejecting my reasoning for wearing them. "You need to get new ones." This was not a request but a demand, and it left me fuming.

Gabe suggested I check the crew handbook for these rules. There were none. A few days later Oscar produced a pair of safety glasses with gray lenses. "Wear these," he said, holding his other hand out for my sunglasses.

"No," I said, swallowing my fear. He was my squad boss, after all, and I was supposed to listen to him. "The handbook doesn't specify what kinds of protective eyewear we have to wear." I defiantly readjusted my glasses on my face.

Terrence had a theory that Oscar wanted to hook up. I brushed it off. There was no way, I thought, that Oscar's nitpicking stemmed from something so ridiculous. On our long hikes in Idaho my mind looped on these incidents, folding in other, smaller events, like one of the younger guys on our crew saying my Pulaski was too heavy for a girl, or derisive comments some of the guys made about Victoria's asthma, and her leadership style. Each looping repetition accumulated more incidents, no matter how small, from this crew but also from my career as a hotshot. They smoldered inside of me, building heat. I couldn't rely on Gabe and Terrence to talk this through, although they were understanding, because in the back of my mind I worried that they, too, would start criticizing me, and Victoria was on the other mod, dealing with her own issues.

Our R & R in Missoula had also disturbed me. The first night there Gabe and I had met his friend at a bar: a guy who worked on a Montana hotshot crew. When he told me his crew had four women I asked if this caused any issues, thinking of everything I'd been told about the risks of having too many women on a crew. But he said there weren't any problems. The women all got along, and because there were four of them no one was tokenized. At the time I didn't consider the word *token* because its meaning was unclear, just like I didn't question my assumption that a hotshot crew could have too many women. But I had been tokenized, especially on Phillip's crew, where everyone assumed I was a diversity hire. Even my mom and Vern had told me that I was only offered a permanent position on Solar Hotshots because of my gender—not my work ethic.

A token is an empty promise that screams to onlookers *we are doing what is right* while also whispering *you don't belong here*. When someone's tokenized, they're expected to accept the status quo—they aren't allowed to be different, or to point out any of the issues they see. If they do, they're often scapegoated. Any so-called diversity hire understands the dynamic, across all professions.

I know the crew was oppressive to some of the guys. Terrence told me many years later that he felt like an outcast on the crew, and

I was one of the only people he connected with. He wasn't interested in sports or *Maxim* or porn but instead preferred independent films and visual art. He wasn't tokenized, but he suffered nonetheless.

By August my body was also beginning to break down. After our first night of drinking in Missoula I walked to a taco shop and stood in a long line, light-headed from my hangover. I remember telling the cashier my order and then waking up in a man's arms. I'd lost consciousness. After thanking him I sat alone at a small table, picking at my food and sipping water, still light-headed and worried about fainting again. I had relayed this to Gabe and Terrence. Maybe that's why Oscar had given me a lighter job.

Something I remember clearly about Idaho is the afternoon we waded in the river—a gift from Ray, our superintendent. Paul, the assistant superintendent, surely would have been pissed had he found out that Ray allowed this, but to my knowledge he never did. Half the crew was with him, and missed out on the fun. Victoria was at the river with us, and Gabe and Terrence, plus a few of the other guys. It started with dunking our hard hats into the river and pouring water over our heads. Then we removed our boots and socks, sighing with pleasure as we sunk our feet into the clear water, rolling our Nomex up as far as they would go. Our legs were pale, imprinted with lines from our socks and boots, our feet marred with blisters. Victoria, Terrence, and I found a small lagoon and took off our shirts, splashing each other with the freezing water, out of sight of the others. Victoria's skin was as translucent as my own, her hands, neck, and face tanned the color of caramel. It was brief but so delicious, a stolen moment of joy.

We drove home through Montana, stopping in Bozeman or Butte for the night. After singing karaoke at a local bar a bunch of us piled into two cabs and, already buzzed, busted through the front doors of a strip club. There were more than ten of us; only the married ones stayed back, except for Terrence. One of the youngest guys on the crew, who had a girlfriend, was persuaded to get a lap dance. Terrence and I bought lap dances for each other. The girl who danced on me was sexy and put my hands on her hips, letting me know it was okay to touch her. I thought about the girls I used to work with in Eugene, and told her I used to be a stripper. She pressed my hand flat on her belly, sending a shot of electricity through me. The softness of it; the way she smelled. The familiarity of a past life.

The guys and I hooted and hollered as the women danced onstage. I wondered if any of these women were strung out, like I'd been. I thought of one of the strippers I had worked with, Ginger, her young daughter sleeping in the bedroom as we partied in her living room. Terrence leaned over and, pointing to one of the less attractive girls, said she looked like a marionette because of the lines down her chin. I imagined strings pulling her legs and arms and hips and suppressed an urge to leave. That's how I'd felt when I danced on the stage, like I was some other person steered by the dollar bills the guys stuck into my panties and bra.

After we got another round of shots a stripper called me onstage. I obliged without thinking. We'd never done such a thing at my old club. Once I was up there she pulled my shirt up, revealing my stomach and bra. I grabbed at its seams and yanked it down, scrambling offstage. No way in hell was I going to dance for the guys I worked with. Oscar's eyes were on me as I walked back to my seat. Across the club, Victoria sat with her boyfriend, another crew member named Hart, and for a moment I envied their attachment.

Back at the hotel Terrence invited me to his room for a beer. The offer was free from sexual innuendo. He was sharing the room with Brad, one of my least favorite people on the crew, a wannabe cop who would later become a border patrol officer. Unfortunately he was also attractive. When Terrence passed out Brad and I flipped the channels until we found some soft porn. Brad had been at the club with us, and we were both drunk. Terrence began snoring, and Brad asked if I wanted to get into his bed. We started kissing, then taking off each other's clothes. The sex was surprisingly good, but I felt nothing for him, not like the stripper's electrical current. Sleeping with him was as simple and satisfying as scratching an itch.

When we were done I snuck back to my room. The next morning I woke up to Victoria shaking me. "You gotta get up, you're late! I was sleeping in Hart's room!" I hadn't set an alarm and scrambled to get my clothes on, stuffing everything into my red bag before running out with Victoria, who was kind enough to wait for me. It was the first time I'd been late for anything on a hotshot crew. We weren't the only ones, but it was still embarrassing. I was paranoid that someone knew about Brad and me sleeping together. When I looked at him we shared a passing smirk, invisible to others. I slept until we stopped at the gas station, where I bought about five beverages, hoping one of them would cure my hangover.

At some point in August, when we were cutting brush, a sharp piece of manzanita pierced my calf. Ray looked at it and told me to keep working, so I did. But my leg wouldn't stop bleeding. Finally Ray pulled me off the line and drove me to a nearby clinic, where a nurse inspected the triangular gash. There was a loose flap of skin hanging from it. She cleaned the wound but told me they couldn't stitch it because too much time had passed since the injury. Instead, we decided to cut off the flap of skin and bandage the wound. Ray took me to lunch as consolation. We ate in silence and then I got nauseous from the painkillers they'd given me, and went to throw up. My face was pale in the mirror. When I came back out he apologized, and said he should have taken me off the line earlier. I told him it was fine. I already had a bunch of scars on my legs.

Chapter Eight

Tears

By the time we got back home it was September, and we resumed morning physical training. Oscar took us to a local soccer field where we ran sprints like I'd done on the California rugby team. Afterwards he noticed I was limping. It was my ankle, as usual. Both my ankles bothered me periodically, but I'd rolled my left ankle in Montana and the swelling never let up. Ray sent me to the doctor, where an X-ray showed a fracture as well as a little bone chip near the joint. "You've fractured this ankle before, right?" the doctor asked, and I shrugged. Probably I had. He told me it looked like I'd fractured it several times. The crew picked up someone to replace me. I wasn't the only one who'd missed part of the season; people got injured all the time. I felt like I'd let everyone down, but I was also relieved.

They stuck me in dispatch for a month, until the season wound down and I moved to Denver. Oscar called me in mid-October. Did I want to come over for a glass of wine? I was reluctant. He was asking me on a date. I questioned him about the power dynamic—his being my squad boss, and he said we'd cross that bridge when we came to it. I told him I'd think about it.

It's not that I wasn't attracted to Oscar—I was. But after we hung up I struggled with how pissed I was about him asking me out. There's a direct correlation between Oscar following me around, nitpicking my work ethic and sunglasses and how much attention I supposedly called to myself, and his asking me out on a date. Oscar took his attraction to me as license to control me. It was the same way Martin had taken ownership of me, stalking me outside of work, or Colin had. When Oscar asked me on a date, it blew up our friendship. A friendship I'd assumed was based on mutual respect.

Victoria and I have talked about it, then and since, and she says that I was so bubbly and beautiful, and that's why it always happened—the men following me around, wanting to sleep with me or date me, and the shadow-side of that: the same men policing me and controlling me. It was within the confines of their supposed affection that I could sense the confines of woman—the man that exists inside that very word and shapes it from within. I'd internalized that gaze, that word, that approval.

But I don't think their treatment of me was attached to my appearance, necessarily. Victoria was beautiful, too. The more these men tried to control me, the more I resisted. My resistance was what they wanted to dominate.

I sent Oscar a scathing email, telling him how transparent he was. Why, I asked him, would I date someone who criticized me so relentlessly? What upset me was that the attraction was mutual. I would have dated him, had he respected my autonomy. But I'd never work with Oscar again.

In early spring of 2007 a guy I'd met offered to take me bouldering in Utah. We drove out to a wilderness area. I'd almost ascended my first boulder when I fell. Although the guy was supposed to be spotting me he stepped back instead. My heel hit the ground, and my knee popped. I felt it bend backwards. When I tried to stand the leg buckled, so I crawled to the car, refusing to lean on the guy who had brought me there. It would be the end of climbing for me.

My mom and Vern had divorced. In some ways Vern felt closer to me because my mom's preoccupation with Todd, her younger boyfriend, made her unreachable. It was the same as when I was little, the way she lost herself in relationships, except now she didn't have to worry about feeding me, or coming home often enough to make sure I hadn't died or burned the apartment down.

I emailed Vern the X-ray and doctor's note, which said I'd torn my ACL clean off. He offered to pay for my ACL replacement surgery, maybe because he'd torn his playing basketball, and he knew I had no health insurance. Maybe because he'd gotten the better half of the divorce settlement—the shared business was now his. The house, too. The surgery was supposed to be routine, but afterwards my knee ballooned into a painful mass, hot to the touch. I kept calling the doctor's office, but the nurse only repeated that it wasn't serious. Several days passed before they finally offered me an appointment. I passed out as the doctor was inserting a syringe for sample collection, and woke up at the hospital, on a gurney. "We have to open up the knee and redo the surgery," the doctor said, hovering over me. My system flooded with fentanyl. The infection had gone septic and required antibiotics so strong they'd collapse my smaller veins, so I needed a PICC line, which is a catheter inserted through a vein in the upper arm. They wheeled me into a room and I watched what looked like a sonogram screen. On it, the catheter snaked through a vein until it was nestled next to my heart.

I had almost died, the doctor told me. Superstrength antibiotics pumped through my bloodstream. For the first couple days nurses helped me to and from the bathroom and a PT made me hobble down the hallway. Every three hours the painkillers wore off and a dull throbbing set in, followed by an intense burning like fire smoldering inside my joint. I gritted my teeth, my hands gripping the bedside until I tossed one way, then the other, then writhed under the sheets, bending my opposite leg and digging my fingernails into my palms in an effort to distract myself until a nurse arrived with that blessed pill.

The doctor said I almost lost the leg; that my knee might never function normally again. It could go either way, really. A lifelong limp or a successful recovery. But I'd never fight fire again. No way, he said. At the time I believed him.

After five days the nurses brought me flowers and a card. I cried when they asked me where my family was. "In Washington," I said. My mom wasn't returning my calls. Vern was, I think, dodging them, lest I ask for more money. Their bouquet was a splash of brightness in my bare room. The nurses were like angels, floating into the room to check on me and soothe me, telling me I'd get a pain pill soon or, finally, giving me a pill and a cup of water. Terrence visited me once, bringing Pad See Ew from his favorite Thai place. I was released after two weeks but had to drive to the treatment center once a day for over a month. I sat with the dialysis and chemo patients, feeling blessed that my IV antibiotics were temporary. Altogether I owed the hospital and surgeon over twenty thousand dollars, after negotiation.

PART V
INTERLUDE

Chapter One

Denver

I spent three years in Denver. My body recovered, and in late 2008 I began therapy. My friendships deepened soon after. Victoria lived in a mountain town north of Denver. We saw each other often, usually meeting in the city when our favorite musicians came through. And there was Julia, who I'd met through my ex (we'd kissed one night outside a bar and become friends), and Dakota, who owned a small art gallery and rode a fixed-gear bicycle, like me. I rode my bike regularly and had a good nanny job. I was still actively bulimic, but I came clean about it to my close friends despite fearing rejection and disgust. Binging and purging was so shameful to me. Many of my friends revealed their own struggles with food and body image. Nearly everyone had a story of parents or peers criticizing their bodies, teaching them that they were flawed and needed fixing in some way or another. My friends became mirrors, reflecting what I couldn't see. And if they deserved love and support, maybe I did, too.

My therapist in Denver had a forthright, open way of interacting with me. In our first session I told her that I didn't like who I was when I drank. But I also didn't like myself sober. "I'm scared of people when

I'm sober," I said. When she asked what I was scared people would see, I said I was a bad person. It was the first time I verbalized this belief. I remember how true it felt, as if there were this rottenness deep inside. If I let anyone too close, they'd see my selfishness and greed. My ugliness.

I didn't expect her to ask me where I was ugly, how I was ugly. But she did. "Do you treat people badly? Do you try to hurt people?" she asked.

"No," I said. "I want people to be happy."

"Think about it," she said. "If this is something you really believe about yourself, where's the evidence for that?"

I came back for another session and said there was no evidence. I was genuinely confused. Why did I feel this way about myself if it wasn't true? We were sitting close together in her small office, our knees almost touching.

"If you really believe that about yourself, then someone taught you to believe it."

I'd only seen my mom three times in the past two years; two of our visits were during the winter holidays. One Christmas she came to Denver and stayed in a fancy hotel. She drank too much at Christmas dinner and, blacked out, called me an ungrateful bitch. Instead of sitting there, letting her words absorb, I got up and walked out of the restaurant. The next day she didn't remember what had happened. I visited her in Seattle the next Christmas. She and Todd had broken up, but he was there when we got snowed in at my mom's house, along with his sister and my cousin Hannah. I found out that Todd had been living with her since she had moved to Seattle. She'd taken a lot of measures to prevent me from knowing this; lies and omissions since before she had divorced Vern. I told her I needed space. It was the first time I had ever stepped away from our relationship.

* * *

In Autumn 2009 my mom started calling me frequently when she was drunk. She left messages, sent emails. She wrote *I'll go disappear now*, and *why do you expect to be treated like gold?* and *if only you knew what I sacrificed for you.* These were the things she'd said all my life, but her words had lost their power to draw me in, though they still stung.

And then my cousin Hannah told me she was telling people she was sick. A week later I got a late-night phone call. This time I answered. She drunkenly wailed, "I have cancer; it's real bad." I was sitting at my desk writing, sneaking a cigarette with the window open. Hannah said she thought it was just a plea for attention, and my gut said something was off, too. I asked my mom questions: what kind of cancer (colon), what stage (three), what does she want to do (no doctors). "You know I hate hospitals," she said. This was true, and had always been true. I decided that I needed to visit her for Christmas.

When I arrived at her rental house in Seattle, she answered the door in an ancient, food-stained black-and-white fleece jacket. Her greasy hair was slicked down, scalp inflamed; her meticulous blonde highlights had grown out. She looked like she'd aged five years in six months—spider-veins laced her ruddy cheeks. Her teeth were yellowed and unbrushed.

The kitchen reeked of stale wine; the fridge empty except for condiments. I followed her into the living room. Everything looked more cavernous than it had during previous visits, the air damp and sour. Bright, twinkling city lights surrounded the black expanse of Lake Washington. String lights framed the picture window as if decorating a portal into an otherworld. Cigarette smoke clung to the ceiling. I'd be sleeping on the couch, my mom said, her eyes betraying all the glasses of wine she must have had before my arrival. A riptide tugged at my feet.

I nearly cried when I saw she'd made toast and bacon, sliced tomatoes, and torn iceberg lettuce for BLTs. That she'd prepared this meal, a favorite of my grandmother's, flooded me with guilt. It was clear she was sick, but something kept nagging at me, telling me she wasn't being honest. We ate in front of the television. She drank two glasses of wine in less than thirty minutes, refilling from a bottle on the table, but barely touched her food, instead drawn to the television's hypnotic glow. This was not the person I had known all my life. After a while she turned to me, eyes blank, and asked me if I remembered her fiftieth birthday party. She mistakenly thought I'd been present. I considered lying, but I said I hadn't. She was taken aback, genuinely confused. "She asked me to pay for my own party," she said. She was talking about Bernie, my aunt. Hannah had told me about this, but I wanted to hear my mom's side of the story. She poured herself more wine and told me she'd asked her sister to throw her a fiftieth birthday party. Bernie was enthusiastic, excited. It was a great party. She'd felt so loved. *So loved.*

"Do you know what she got me?" she asked. "Have you seen it?"

"No," I said, and she got up, stomping into the kitchen. Drawers slammed. She returned holding a small ceramic knife with a turquoise handle in front of my face. I imagined her slicing my cheek. Slowly, I reached up and took it from her, resisting the urge to slide it beneath a couch cushion. "That's it!" she shrieked. "That's all she fucking got for my fiftieth birthday!"

"But she threw you a party," I said.

"Yeah," my mom said. Now I recognized her—the baritone voice, the downward curve of her mouth, the unyielding stance, as if she were preparing to pounce. This was the monster from my childhood; the person I feared most. "She handed me a bill! What kind of sister does that?" Red splotches erupted on her face. "I would never do that. I would never—" her breath caught, and she took a ragged inhale, then howled, reaching for me. I flinched, thinking she was going to hit me, but she nuzzled her head into my chest and sobbed. I smoothed her hair.

"Mom," I said. "You can't do this."

"Do what?" she asked, her voice small and muffled.

"Hold this anger inside you."

"But I would never do that. I would never—"

She righted herself, face contorted. I could see that she was winding up again. "I'm so sorry, Mom," I said, thinking the words would calm her. I put my hand on her shoulder. "Let's go to bed, okay?" Her lips tightened back into a white line.

"I understand. You don't want to spend time with me. You can sleep on the couch," she said, wobbling to the bathroom. While she was in there I searched every drawer for any evidence of doctor's visits or medication. I rifled through the piles of paper on the dining room table, mostly credit card bills. Several denials for extended unemployment. These were all out in the open, where I could see them. How many credit cards did she have? My mom had been living off the highest level of unemployment for over a year. I knew she had gotten a divorce settlement but would only find out later that she had spent half a million dollars in three years.

When she was in her bedroom I crawled underneath the blankets and called Greta to tell her my mom was sick. But could people with stage three colon cancer drink so much? "I don't know if she has cancer," I said. Greta told me that she'd had the same thought the moment I told her about my mom's initial phone call. But neither of us could say the word *lying*.

I lay under the covers late that night, mind racing. Murky streetlights cast the room a diaphanous pale gray, my mother's bedroom door a menacing dark triangle. I knew how fast her rage could shift focus. She'd had night terrors when I was younger. What if she had a night terror and tried to kill me?

I thought I was being irrational. I didn't know she had recently bought a gun.

* * *

On Christmas I insisted on taking a cab to dinner. In a picture she took of me I'm smiling, holding a tiny, pronged oyster aloft. I'm wearing her tanzanite necklace, one of the many pieces of jewelry she gave me during my visit. My bleached hair is cut pixie style. She was drinking martinis and had been blacked out since before we left the house. She had fish and chips and finished everything, but I was so alert to her shifting moods that I don't remember what I ate. We ordered dessert. I encouraged her to get coffee, but she got wine instead.

I was eating my bread pudding when she reached across the table to slide my plate away from me, eyes narrowed as she asked me if I really needed dessert. "I know you threw up your dinner," she hissed. She was right. I didn't respond.

"All those books about kids with eating disorders always blame the parents." She shoved the dessert back towards me. "They say I'm supposed to change. That's bullshit. You're the one that needs to change. You need to stop blaming everything on me and take responsibility for yourself." Like sharpened metal these words emerged from her mouth. I stood up and walked out of the restaurant.

Outside, I leaned against the heavy glass, solid against my back. A family was exiting a taxi; two parents, two adult children a few years younger than me. Or perhaps an adult child and their partner. They interacted with such ease, the mom reaching out to her son, adjusting his scarf. I turned and looked at my mother, alone at our table. My heart naturally reached out to her. She held her head rigidly, half-smiling, her eyes unfixed. Masking an open wound. I couldn't help but feel responsible for her, and for the wound itself. I took a few breaths and followed the family in, smiling at our server as I passed him. When I sat at the table I was met with my mother's powerful gaze. The gaze said: You are mine.

I decided I had to move to Seattle. Hannah and I discussed a possible intervention. When I had asked my mom about her illness, she was evasive, at first claiming not to remember where she was diagnosed. Maybe we could recruit my mom's two brothers. Convince her to go to the doctor, or, at minimum, get some sort of help for her drinking. I was hopeful. In Denver I packed my things into my car, said good-bye to my nanny family, my friends, and my therapist. I was driving through the middle of Wyoming when the Park Service called with a job offer—I'd applied for a job in Alaska. Victoria had given me the info; she'd spent a summer working there, not as a hotshot but as a helicopter crew member. My knee wasn't strong enough for hotshot-ting, but surely I could be a helislacker. I made a deal with myself: We'd have the intervention and if I could get my mom to therapy or convince her to bring me along on a doctor's visit for a firm cancer diagnosis, I would consider staying in town to help her. If she didn't, I would leave. I accepted the job offer. It was an escape route.

I told Hannah about the job, via text. She texted me back. *My mom doesn't think we should do the intervention.* I pulled over and called her, trying to change her mind, but she didn't want to deal with it. Neither did her mom. And they didn't have to. I fumed for the rest of the drive, and cried. My uncles were strangers to me. My grandparents were dead. My mother's friends were convinced she had cancer. And I was alone in this. Whatever it was.

Chapter Two

Seattle

When I go through my journals from this time, I'm always surprised at how hopeful I was, almost delusional. I wrote about taking writing classes, making friends, connecting with my roommates, finding another therapist. Interspersed with the hope is a discordant despair appearing only every few pages. My mom's abandoned *Law of Attraction* philosophy must have sunk in somehow—or maybe I was just trying to keep myself from drowning. Whenever I asked my mom about seeing a doctor she simply said, "No doctors." She kept saying she wanted to die in peace.

In early March 2010, she and I met her friend Pauline for lunch. Pauline offered to help her apply for a job at Boeing and my mom snapped. I'd never seen her treat her friends like she treated me. She disappeared to the bathroom, and Pauline commented, "I've never seen her like this. It must be the brain tumor." My mom had told Pauline she had stage four brain cancer. When we left, my mom stumbled to the car. I insisted on driving. Once we were on the road, I asked her about the brain tumor.

"It hasn't been diagnosed yet. But I can feel it." She rubbed her skull with two fingers. "Want to feel it?"

"Wait, so you told her you have stage four brain cancer, but you haven't had it diagnosed by a doctor?" I stared ahead, trying to concentrate.

"I know I'm dying," she said.

I continued to press her, asking again if she had really been diagnosed with colon cancer. She banged her fists on the dashboard, angered by the questions. We were driving across a bridge I had crossed countless times, and I remembered a recurring dream from childhood, us in her old Nissan Sentra, flying off this bridge into the lake.

"Fuck you!" my mom finally screamed. My ears rung. I clung to the steering wheel. She yelled again. "You're not my daughter. I don't want to be your mother anymore. We have too much history. We should just divorce." She banged the dash again, slamming her hands three times, as if she were an animal trapped in a cage. "Like me and Vern. This isn't working out."

I couldn't breathe. "I'm trying to drive," I said, a sob punctuating my sentence. I rolled down my window to get some air, wiped at my face. We were almost across the bridge. "You can't let me move all the way out here and then just say that. I'm your daughter. I came here to help you!"

I cried quietly until we arrived at my mom's house. We both went inside. I knew my mom—a big outburst and then the energy was gone. By the time we sat on the couch she didn't even look upset. "Mom," I said, leaning towards her. "What do you want me to be?" I hiccupped. "I'll be anything. I'll do anything you want me to do. What do you need from me?" I was completely serious. It was the question I'd been asking silently all my life. She shook her head, her expression a combination of pity and despair.

"I don't know," she said. I wanted a coherent answer. It didn't occur to me that she was incapable of providing one. That I had spent all my life trying to be what she wanted, when neither of us had ever known what that was.

In the dark early mornings after my housekeeping night shift I often drew a bath. Afterwards, skin still hot, I'd crawl under the thick down comforter. I dreamed of my mother lying in a shallow grave, reaching up towards me. In the dream I kneeled down to help her out, but she grabbed my arms, pulling me down instead.

My mom invited me over for a farewell dinner in early April. She'd bought crab, a rare treat. In the kitchen she apologized for how hard it had been, my being there. I said it was okay. I touched her arm, but she didn't turn. Her fleece jacket was like armor. She was unreachable.

I told her I was coming to visit in June; I'd already bought the ticket. By the time we said goodbye it was dark outside. At the front door I handed her the card of a therapist I'd spoken with. "I'll stay if you go see her," I said. She shook her head, setting the card on the counter. When we hugged our cheeks pressed together. Both of us were crying and our tears intermingled.

"I love you so much," I said.

"I love you too," she said. I kept turning back to look at her as I walked to my car. The new owner would pick it up the next day, right before my flight. I waved. She waved back, the outline of her body dark against the warm kitchen light. It was the last time I saw her.

PART VI

The Last Frontier
(2010)

Chapter One

Auroras

My new neighbor Gracie picked me up from the tiny airport in her old yellow Datsun. Her face was clean of makeup, her reddish hair unbrushed and wild. I told her that the stunted spruce trees looked like little green elves on the flat landscape. She told me it was taiga. "You're gonna like it here, I can already tell," she said. I liked how secure she seemed, with herself and with this place. Fairbanks.

When she dropped me off at my yurt she showed me how to work the pump sink and where the outhouse was. She and her partner, Doug, had chopped some wood for me, and she asked if I knew how to work the woodstove. I did. "It gets cold in here," she said.

Gracie's friend lent me her Subaru. It had a large, horizontal wood block of floodlights taped to its roof. Moose lights. They illuminated the snowy roads, like a white half-tunnel made of snow and ice, the sky a black ceiling. It was disorienting and a little bit exhilarating, to think that if the car suddenly broke down I'd be stranded on a strip of ice, itself on a chunk of ice, surrounded by wilderness.

Soon after my arrival I trekked with Gracie, Doug, Leslie, and Ahmed to a frozen pond. The auroras were out. The auroras. The sound of those two words summoned postcard pictures. I'd always wanted to come to Alaska.

Above the frozen pond the sky resembled the bottom of a well, the stars scattered like debris of light. My four new friends, three of them graduate students in anthropology at UAF, all slid onto the shiny ice in their shoes. "Come on!" Gracie called. I tried, but kept picturing the ice cracking beneath me. I'd seen too many videos of people falling through ice and drowning, or dying of hypothermia, so I stayed near the edge and drank the cup of blueberry vodka punch Gracie had handed me. "I'm okay," I said. They all stood in the middle of the pond. "I don't want to hurt myself before I start work." I looked up to see a slip of green like watercolor. It spread outwards, dispersed, and narrowed into several diffuse bands of light. "Oh, good! The auroras!" Gracie yelled, looking to make sure I was watching. I gasped and watched the bright emerald waves shimmering above me. Gossamer curtains, violet and fuchsia, danced across the sky. This was better than any pictures or videos. It was God pressing their finger into the sky. Brilliant neon lights fluttered down like iridescent rain. I thought of my mom then; she was probably sitting in front of her television, on her third bottle of wine. Maybe blacked out. I thought I must be an awful person to be underneath such a beautiful sky while she was stuck inside her house, by herself.

The following evening I went to Leslie and Ahmed's insulated yurt; Gracie and Doug knocked on my door as they passed, and we stomped through the snowy pathway through the stunted trees. In the warmth of their little home, surrounded by neighbors who wanted to know me and showed affection for me, I remained guarded. I stayed as long as I could, then scuttled back to my yurt in the snow to sit on my plank bed again. I couldn't understand why it felt so hard to be with others; why I couldn't accept that my presence was invited, even encouraged. It was this old self—this self I rejected, and who'd been rejected—pressing up against the warmth of potential friends and community. There was a part of me that resisted it and tried to shape the welcoming space into a rejecting one. For the first time I saw what I was doing, but I couldn't stop myself.

Chapter Two

Wolf

I was no longer a hotshot, and there was no hotshot base here, just a big brown building filled with administrators, some fire personnel, and ecologists. My position at the Park Service was officially a forestry technician, an umbrella term applied to many wildland firefighters. I would be doing primarily what's called fuels work and assisting with helicopters.

My new boss, Stephan, shook my hand and showed me around the offices. I was still a GS-4 despite my six years of experience. I hadn't applied to other jobs at all. Stephan showed me the group office, where I'd be sharing space with four guys. Everyone had their own computers. I'd never had my own workspace on the hotshots because my position wasn't important enough. Stephan told me we'd have our refresher training and upcoming opportunities for prescribed burning on the weekends. He also introduced me to Kit, a woman in her thirties who would be working with us. She was a helicopter manager. I sensed tension between us right away—that familiar undercurrent of competition that sometimes occurs with women in male-dominated fields.

Fairbanks is the primary base for Alaska fire operations because of its central location. The Alaska Interagency Coordination Center (AICC) is in Fort Wainwright, a military base in Fairbanks. The military connection is no mistake: Alaska's fire suppression policies were mostly written in the 1940s and '50s. Because Alaska was colonized later than the lower forty-eight states, fire suppression came later, on an accelerated timeline. When Henry S. Graves saw fire in Alaska in 1915 (five years after he took over the USFS from Gifford Pinchot) he immediately called for a suppression arm. From his perspective, fire was destroying massive stores of timber, and these timber stores could save the United States from the "timber famine." Indigenous Alaskans were blamed for fires, despite the near-constant presence of lightning during Alaska's fire season, which historically lasts from May to September.

Data collection on fire frequencies and regimes started in the 1940s, though arriving colonizers did remark on the presence of smoke and fire in the late 1800s and especially during the gold rush era at the turn of the twentieth century. Southwest Alaska, which is far from Fairbanks, doesn't burn often. Most of it is coastal rainforest. Lightning strikes typically only ignite fires where the coastal rainforests are transitioning into taiga (which it does as one moves northward, before transitioning into tundra). Public southern lands, where fires occur less frequently, are mostly National Forests, but much of Alaska's interior is under the jurisdiction of the Bureau of Land Management, which also oversees most of the Great Basin in the lower forty-eight. The BLM and AFS (Alaska Fire Service) are one and the same in Alaska. Their interchangeable titles can be confusing.

National Park Service jurisdiction in Alaska is small compared to the BLM's. Most people think of Denali National Park, or the southern parks like Katmai and Glacier Bay, but the Fairbanks office oversees the interior and northern parks, including Gates of the Arctic and Wrangell-St. Elias. When I took the job, I'd imagined lush wilderness, but the Park Service building was plain, with rows of windowless offices, and the town itself was small and flat. It grew on me quickly, though.

In mid-April I was driving south to Palmer for helicopter training, through Denali, with Ted. He was one of my co-workers, about six years younger than me. A preppy kid with an arrestingly cute face punctuated by dimpled cheeks and an easy smile.

Ted asked me what it was like to be a hotshot, because that's what he wanted to do after his year at the Park Service. We were getting along, so I told him how great it was to work in the wilderness; how exhilarating it felt to be pushed to your physical and mental edge, and that most of the people I'd worked with were kind and good.

A faint layer of powdery snow created a bright white tapestry patterned in mustard yellow and mossy green undergrowth. Stunted spruce and miniature shrubbery dotted the landscape; the mountains, snowcapped, stood high and sharp against the endless blue sky like pinned-up posters. Lichen and moss etched gray boulders in shades of green. I was staring at the landscape when I saw the gray wolf, sitting at the edge of the road, watching our van approach. I pointed her out, then looked into her gold eyes.

Neither of us had seen a wolf in the wild. It was as if she had been waiting. Her fur blended perfectly with the branches of the not-quite-blooming shrubs. She could have stayed hidden, but she let us see her. Her eyes looked like eternal witnesses; like they held all the world's secrets. I'd seen a captive wolf at the Defenders of Wildlife conference. This one was different. Glowing with pure presence. I wondered what we looked like to her.

Chapter Three

Mud Season

S pring arrived in Fairbanks near the end of April. The days lengthened. The snow melted. Almost overnight the birch and aspens bloomed a dazzling green. This was the mud season, also called greenup. The first weekend of May I burned with Stephan, Kit, Ted, and Hansel, my Park Service co-workers, along with a bunch of AFS people of varying positions, including a few smokejumpers. We drove outside of town and parked, trying not to get our trucks stuck in the mud, before getting the drip torches and fuel ready.

Prescribed burning is different than burning on a fire. The goal of prescribed burning is to cleanse the environment, usually with low severity fire. It's always planned and timed for conducive weather. Most often small sections are burned one at a time. This is called "box and burn," and lessens the chance of fires escaping.

My Park Service co-workers weren't as comfortable with burning as me and the other firefighters. They all had college degrees but lacked tangible firefighting experience. Kit was clumsy and out of shape. I couldn't help judging her, as any hotshot would. She had trouble carrying the heavy drip torch and started dragging it on the ground, and she couldn't follow the directions of the smokejumpers as to where to burn. When they got frustrated she giggled. I'd once giggled like that. At the time I was annoyed with her for being so nonchalant with something that was, to me, a serious endeavor. I worked alongside the smokejumpers, finding ways to slip hotshotting into the conversation as a way of separating myself from my Park Service peers. I'd internalized the macho attitude that had suffocated me for so long, but I also knew that Kit wouldn't have accepted my help had I offered it.

When one of the veteran smokejumpers asked me if I wanted to try out for smokejumping, I said maybe, but I knew I wouldn't. Victoria was a smokejumper now. I figured my knee ruled it out. Qualifying as a smokejumper is more difficult than hotshot training. The physical requirements are grueling: they had to run 1.5 miles in under ten minutes, do ten pull-ups in a row, thirty-five push-ups, and sixty sit-ups. Whereas the hotshot pack test required us to carry a forty-five-lb. pack three miles in under forty-five minutes on flat ground (relatively easy for most people), smokejumpers had to carry 110 lbs. the same distance in under fifty-five minutes. And those are minimums. Most smokejumpers spend at least a couple years hotshotting before they try out, and many fail, but the guys I burned with in Alaska told me smokejumping was easier than hotshotting. You got to work independently, without some superintendent breathing down your neck.

I was almost in disbelief that we could burn in a grassy swamp. Instead of using a road as a fuel break, we used a stream. Some of the AFS people and smokejumpers carried flappers—big squares of rubber attached to long metal poles. If you flap them onto burning materials, especially in swampy, watery areas, they can extinguish fire that's burning too hot or in the wrong direction. It's necessary in an environment like the boreal forest where it is almost impossible to dig fireline because of the deep organic layers and permafrost. We spent the whole day burning, about ten hours. After the first couple hours my boots were soaked through. The fire crackled and hissed in the grass, burning steadily despite the moisture.

The moisture-soaked boreal forests of Alaska share surprising similarities with South Florida's palmetto swamps and longleaf pine fire regimes. Although they're very different ecosystems, all three are shaped by lightning. They depend on fire for their survival, and contain diverse, fire-adapted species. Palmetto swamps, also called cabbage palm habitats, are wetlands. So are Alaska's boreal forests, which contain peatlands, marshes, and swamps, and upland forests composed of black-and-white spruce. People don't necessarily think of these boreal forests as wetlands because they're frozen for over half the year, but in some areas wetlands and peatlands cover over half of the landscape, acting as natural firebreaks and aiding in the creation of fire mosaics. Boreal peatlands have excellent carbon storage capabilities, but burning releases their carbon into the atmosphere, whereas palmetto stores carbon in underground rhizomes. Palmetto swamps are highly volatile—palmetto has a flammable waxy cuticle and burns intensely, but its underground rhizome survives and sprouts after fire. Saw palmettos are a keystone species. Their flowers attract pollinators and their fruit, called drupes, are eaten by black bears, foxes, raccoons, and other mammals, as well as reptiles and birds. Hundreds of insect species depend on saw palmetto for survival.

Unlike boreal forests, palmetto swamps have a dense understory. The two have vastly different fire return intervals—Palmetto swamp has historically burned at low severity every 1–7 years, during the winter months, whereas the boreal forests of interior Alaska have historically burned every 75–150+ years, in summertime. Boreal's long interval doesn't mean fires only burn every 75–150 years. Fires occur often, contributing to a diverse mosaic. Boreal fire intervals have shortened due to climate change, making it difficult for serotinous cones to properly propagate, but palmetto swamp intervals have lengthened because of the presence of humans, who start fires accidentally and make it challenging to conduct prescribed burns; housing complexes and population centers have fragmented the ecosystem. In both habitats fuel accumulation hinders the flow of water through the land, reducing soil fertility. Both crave fire as much as water for cleansing and replenishment.

Florida's northern landscape is much different than the palmetto swamps, but also fire-adapted. It was once almost entirely composed from the longleaf pine ecosystem, which stretched from southern Virginia to eastern Texas along the coastal plain. The trees were logged and shipped back to England beginning in the 1600s, by the Jamestown Colony. Their sturdy wood was prized for the construction of ships and houses. The longleaf logging enterprise lasted around 300 years, and revenue outpaced cotton for fifty of them. As with cotton harvesting, enslaved Africans were exploited in this endeavor, increasing profits for European colonizers.

Longleaf pines, also a keystone species, are especially unique, because the youngest of the trees, in their "grass stage," can survive fire at a very young age, unlike other pines. This is because of their compact singular stem, which sprouts up from the ground after fire, and their deep taproot. Without branches, like other pine species, they're less liable to burn. In their grass stage, baby longleaf pines also send much of their growth underground. Its long needles protect it from fire.

Before fire suppression, a longleaf pine ecosystem would typically burn every 2–3 years. Although prescribed fire is more widely accepted in northern Florida than other regions, the Forest Service is often unwilling to conduct prescribed burns in the dry season, when longleaf needs to burn in order to propagate properly. This hinders longleaf pine restoration. Loblolly and slash pine plantations have succeeded much of its territory; their plantations are more susceptible to pests and disease and less ecologically diverse than longleaf pine habitat. Usually the trees are planted in uniform lines. Longleaf pine and Alaska's boreal forests have been degraded by fragmentation—in Alaska this is primarily due to logging. In northern Florida (and throughout the longleaf territory), logging, population growth, and fire suppression have all contributed to fragmentation.

Climate change, too, is transforming these landscapes. Drought increases palmetto swamp and longleaf flammability, heightening fire severity. Fire management specialists and scientists are using GIS to map these changes. They've discovered that frequent prescribed burning throughout Florida reduces fuel loading and helps maintain ecological integrity, while longleaf ecosystems need additional restoration and maintenance.

Typically, interior Alaska fire seasons were influenced by precipitation levels: Dry seasons produced more fire. But core samples from two glaciers, along with fire history records, indicate that fires are now also influenced by rising temperatures. Winter and spring temperatures in Alaska have increased nearly three degrees Fahrenheit since 1925, leading to less snowpack, melting permafrost, and receding glaciers. Fire seasons have lengthened, resulting in more ignitions and more time for fires to grow, ultimately reducing the fire mosaic and diversity.

Chapter Four

Rupture

Along our melting muddy dirt road the translucent aspen leaves flowed like a singular ocean wave, pulsating with the wind, chartreuse against the dark blue-green of the spruce trees and white of the sky. It was early May. I inhaled as soon as I stepped out of my new-to-me Ford Ranger, which I had bought for a few hundred dollars. Wet moss, mud, and the cottony scent of birch and aspen enlivened me. The particular smell of woodsmoke, dry wood, and incense that I'd come to love and think of as my own greeted me inside my yurt. Although the days were getting warmer, I started a fire in the wood-stove and turned the little FM radio to NPR.

I called my mom, but she wasn't answering her phone. I was sure something was wrong. Pacing my yurt, I sent several texts. *Mom, please call me, I'm so worried right now. Where are you?* I imagined her fallen down the stairs leading to the basement, or in bed struggling to breathe, consumed by the cancer I'd doubted she'd had. I listened to her automated voicemail repeatedly—the pause where her voice came in to say her name. I left another message. "You always call me back," I said, which was mostly true. "Please just call me or text me and let me know you're okay."

I sat on my little wooden bed, on top of the small Therm-a-Rest and quilt Gracie had given me, and called my mom's longtime friend Karla, a flight attendant. We hadn't seen each other in a while, but my mom had given me her number. "She's fine," Karla said. Frustrated, I tried Pauline, the one who'd told me about my mom's brain tumor, begging her to check on my mom in the morning, as early as she could. I didn't want to upset her, but I knew something was wrong. She promised to go first thing in the morning, with her husband. "She's fine, honey, I'm sure she's fine." Her words were unconvincing. I collapsed back onto the bed, staring at the latticework that formed my yurt, grainy and fraying. A thin layer of woodsmoke hung above me, interlaced with the sweet smell of incense. Although I didn't believe in any god, I had prayed when I lit the incense, promising to move back to Seattle if she was alive, to call an institution. I should have done more, I thought. How stupid of me to have left her alone.

Midnight settled around me, an oozing diaphanous half-light suffused with shadows, tinged with the sun's lingering gold, ushering me into some liminal realm. Tears pooled in the crevices of my ears; I shifted my head side to side so they could soak into my blankets. *She is dead*, I thought. *If she is dead, please let it have been peaceful. It must have been cancer. She was telling the truth. How terrible to have to endure my doubt; to feel so alone in her suffering.*

I drifted in and out of sleep, longing for an escape from this panic and helplessness, sleeping ten or twenty minutes, waking each time to reality, which felt less real than dreaming. With each waking I checked my phone and called hers again. No change. The infinite night wound itself around me, suffocating.

I awoke to the returning light. Still too early to call Pauline again. Slipping back into half-sleep, I dreamed I was naked in a freezing river, trying to swim through a thick layer of ice, chopping at it with my hands and arms until they were red and bruised. Beyond the river was an ocean, its deep blue waves multitudinous and foam-peaked, full of sharks. The ice was thick and opaque, whiter than ivory. I shoved the floating chunks away, their sharp edges cutting into my numb skin. I couldn't feel my body at all. I paused, glanced up. There on the shore was a red fox, her copper fur blazing, gold eyes lined in black. She was watching me. Behind her was my mother's house. But not her house. Beyond was emptiness, but not emptiness. An indiscernible blurry landscape.

When I woke up again I was sobbing, sure she was dead. The feeling burned like a lost layer of skin. It was five a.m. Seattle was one hour ahead of Fairbanks. I prayed to my absent god that Pauline would call soon. When she did, I was collapsed over my legs on the edge of my bed. Pauline said they were on their way to my mom's, then called thirty minutes later. "We're here," she said breathlessly. "Her car's in the driveway but she's not answering the door. What do you want us to do?"

I pictured her and her husband Jeremy standing at my mother's front door, peering into the window. "You can either call the police or go inside. Whatever feels right to you." They surprised me by opting to go inside. Pauline narrated: "Jeremy is crawling through the doggy door. He's inside. Okay, I'm inside now. We're in the kitchen." As she spoke I watched the house unfold in front of me. I knew it so well: the tiny dog door, the kitchen with its linoleum floors peeling up from the corners, its sticky drawers. "We're in the living room." The stained gray carpet on the floor, my grandparents' dining table to the left, a china cabinet behind it, and on the right some pictures, a chair, the antique tiki lamp with its hula girls. "We're opening the door to her bedroom, we're going in—" And then she screamed. My legs collapsed. I wanted to throw my phone across the room, but I inhaled and asked her to give the phone to Jeremy.

He said to come home. He didn't say she was dead, but I knew. My teeth chattered. I threw some things into my suitcase, then texted

Stephan to tell him my mom had died. Soon after, Kit called me to offer a ride to the airport. Then I called Karla and told her she was dead, gave her Pauline's number. "Get on a flight," she said. "Tell me which one and I'll meet you at the terminal when you arrive." Her firm voice comforted me. There was an afternoon flight. Kit was already on her way but I didn't ask her to come later. I couldn't be in my yurt anymore. I needed to be going somewhere. To my mother.

At the airport I sat at a table and built a mountain of tear-stained napkins. I called everyone. My mother has died. Greta cried when I called her. "At least it was cancer," I said. I was so relieved that she hadn't been lying, so glad that she'd died peacefully, so regretful that I'd doubted her. "Thank god," Greta said, intuiting what I meant. "Will you let me know about the memorial?" she asked, and I said yes and then thought, oh god, a memorial. I had no money. Nine hundred dollars in my bank account. Over the past several months my mom had given me a couple thousand dollars. *Don't spend this, there's not much more.* But it was gone.

I carried my pile of wet napkins to the garbage can and sat near my assigned gate, against the wall. I called at least twelve people to tell them my mom had died, but didn't believe it myself.

On the plane I gazed out at the sky, layered in pink and baby blue. I let my vision blur and imagined that my mom was out there. Her spirit was free; there was no more pain for her. I let her go.

Chapter Five

Mother's Day

I arrived at my mother's house on Mother's Day. The first thing I noticed was a mattress leaned against one of the tall bushes, its corner stained copper and red. Jeremy was waiting for me and Karla near my mother's blooming peonies, their heads drooping on the concrete. His hands were shaking.

"Your mom shot herself," he said. I went mute, so he continued. "It makes sense, I think, because of the cancer."

"She didn't have cancer." The words erupted from my throat. Tension expanded inside me, until I couldn't take a full breath. "I've known it this whole time."

Now I knew why Pauline had screamed. The past six months coursed through me, everything rearranging itself with this new information. I could see the purity of my sadness, a purity that came from knowing my mom was telling the truth. It slipped away, replaced by something solid and hard.

I found a glass of white wine on her bedside table, a dead fruit fly floating on its surface. Beside it was a piece of printer paper with her handwriting. Big, bold, messy letters. *This takes courage. I am not a coward.* The Sharpie lay on the table. Her bed frame was empty. She'd written the note as I'd sobbed in my yurt. These were the things the investigators had left intact.

The coroner's assistant, Cassandra, handed me a checklist, followed by my mother's suicide notes, one after the other, all written on yellow legal paper and addressed to various people. There was an envelope with my name on it, underlined xoxo, all in my mother's sprawling handwriting. Cassandra counted out the money my mom had left inside. Two thousand dollars. "I'm going to leave you two for a few moments."

I spread everything out in front of me. Karla picked up one of the smaller notes and said my aunt's name. I opened the white envelope with my name on it. Inside, with the money, was a note addressed to me.

I'm sorry I lied about the cancer. The truth is, I'm running out of money, and I'm too old to start over. I'm sorry I lied about Todd. I don't know why I did that, and it caused our relationship so much harm. You were always the sweetest little thing. The sweetest little girl. I know you'll be better off without me. Your friends are your family now, and I know my friends will take care of you. Don't be sad for me. I don't want to be here anymore. I'm too old to start over. Love, Mom.

"I can't believe it," I said. "She really did lie." There was no satisfaction in being right. She hadn't said one nasty thing about me in her note, but her house was saturated with rage.

When Cassandra came back into the room I asked for an autopsy. "In her notes she said she lied about having cancer," I said, and Cassandra asked if there was a particular cancer to look for, and I said colon, but could she please look for anything that may have caused an onset of mental illness? When she asked me what I wanted to do with the body I said cremation. I couldn't afford a burial, a coffin, a headstone, and my mom had never told me what she wanted.

* * *

Over the next few days everything spun around me and it felt as if I was the only solid thing in the world. I spent each night at Karla's condo in the suburbs, waking each morning to peanut butter toast and coffee. At my mother's house, she helped me sift through all the piles of paper and I called my mother's friends one by one, inviting them to an informal memorial.

Everyone wanted things from me. If not physical things, energetic things, or at least an explanation. They wanted answers and thought I had them. And maybe I did, but I knew I couldn't tell them what I thought. That she had done this because she was angry, trapped. That she had done this to me. That she had lied to lure me back into her life. This is only one of many truths.

I wondered what I would say when people asked me what my parents did, where my family lives, who I come from, who I was. Because who was I, without her, without trying to be what she wanted?

Vern came up from Olympia for lunch; he cried when I told him. He said he wasn't going to attend the memorial, that he was going to tell people she died of cancer. My aunt and cousin also wanted to cover up the suicide, but I refused. Lying would rot me from the inside. It had killed my mother. I promised myself I would never lie again, no matter the cost.

Greta arrived, carrying flowers as she climbed the long set of stairs below my mother's porch. The flowers made me want to cry except I couldn't cry. She was weeping. I hugged her rigidly, as if her despair were a contagion. If I contracted it, I'd never be okay again. My aunt Bernie shadowed me, asking for my mom's things until I finally had to tell her to stop.

The autopsy made it official: no cancer.

My whole life I'd lived in my mother's tightly controlled reality. So many times I'd tried to share this world with others. They never believed me. Now everyone could see it, but they struggled to believe that my mother was someone who could sustain a lie for so long, deceiving everyone, maybe even herself. Karla kept asking how my mother could leave me to deal with everything. I was having the opposite experience. My mother was absolutely someone who could do this. But it would take me years to accept it completely.

I held a small memorial at her house. Ghoulish, in a way, but I had little money left. I half-wished people brought money to memorials. One of her brothers paid for her cremation. The other one didn't come, and never returned my call.

People spoke about her, generic things like how great she was, how funny, how charismatic. Her sister didn't speak. An Olympia friend, drunk, wagged her finger in my face. *You should be more like your mom.* I wanted to punch her. I wanted to punch them all.

Instead, I stepped in front of everyone and read an E. E. Cummings poem I had sent her for Mother's Day, the card arriving after I did. "[i carry your heart with me(i carry it in]." I read the poem and felt my mother's heart beating in my heart. For the first time my stoicism melted away and I sobbed, almost unable to finish the poem. I remembered the last time I'd hugged her, the last words I'd said to her. *I love you.*

After the memorial I walked into my mother's bedroom and stepped inside of her empty bed frame. Something on the ceiling caught my eye. I thought it was glow-in-the-dark stars, but it was brain matter. The room spun and I leapt out of the bed frame. Karla was outside the bedroom door holding a quilt. "Do you want this?" she asked, handing it to me. I said yes, and took it, only to realize it was stained with blood.

You saved my life. That's what she used to tell me. *When the nurse set you on my chest and you looked up at me with your big blue eyes, you were the most beautiful, most intelligent little being.* Two years after she died, I found a picture of myself as a baby. On the back, my mother had written that she loved Stacy. This was my childhood name until I was twelve, when I asked to be called Janet, my legal first name. I loved Stacy, she wrote, but I don't love Janet. I burned the picture on a cliff above the Pacific Ocean.

Chapter Six

Kindred Spirits

The night I returned from Seattle, Gracie and Leslie picked me up from the airport. Leslie pulled the passenger seat forward and climbed in behind it.

"You don't have to sit in the back," I said, and she laughed.

"Do not try to accommodate us."

I got in the passenger seat, setting my mom's purse on my lap. I'd emailed Gracie a few days ago, when I'd gotten the news from the coroner, telling her that my mom was lying, and that she'd shot herself. Her reply had been forthright and kind. *I had a friend when I was younger whose mom had killed herself. That is so hard.*

"You have just been through the ultimate," Leslie said from the back seat. "I hope it's okay that Gracie told me."

"I'm glad to be back," I said. I was grateful Gracie had told her, so I wouldn't have to.

"We have gin and tonic at the cabin. Doug bought you a pack of American Spirits," Gracie said. "We figured you might like at least one of those things."

* * *

For the first time since my mom's death I felt seen. Neither of them needed me to take care of them. They didn't look at me with pity. I had been performing in Seattle, for everyone. I didn't need to do that here, with them.

They parked near my yurt, where it smelled like earth and new growth. The snow was gone. We sat on the stairs, where Gracie's dogs ran up to greet us. Doug and Ahmed showed up with the gin, tonic, and cigarettes. For the first time, I thought I would be okay. I felt a closeness to these two women I barely knew. We made a few drinks, passing them around, and I smoked. The guys asked how the weather in Seattle had been. They told me about hunting for moose and said the summer fires had begun.

After my first drink, Gracie hugged me and said, "If you need anything, just shout. We're gonna leave you alone now, I'm sure you need to decompress."

They all hugged me and went home, the dogs following them. Only a few hours later Stephan called. Was I ready to go on a fire? I said I was. I didn't know what else to do.

Chapter Seven

This Isn't a Fucking Hotshot Crew

The next day Stephan dropped me and Cole off at the AFS offices, and a Native Alaskan showed up with a white van and loaded in several of us. Cole, a chubby white guy with short brown hair, had started at the office while I was gone; I hadn't met him yet, and he didn't introduce himself or make eye contact. We drove several hours to a helicopter base in the middle of nowhere, but everything was socked in with smoke, reducing visibility. All flights were grounded until it cleared. When I unloaded, I heard someone call my name and turned around. A girl with dark blonde hair was running up to me.

"Hi!" she said, holding out her hand, "I'm Margaret. I work in the south zone. In Denali?" She was smiling, and her hazel eyes were open and friendly. I shook her hand.

"You work for Stephan, right?" she asked.

"Yeah," I said.

"You used to be a hotshot," she said, and I nodded. "Wow, that is so hardcore. I could never do that." I wanted to tell her that she could but she turned around. "You should set up your tent near mine, it's over here."

I followed her through some birch trees and saw a few tents set up in a break between the trees. The ground was soft and dry, covered with moss and lichen. "It's a perfect spot," she said, "and the mosquitoes don't seem to be bad here. I have to go back to the cabin really quick, but that purple tent is mine." She pointed to a tiny purple tent that was identical to the one I'd been issued.

"I have the same one," I said, and she laughed. I set mine up quickly, then walked over to a stack of MREs, grabbing one for lunch.

"I guess we're not going anywhere today," Cole said from the steps. His back was turned.

"I guess not," I said. "I met Margaret. Have you worked with her?"

"Worked with her last year," he said. "She's cool. She's gonna be a pilot in a few years."

"That's awesome," I said. He shrugged, and didn't reply.

We were charged with untangling truckloads of dirty, tangled hose, and I rolled them up with Margaret and Cole, each of us taking turns jumping into the truck and throwing the hose down, unrolling it and rolling it carefully back up again. I found myself jumping into the truck more often than they were, and throwing the hoses out faster.

"This isn't a fucking hotshot crew, Ana," Cole yelled up at me, out of breath. "We have the rest of the day."

"Sorry," I said, slowing down to what felt like a snail's pace. After a while I hopped out of the truck.

"You can go up there and do it, then," I said to him. "It's boring if I have to go slow." I didn't like the way he spoke to me, and had the urge to hit him in the face. He was a GS-6, technically my superior. Margaret had told me not to worry about him, that he was always moody. We unrolled the hoses together, Cole throwing them out of the truck one by one, until it was time for dinner. The three of us unwrapped MREs and compared meals; I had chicken tetrazzini, Margaret got raviolis, and Cole dug through two boxes of the meals and opened a third, searching for beef teriyaki. He grunted when he couldn't find it and went into the birch trees to eat alone.

"Did you work with him last year?" I asked Margaret, who was heating her main entree with the included flameless heater. I ate mine cold, like I'd done on the hotshots.

"Yeah," Margaret said. "He's not a bad person. He'll warm up to you. But he doesn't like his job very much."

"I've worked with guys like that before, on the hotshot crew."

"Did you like working on a hotshot crew?" Margaret asked, eyes big. She was much younger than me, I realized, and very genuine.

"Yes and no," I said. "I liked working hard, and I liked the camaraderie. But it wasn't easy to be one of the only women."

"Were you usually the only one?"

"For my first year. Then there was always two of us."

"Wow," she said.

"It's not that hard," I said, "I mean, it was hard, but any woman could do it. It just takes a lot of work."

"I don't think that's true. I'm pretty sure I couldn't do it. You must have something special. As a person. I mean, Cole could never be a hotshot."

We sat, eating together, as dusk fell down on us, but the sky never got dark. At ten o'clock, we all went to our tents and crawled inside. I was grateful for a tiny space to call my own, and fell asleep easily.

The next morning Cole woke me up. "Tear down your tent," he said, "we're headed out in two hours. Flying into H-13 before the inversion lowers again. We have a ton of supplies, they've been socked in for six days, who knows how long we'll be out there. I'll be training you."

For a moment I wished I'd turned down the fire call; I could be in my yurt right now, or in the office, bored on the internet. Somewhere safe. I threw everything into my red bag, keeping my helicopter bag out. I'd be training as a helicopter crew member. Despite having flown countless times as a hotshot I knew very little about helicopters, except that you had to crouch down when you loaded and unloaded. Now I was supposed to wear an actual helmet and hook it up to my radio so I could hear the pilot. The extra gear and responsibility felt like too much to handle, but I carried my two bags across the road to where the helicopters were waiting and met the pilot before loading into the helicopter.

"Four souls on board," he said over the radio, "En route to H-13." Four souls. I thought of my soul as we rose from the concrete. There were miles of tundra, grass, and water reflecting the sun like little mirrors. The helicopter lurched forward and I could feel the air coming in through the door on my side. I had a sudden urge to open it. What would it feel like to fall out of the door and into one of the glassy mirrors of water? I thought of my mom, and remembered she was gone.

We flew until I began to feel a little sick and wanted to land. After about forty minutes, we finally reached our destination. As we got closer, trees appeared: tall white spruce clustered along a winding river. The helicopter landed on a sand bank; two men with red hard hats guided it in. I followed Cole out to the edge of the sand bank as a helicopter crew member unloaded our bags, along with boxes and bags and rolls of hose. When they departed the rotors sprayed the beach with sand, which got into my mouth and eyes. One of the men who had guided the helicopter in came up to us as we walked up the sand bank. He was Darren, a hotshot and the division superintendent, detailing out from his crew to obtain the certification needed to work as a captain. He spread a map out on the sandy dry riverbank. They were doing little more than monitoring the fire, which had burned through a couple native allotments (land that was "given" to Indigenous Alaskan people after it was taken from them), and they wanted to do some suppression work to prevent the allotments from burning.

Cole introduced me as his trainee, and I wanted to clarify that I was a former hotshot, that this jerk had nothing to teach me, but I smiled instead. "Man," Darren said, "this inversion just lifted today. We haven't been able to do anything. Not sure how long it will stay like this but fire activity's picked up quite a bit. Another helicopter's gonna show up in about a half hour and drop a net of supplies. You two want to wait for that?" Cole nodded, and they studied a map together. Apparently the inversion layer, which is basically the settling of thick smoke, had kept helicopters out for almost a week. It made sense that fire activity had picked up because there was now more oxygen in the atmosphere.

I listened as Darren told us there had been bear activity, and a "shooter" was arriving soon, along with two EMTs. They expected the inversion layer to settle again, and the EMTs were insurance against possible injuries if the helicopters were grounded. After getting us oriented, he left me and Cole to sort through the supplies while waiting for the second load. I'd never taken inventory before, and Cole was supposed to teach me how to do it.

"Take your pad out," he said. "Write how much there is of each thing. Be accurate, because people's lives depend on it, you know?" He raised his eyebrows at me and I nodded. "Give a holler if you need anything," he said, and took out his iPhone, swiping his fingers across it until I heard marching band music. "This is me," he said, smiling for the first time.

"What?" I asked, already making a hand-drawn graph for inventory.

"I played tuba. In the Ohio State Marching Band. Best band in the country."

"Cool," I said, barely looking at him. The music accompanied me as I took inventory. I double- and triple-checked everything, scared of miscounting.

Chapter Eight

Skinned

The Toklat Fire had already burned fifteen thousand acres, about the size of Manhattan at low tide. Our division was located along the southeast corner of the fire, along the Kantishna River, at the helispot we were to manage. I had never felt so isolated on a fire. There were six of us in our camp, including the shooter and EMTs, who arrived that afternoon. A twenty-person crew was camped about a half mile from us. I heard them speaking Inupiaq over the radio sometimes. They were a Native Alaskan Type II crew stationed out of Minto, about sixty minutes northwest of Fairbanks. Most of my days were spent on the embankment with Cole. The inversion layer, as predicted, settled again, and we often had little to do. Usually we sat beneath a cluster of birch trees. He listened to his marching band music constantly and barely spoke to me. He knew my mom had died; everyone from my department knew it.

During the day I'd walk to the riverbank, where all the animals of the forest converged, and study the gently rounded paws of a bear, giant moose tracks, rabbit, fox, and the tiny circular prints I'd later learn were those of a porcupine. I watched the sun's silvery reflections catch on the tiny particles of glimmering rock and silt. Sometimes

I imagined walking into the middle of the river, fully clothed, and letting it carry my body away. More than wanting to be in a different place, I wanted to be held and supported. I missed Gracie and Leslie. There was no space for support here.

When the air was clear we unloaded and loaded. Loaded and unloaded. Added and subtracted. Even with our chin straps tight the violent rotor wash threatened to yank our helmets off. Cubees got stacked into pyramids, along with MREs, huge bags of hose, fifty-lb. helicopter nets and metal hooks, toilet paper, bath-in-a-bags, flagging tape, chainsaw supplies, and fuel. We dragged the heavy food boxes into the shade so the perishables wouldn't go bad. I caught myself trying to outpace Cole, which wasn't hard. Darren always spoke to him instead of me, and I resented it, feeling that familiar invisibility return. It was as if a layer of my skin had been removed. Everything touched me, and everything hurt.

While Cole snoozed under the shade of the birch trees I started spending more time on the embankment, partially to escape his music and moods. I used the stacked cubees as a back rest, and propped up my book so I could underline its passages with my Park Service pen. I was reading *When Things Fall Apart* by Pema Chödrön. Sometimes I set the book down and listened to the low drone of the insects intermingling with the high whine of far-off chainsaws until it all became a long, monotonous hum, like the om I'd learned at my grandfather's Buddhist temple. Everything blended into everything. I was part of that sound. There was something in me that was totally exposed. The pain heightened my sensitivity to beauty. I watched as the clouds fell into a pattern with the day's progression, starting as little gauzy puffs before building into robust fluffy white clouds, then thunderheads. Before rain developed, they collapsed and dispersed. After a while the gauzy puffs would reappear, drawn aloft by the wind.

*   *   *

It wasn't long until we attracted a bear. I had dug a "refrigerator," which was a hole in the duff down to the permafrost. It took me about forty minutes with the Pulaski. First I chopped a rectangle into the top layer of peaty soil with the axe end, then dug it out with the adze end. Then I dug and dug until I reached frozen ground. We stowed our perishables in there, covering them with the intact rectangles of moss and roots. Although we had MREs, we only used them as a last resort. Alaskan food boxes were legendary in the firefighting world, filled with steaks, chicken, fresh veggies, pasta, and fruit. Federal rules stated that we must hang our trash, but we didn't hang it high enough.

A bear came to our camp on the fifth or sixth night. We shooed it away. The next night I started awake. I had cried silently for several hours before falling asleep, so it must have been very early morning, but the gold dusk gave no indication of the time. I held my breath and heard rustling. Quietly, I sat up and peeked under the fly of my tent. The dusk was a sheer dark curtain over my eyes. A smallish black bear was nosing through the trash. Maybe three hundred pounds. It poked and pulled apart the plastic and burlap with its hand-like paws.

"Hey!" I yelled. The bear glanced up, then continued rooting in the trash. "Hey!" I yelled, louder. I unzipped my sleeping bag as loudly as I could, hoping to wake someone. When I poked my head out the bear and I stared at each other. Moss and sticks dug into my bare knees. "Hey!" I yelled, louder again this time, and clapped my hands. They'd shown us a bear video during our first week of training. The people in it had clapped their hands and yelled at a grizzly to scare it away. The black bear didn't run, but glanced down the game trail, then turned back to look at me, then the garbage.

I kicked my right foot out of the tent and stood up. "Hey," I yelled as loudly as I could, clapping again. Darren must have heard me or the bear near his tent, because he yelped, sounding scared and half-asleep. I yelled for the shooter—a smokejumper with shotgun certification. He emerged shirtless, in long johns, slinging the strap of his shotgun over his bare shoulder, before yelling and walking towards the bear, who backed up and turned, lumbering towards the trail. The shooter vanished in the shadows, then reappeared. "Back up!" he yelled at all of us. We waved our arms and yelled at the bear, who was following the shooter back into camp. It hesitated, eyeing the trash bag, which we'd stupidly left on the ground.

The shooter led the bear out again, his shotgun pointed, and we all followed him as if gravitationally attached. When he was out of sight I heard the shot, a crack like thunder. Then another, followed by a few dull thuds which vibrated beneath my feet. A sound like a child's cry, high-pitched and delicate, filled the forest.

In the morning I walked down the game trail with the shooter and one of the guys from the Minto crew. We found the bear lying at the bottom of a small hill, on its side. The guy from the Minto crew asked if I'd ever seen a bear skinned before, and I said no. "It looks just like a human," he said. I touched the bear's face. Its fur was rough and coarse; its flat pink tongue tucked neatly inside its teeth. Only a few hours ago the bear had been alive. Now it was gone. Since I was little I'd believed in reincarnation, and I wondered what the bear would be reborn as. Was its spirit floating around us, as my mother's spirit had been during the week after her death? I couldn't feel her presence anymore. Not in Alaska. But I thought about her all the time.

A boat arrived one day to drop off some smokejumpers. Its driver, small and white-headed, got out too, and after Cole and the smokejumpers shook hands, Cole yelled to me that he'd be right back, taking the three men and leaving the boat operator on the shore. The man had to be about seventy. He was wearing Carhartt overalls and a T-shirt, not Nomex. He walked up to the embankment, sat by me and offered me a chew, which I took. His name was Mike. He asked me about the bears, and if I was from Alaska. I told him no. "Why'd you decide to come up, and where from?"

"That's a long story," I said. Mike held up his hands as if to say, *What else are we going to do?* I felt this constant compulsion to tell people about my mother's death; to see their reactions, to make it real for myself.

"It's kind of sad."

"I've heard sadder, I'm sure."

I told him everything, all in one long exhale, as if I'd been holding my breath forever. When I finished I kept my chin tucked into the gap between my knees. I slowly turned my head towards Mike. I was scared he was going to make an excuse to get up and join the other guys. A few people, when I'd told them, had acted like they immediately had something to do, somewhere to go, as if my mother's suicide was somehow a sickness that could be passed on to them. He looked into me with neon blue eyes. "That's a heavy load to carry," he said, and we sat there together in silence, watching the river.

Chapter Nine

Glaciers

I spent three weeks on the Toklat Fire. With overtime I made about six thousand dollars. I considered leaving then, and moving down to Seattle so I could take care of my mother's things, which were packed away in a storage unit. But I knew I needed more money. I left on an assignment to Yukon-Charley Rivers National Preserve with Stephan, driving to a town called Eagle before taking a long boat ride down the Yukon, where I saw bears and moose and some wolves. The water was smooth and easy to navigate. We passed some kayakers, but there weren't many people around at all. There were no real roads that led into the preserve; the river was the only way in, other than by helicopter or small plane. Kit, Hansel, and Ted had taken the helicopter.

We passed jutting cliffs striped in bronze; silver, gold-colored rocks; and miles and miles of beautiful green forests rarely explored by people. I sat out in the fresh air and then behind the glass of the two small seats when it got too cold. In the distance we could see little fires, most of them unmanned. Finally we arrived at Coal Creek, an old prospecting site from the early 1900s, where all of us stayed in little cabins surrounding a small mess hall, all part of Coal Creek's historic mining ephemera, which also includes a dredge, quarries, and scattered historic homesteading sites. First I shared my cabin with Kit, then Ted, who I ended up sleeping with a few times. The sex wasn't good, but it wasn't sex I wanted.

We took the helicopter out to abandoned cabin sites, clearing brush and completing maintenance for preserve visitors. Cole arrived and started teaching me how to fell large trees, so I could get my Faller C, the highest level. We all hiked up into the forest. I could tell he enjoyed cutting down trees, and it seemed to make him a better teacher than he'd been earlier. I was riddled with anxiety, and he spoke softly, letting me know everything would be okay.

While I was in Seattle I had missed ATV training, and I insisted that Stephan train me, because all the guys were driving ATVs everywhere. I didn't want to spend my summer depending on others to cart me around. Driving an ATV was more fun than I had expected, but Stephan would later tell me that I was "too aggressive" for insisting on the training.

My co-worker Hansel and I flew back to Eagle with Stephan a couple weeks later, and then drove together to McCarthy, an old mining town only accessible by dirt road or with aircraft. The town sits at the southern edge of the Kennicott and Root Glaciers, and serves as the gateway to Wrangell-St. Elias National Preserve in southeastern Alaska. Hansel and I shared some beers at a local bar. For the first time I felt a connection with him. He enjoyed photography and showed me his pictures, which were quite beautiful. We'd never had a full conversation before then. Together we hiked up to Kennicott and visited an old mine and some gift shops. It was drizzling, the gray clouds low and heavy. In the evening we went to a midnight bonfire beneath Root Glacier, which looked like a giant iridescent opal in the pink dusky light. I really loved the small-town vibe there, and the endless days.

*　　*　　*

Whenever I was alone in the woods I thought of the bear in camp. My fear was both realistic and outsized; my mom's death and the bear's death had collided and merged in my mind. I kept worrying about dying. I was only starting to process the gravity of what had happened.

The prop plane that I boarded with Hansel was just large enough for three people, including the pilot. We donned giant earmuffs to block the engine's high whine. As we made our way to Wrangell-St. Elias, I peered out the small window, awed by the glaciers: massive and white with long brown striations of earth running through them. In Wrangell we linked up with some fire-ecologists who were gathering data from plots they'd been monitoring since 2004, when a high-severity fire season had taken out miles of black spruce habitat. They were trying to measure post-fire regeneration and assessing to see if coniferous black spruce habitats are replaced by deciduous birch and aspen habitats after high-severity fire. Black spruce is more flammable than birch and aspen, and releases more stored carbon into the atmosphere when burned. In the boreal ecosystem European aspen are a keystone species, supporting a wide range of mosses and lichen as well as invertebrates, birds, and mammals. Slugs and snails thrive in their leaf litter, and dead and decaying trunks host multiple fungi species. They also store most of their carbon in large underground root systems. If the spruce trees were replaced by deciduous stands of aspen and birch, that could reduce the chances for high-severity fires and restore carbon stores more dramatically, but there are drawbacks to this.

I helped analyze post-fire growth in some of these plots in 2010, but they were measured from 2004 to 2017, and it was found that by 2017, only 28 percent of the plots had returned to spruce-dominated ecosystems. Many of them were of mixed spruce and deciduous ecosystems by 2017. It's likely that this has been the natural fire cycle throughout boreal forests and taiga for at least hundreds of years—high-severity spruce fires which lead to stand replacement by deciduous trees and better carbon stores, succeeding again to spruce, and then repeating. The current question is how deciduous ecosystems will be affected (and perhaps become more highly flammable) with increasing temperatures. From 1970 to 2000, fires burned twenty million acres in Alaska. The same amount of acreage burned in only ten years from 2000 to 2010. Temperatures in Alaska are increasing. In June 2022, almost two million acres burned in a single month, but the 2024 fire season was relatively normal. Through the analysis of statistical data, scientists predict that burned area in boreal forests of Alaska may increase as much as 126 percent. They advise agencies to extinguish overwinter fires, which smolder through winter and have the potential to reignite the following summer, because smoldering activity can release large amounts of stored carbon. Prescribed fire and thinning reduces the impact of larger and more destructive wildfires.

Scientists also suggest that fire management officials reseed forests with species better adapted to the changing climate, which may include hardwoods like aspen and birch, but this is not a catchall solution. Spruce-dominated forests insulate permafrost by supporting thick layers of organic matter like moss, and consume less water than deciduous trees. Fire suppression in Alaska may need to be implemented on a larger scale in order to preserve black spruce habitat, mitigate melting permafrost, and reduce amounts of carbon released by larger, more frequent fires.

Chapter Ten

Thirty

I had received my Helicopter Crew Member and Faller B certifications by early August, when I flew to a remote fire and trained as a helispot manager, conducting all operations at a small helispot somewhere in interior Alaska. Training was much easier without Cole—I was camped with three AFS guys, all of them older than me, and they were mellow and kind. I directed the helicopters in and out, kept inventory, and read *East of Eden* when things were slow. Helislacker life was much nicer than hotshotting. It also brought more opportunities. By the end of the week my training booklet was complete, my evaluations solid. When one of the AFS guys asked me if I'd like to train as an Aircraft Base Radio Operator (ABRO), I said yes, and flew by helicopter to an outpost hotel/restaurant located on the Dalton Highway in north Alaska. This was my favorite part of the summer, because my trainer was a woman, Clara, only a couple years younger than me.

There was a diverse mix of AFS and Park Service folks stationed at the base, none of whom I'd met before. The women who owned the outpost were both in their fifties; sweet Alaskan women. For the first time all season I got daily showers and slept deeply. Each day I sat down at the radio and Clara taught me the ABRO language. We relayed communications between all personnel across the fire. She told me about her Mormon upbringing in Utah and I talked about Buddhism, and she talked about her smokejumper boyfriend and I told her about the guys I worked with, like Cole. It was the first time all summer I had made a real friend.

People from all over stayed at the outpost: men on motorcycle trips and truckers and some adventurous tourists. I met a woman from Seattle and she asked me about my parents. I was honest, as I always was, and said my mom died by suicide. She told me her first husband had killed himself. "You never get over it," she said, and patted my knee. "Be gentle with yourself. Whatever guilt you're feeling, you have to forgive yourself." I had never considered being gentle with myself or realized I was punishing myself. I thought constantly of everything I should have done, or known. Her words didn't stop me from doing this, but it was the first time I knew that I wasn't alone.

I had my thirtieth birthday out there. My journal entry from that morning is about my mom. *I'll never know what to believe.* I wondered if I was shutting myself off to the world, and to relationships, friendship or otherwise. I was, and would for many years. Some veil was lifted when my mom died, revealing pure chaos. I didn't know who I was without my mother, and there was no one who could fix it for me. I was full of rage and grief—too much to process. But there were glimmers of connection, and I held them close to me, collecting evidence of goodness amidst the chaos.

The entire base had planned a surprise party for my birthday. The outpost women baked me a red velvet cake and we all dressed up in costume. I used my pillow to make a beer belly for my trucker costume. One of the Native Alaskan guys brought me canned smoked salmon but told me not to open it because, he said, the bears would come running. We drank wine in the evening, and blasted music. This was so entirely unexpected, and I was overcome with gratitude for every single person who made it happen.

It may have been around this time that I decided to quit fire. Despite all the training I now had, I knew it was time for me to leave. For my entire career, I'd been searching for something sacred—a closeness to nature and sense of familial connection, but I never found it. I went from crew to crew and job to job, trying to repair this deep wound inside me. Firefighting had given me definition as a person. I loved telling people I was a firefighter, seeing the shocked looks on their faces and defying what the world thought I could do or be. But something inside me, a part of me that had been silent since childhood, said I didn't need that anymore. This quiet voice was first a whisper, almost indiscernible, but it became stronger over time.

In late September I left Fairbanks, and fire. I loved Alaska, but also knew the dark and frigid winter would be unbearable. I had my mother's things to deal with. But my time there helped me surrender to what was the beginning of a personal transformation. I learned that sharing myself with others is a way of holding the world together, like the vast root networks connecting a forest.

Epilogue

After leaving Alaska for Seattle in 2010, I was immersed in the grief and trauma that followed my mother's suicide. The movers transferred her possessions from the storage unit to my small basement apartment. The objects felt foreign, energetically threatening. Panic attacks seized me night after night, until I began sleeping with my open laptop, silently playing cartoons. Their bright colors comforted me. I sought therapy. In that little room, my therapist sitting across from me, I learned that I'd been dissociating for as long as I could remember, watching myself through what felt like the lens of a video camera instead of fully experiencing my life. Everything I'd compartmentalized for decades spilled over and threatened to drown me. My mother did not feel absent, but more present than ever. I saw her all around town. Memories from my childhood surfaced. I longed for my grandparents; for connection of some sort, but connection was also terrifying. I no longer knew who I was without my mother's opinions and demands to shape me.

Despite the intensity of my experience, or maybe because of it, I registered for community college and started imagining myself as a writer. For a year and a half after my mother's death I was barely a person—her suicide obliterated me. But I learned to hold it all together:

the obliteration, the terror, and the constant beauty that surrounds us, if we're willing to see it.

I applied to college in the winter of 2012. There was only one acceptance, but it was the one I'd hoped for: Syracuse University. In autumn of 2012 I began life as a thirty-two-year-old undergraduate. I was broke and adrift, but slowly I found myself. Not as a firefighter, but as a human. And a writer. I learned to feel myself from the inside out, rather than defining myself through the eyes of others. And I came to believe that my own stories were worth telling; that I was not alone in any experience. In 2015 I was accepted into the Syracuse MFA program. A long-held dream came to fruition.

For years I needed to tell people I was once a firefighter, to feel that sense of admiration and approval. Now I tried to forget fire. Not because I wanted to leave it behind, but because it was too painful to think about how much I'd loved being a firefighter, despite its challenges. I avoided the news during fire seasons and slowly lost contact with most of my former co-workers. At the MFA program I wrote autobiographical fiction, mostly about my experiences with homelessness and addiction. When one of my mentors asked why I didn't write about firefighting, I had no coherent answer except to say that it felt too complex. Too charged. Too riddled with shame. In my mind, I had never been the right kind of firefighter. She urged me to try, and I wrote an autobiographical short story. Hearing my cohort discuss the work as fiction was illuminating. They saw things I couldn't, and through their eyes I learned to accept that I would have been the right kind of firefighter if there had been a place for me. The culture itself was the problem.

Agencies like the Forest Service and Park Service need people who think differently. Who don't fit in. There are tens of thousands of federal employees who are dedicated to improving the ecological health of lands throughout the U.S., yet federal agencies still struggle to retain diverse personnel or address issues of systemic prejudice and bigotry. They struggle to change environmentally harmful policies, especially when it comes to fire management. Fire policy and fire management culture within federal agencies is often undergirded by a fear of vulnerability, and transformation is impossible in the absence of a true willingness to be held accountable for past and present harms.

Although it's been almost fifteen years since I worked as a wildland firefighter, minority groups, including women, BIPOC, LGBTQIA+, and disabled people still face the same hurdles I faced. A 2019 survey conducted by the Pacific Northwest Research Station found that 75 percent of women in fire have felt out of place because of their gender. Around 35 percent said that race, gender, ethnicity, sexual orientation, age, disability status, and family caregiver status had prevented them from advancing in their profession. As of 2023, only 13 percent of wildland firefighters are women, and only 4 percent of those women are permanent wildland firefighters. There are people working to change this, but that change rarely comes from within the agencies themselves.

In 2016, Lenya Quinn-Davidson and several other women in fire held the first ever WTREX (Women-in-Fire Prescribed Fire Training Exchanges) in Northern California. Since then, the program has expanded, with events being held in several other states as well as Canada and South Africa. This is heartening. But what happens when women trained through this kind of mentorship become hotshots, or work in a hostile district? They're still vulnerable to discrimination and harassment.

It's my belief that this harassment, discrimination, and the risk of violence will never go away until we address the power structures within these agencies, which allow those at the top, like superintendents and district rangers, to dictate the cultures of their crews and districts. Reporting options are limited and difficult to navigate, and often run through agency channels rather than through external ones. Federal agencies are slow to act when misconduct is reported, and perpetrators rarely face punishment. Often reports are leaked, endangering victims. Those who report misconduct are moved to new crews or districts. Or they quit fire altogether, while perpetrators continue in their positions.

Google "sexual harassment in wildland firefighting" and you'll find endless accounts of women who have endured much worse than what I endured. Lewd voicemails and phone calls. Sexual assault. Stalking. Threats of rape and death. These are the visible and more tangible forms of violence and discrimination, but encounters with sexism and bigotry can also be insidious: crew members subtly pitted against each other, exclusion from promotions, the silent treatment, and comments revealing cultural assumptions about gender, race, and sexual orientation. No matter one's demographics, anyone straying from the status quo is liable to endure subtle hazing and exclusion, even if it's well-intentioned or neutral. To create a safe working space in these high-stress environments requires open communication, a willingness to be wrong and learn from one's mistakes, and continuous dialogue. Each crew is an intermingling of people with various cultural beliefs and backgrounds. Avenues for safe and healthy conflict resolution are imperative. Thus far, there's little training for this. It's barely part of the overarching conversation in the field.

Over the last several decades hundreds of lawsuits have been brought forth. When I was employed as a hotshot in California, known as Region 5 within the Forest Service, the entire region's forests were under court oversight for misconduct, the result of a class action lawsuit. Yet I felt discouraged from making a report when I spoke with human resources on Solar Hotshots, and I didn't know of any oversight at the time. The class action lawsuit preceding mandated oversight was filed by Lesa Donnelly, who continues filing class action suits with hundreds of new allegations. Donnelly is a former USFS employee who worked in Region 5 and now represents women currently and formerly employed in Region 5 in an ongoing class action lawsuit.

Although there's been some improvement, little has changed on a fundamental level. There are many women and minorities who have had positive experiences working as wildland firefighters. And there are many who have not. I've had both, and neither cancels out the other. Based on the evidence of lawsuits and reports, which continue as of this writing, the problem has yet to be properly addressed. I can only speak from my experience: The harassment I endured on my first hotshot crew permeated my entire life in ways I couldn't comprehend. It took me over a decade to understand it was part of a pattern, and I have not fully recovered from that experience. I'm not sure I ever will. I questioned my worth not only as a firefighter but as a human being. There are few things more terrifying than being trapped in the wilderness with men who clearly wish you harm or, at the very least, are unwilling to risk their own status to protect you.

What is the solution? I won't claim to know the answer, but I think there needs to be a zero-tolerance policy against harassment and violence, whether we're talking about a subtly sexist remark or sexual assault. This might result in a loss of leadership, but there's not a lack of qualified personnel to step up. This could positively shift the culture. Really, anything is better than continuously excusing this behavior and punishing victims. Women are as capable as men when it comes to fighting fire, and should be treated as such. Full stop.

As much as we need to reassess policies regarding harassment and discrimination within federal agencies such as the Forest Service and Park Service, we also must reassess our conceptions of wilderness and nature as separate from civilization and acknowledge how these ideas came from the violence of colonization. When whites first arrived in the "New World," they saw inhabited lands as wilderness. Wilderness meant savage and barren. The sophisticated land-tending and agricultural practices of Native Americans were overlooked in favor of more destructive European agricultural practices. Land was commodified and assessed for monetary worth; healthy old-growth forests were transformed into board feet that was then sold and shipped around the world; mountains were torn open and plundered for materials; waterways were dammed; animals killed for sport or fur. Land was something to be owned and altered, not something within which one lived in harmony with their fellow inhabitants.

The first artistic renditions of the Western United States were primarily landscapes emptied of the people who lived there. We can juxtapose these renditions with European ideas of "civilized" life, because through this colonizing perspective the landscapes are indeed separate, to be dominated by humans. Over time, American ideas about wilderness have led to what is essentially the neglect of the many and varied ecosystems. I grew up seeing myself as separate from nature, not understanding that the parcels of wetlands and trails of my childhood were as sacred as any national park or wilderness area. Nature was woven into my everyday life, as it still is, no matter where I live. It's the blooming trees outside my urban window; the hardy plants poking through concrete; berry bushes fruiting along roadsides; streams gurgling behind apartment complexes. For much of my life this idea of myself as separate from nature robbed me of a sense of community and connection with the natural world. With our world, that we share with all living beings, down to the tiniest organisms.

We now know that the New World's "wilderness" was indeed cultivated by Native Americans, stewarded by people who rightly saw their place in the world as part of an ecological family, who had a reciprocal relationship with their surrounding non-human relatives.

In the late nineteenth and early twentieth centuries, with the advent of romanticist ideals of sublime nature, conservationists systematically stole land from Native Americans in the name of preservation. Somehow wilderness became something outside of ourselves, to be visited and enjoyed, usually by city-dwellers and those with economic means. The first National Parks in the United States were established with the violent removal of Indigenous Americans. There is no justification for these tactics. At the same time, had they not been established, it's likely that the land would have been deforested, mined, or otherwise exploited. We can hold two truths at once: that the lands were stolen, and that they were rescued from a harsher fate. Federal agencies need improvement, and they're a force for good, in need of protection from privatization.

The natural world is interwoven throughout our "civilized" and "mechanized" world. We can find refuge in nature anywhere. We need not seek it out, and we must realign our cultural paradigm of separateness and understand our responsibilities to local communities beyond preserved land, while continuing to protect nature from those who wish to exploit it. We are part of nature rather than apart from it. There is no need to visit Yosemite or Yellowstone to experience a place that is natural, sacred, and worthy of care and tending, because every place is. Before the arrival of Europeans, cities and towns populated the United States. It wasn't the wild landscape many of us imagine. Each tribal community had a particular culture. We cannot predict how those cultures may have developed without colonization, but those cultures and practices are still very present in the United States. Present, but marginalized. The sooner we can honestly reckon with the truths of the past and present and see ourselves as innately inside of nature, the sooner we can begin healing the landscapes suffering due to what is, essentially, abandonment. Many Indigenous tribes throughout the United States are working towards this as I write these sentences. Federal land agencies need to relinquish their stranglehold and let tribes lead the way forward. Reintroducing fire is an essential part of this process.

I am not suggesting removing laws protecting lands from extractive endeavors; only that all lands need protection, equally. Extractive pursuits and agriculture must be practiced with an eye towards stewardship rather than ownership. In her book *Gathering Moss*, Robin Wall Kimmerer writes, "In Indigenous ways of knowing, it is understood that each living being has a particular role to play. Every being is endowed with certain gifts, its own intelligence, its own spirit, its own story." How can non-Indigenous people shift their ways of thinking to include all beings as worthy of care and tending? When we can understand the land as a part of us rather than separate, the potential for healing is infinite. This may sound idealistic, but more profound changes have happened throughout history. It is entirely possible to fundamentally change our relationship with the world, and ourselves, simply by changing how we perceive our place here, within nature.

Acknowledgments

This book would not exist were it not for the many people who encouraged me to become a writer. I am deeply grateful to my grandmother and grandfather, both of whom helped me believe in myself, and to my parents. My mother, whose life was profoundly affected by addiction, abuse, and mental illness—I am grateful to have learned from your mistakes, and more than anything I hope your spirit is without pain. My father, who taught me that not every longing can be fulfilled. By necessity I have learned to claim responsibility for myself, my actions, and my autonomy, despite our inherited traits of denial and deceit. I know I am not the only one attempting to heal my lineage—there are so many of us, and I am grateful for this fact. My friendships, both long-lasting and short-lived, have provided sustenance. In particular I thank Elizabeth Johnson, Kate Rafferty, Jessica Poli, Erinkate Springer, Kate Palermo, Mim LaSala, Michael Keen, Shauna Roloff, April Hail, and Tim Dyke. To my mentors and teachers, Arthur Flowers, Dana Spiotta, Minnie-Bruce Pratt, George Saunders, Ravi Howard, Jeff Harrison, Brooks Haxton, Stephanie Shirilan, Sarah Harwell, Eleanor Henderson, Roger Hallas, Molly Hand, Maxine Montgomery, Luis Alberto Urrea, Marty Albee, Mrs. Maurer, Mrs. Bryant, Mrs. Paulsen, Britt Nederhood, and Eric Chase: thank you. Thank you to my mother's friends, Cynthia

Hughen, Patty Johncox, and Lori Thomas, for helping me find my way. And to the many, many people who have provided me friendship, love, and support, I am deeply grateful to you.

I am also indebted to my MFA cohort at Syracuse University, particularly Alexandra Chang, Alexander Sammartino, and Joel Cuthbertson, as well as everyone who came before and after me, all of whom touched my life in so many ways. Much gratitude also to the Tin House workshop crew. To Mark Halliday, who accepted my first short story for publication and encouraged me to complete my undergraduate studies, I cannot overstate your impact on my life's trajectory. Thank you to all of my teachers at Avanti High School, who helped me see my own potential, to my community college instructors, and to the MFA program and English department at Syracuse University.

There are many who have helped this particular book come to fruition. My agent, Chris Bucci, who helped shape the proposal. My editors, Amy Hundley, who believed the proposal could become a book and pushed me to create something better than I could have ever imagined, and Joseph Payne, who worked alongside us and helped make it happen. And to everyone at Grove Atlantic: John Mark Boling, Natalie Church, JT Green, Jisu Kim, Mike Richards, Rachael Richardson, Deb Seager, and the amazing cover designer(s). Thank you also to my beta readers, Erin Gravley, Sarah Jaffe, Denise K. James, Rey Katz, and Jess Martin.

I am deeply grateful to the Indigenous writers whose work informed this book, especially Robin Wall Kimmerer and Roxanne Dubar-Ortiz. And to everyone who shared their time for interviews and inquiries, including Frank K. Lake, Stephen Pyne, Mary Huffman, Margo Robbins, Dr. Bruce Means, Ryan Means, Zeke Lunder, Christopher Adlam, and Lenya Quinn-Davidson.

Many writers have inspired my work: Terry Tempest Williams, Cheryl Strayed, Toni Morrison, Barry Lopez, Leslie Marmon Silko, Pam Houston, James Baldwin, Linda Hogan, bell hooks, Rebecca

Solnit, Kiese Laymon, Mary Hunter Austin, Tobias Wolff, David Wojnarowicz, Mary Karr, Lidia Yuknavitch, Harry Crews, and Jesmyn Ward, to name only a few.

Finally, I am profoundly grateful to everyone I worked alongside as a wildland firefighter, especially those who provided support and friendship. To everyone working in wildland fire—especially those going against the grain, lifting each other up, valuing difference, and advocating for positive change—thank you. And to all the folks whose childhoods were transient, traumatic, and chaotic: You're not alone. Keep going.

Glossary

Aerial ignition: Ignition of fuels by dropping incendiary devices or other materials from aircraft. These include the "ping-pong system," which is a mechanized method of dispensing DAIDs (Delayed Aerial Ignition Devices) at a selected rate. The DAIDs are polystyrene balls, 1.25 inches in diameter, containing potassium permanganate. The balls are fed into a dispenser, generally mounted in a helicopter, where they are injected with a water-glycol solution and then dropped through a chute leading out of the helicopter. The chemicals react thermally and ignite in 25–30 seconds.

After action review (AAR): A structured review or de-brief process of an event, focused on performance standards, that enables participants to discover for themselves what happened, why it happened, and how to sustain strengths and improve on weaknesses. After action reviews, informal or formal, follow the same general format, involve the exchange of ideas and observations, and focus on improving performance.

Agency: An administrative division of a government with a specific function, or a non-governmental organization (e.g., private contractor, business, etc.) that offers a particular kind of assistance. A federal, tribal, state, or local agency that has direct fire management or land management responsibilities or that has programs and activities that support fire management activities.

Air attack: The deployment of fixed-wing or rotary aircraft on a wildland fire, to drop retardant or extinguishing agents, shuttle and deploy crews and supplies, or perform aerial reconnaissance of the overall fire situation.

Air stability: According to the American Meteorological Society, the ability of the atmosphere at rest to become turbulent or laminar due to the effects of buoyancy. Air tending to become or remain turbulent is said to be statically unstable; air tending to become or remain laminar is statically stable; and air on the borderline between the two (which might remain laminar or turbulent depending on its history) is statically neutral.

Airtanker: Fixed-wing aircraft certified by FAA as being capable of transport and delivery of fire retardant solutions.

Allowable payload: The amount of weight that is available for passengers and/or cargo on an aircraft. On the load calculation form it is the operating weight subtracted from the selected weight.

Anchor point: An advantageous location, usually a barrier to fire spread, from which to start constructing a fireline. The anchor point is used to minimize the chance of being flanked by the fire while the line is being constructed.

Backfire: A fire set along the inner edge of a fireline to consume the fuel in the path of a wildfire or change the direction of force of the fire's convection column.

Backfiring: A tactic associated with indirect attack, intentionally setting fire to fuels inside the control line to slow, knock down, or contain a rapidly spreading fire. Backfiring provides a wide defense perimeter and may be further employed to change the force of the convection column. Backfiring makes possible a strategy of locating control lines at places where the fire can be fought on the firefighter's terms. Except for rare circumstances meeting specified criteria, backfiring is executed on a command decision made through line channels of authority.

Backing fire: That portion of the fire with slower rates of fire spread and lower intensity normally moving into the wind and/or down slope.

Belt weather kit: Belt-mounted case with pockets fitted for anemometer, compass, sling psychrometer, slide rule, water bottle, pencils, and book of weather report forms. Used to take weather observations to provide on-site conditions to the fire weather forecaster or fire behavior analyst.

Observations include air temperature, wind speed and direction, and relative humidity.

Bladder bag (piss pump): A collapsible backpack portable sprayer made of neoprene or high-strength nylon fabric fitted with a pump.

Blowup: Sudden increase in fireline intensity or rate of spread of a fire sufficient to preclude direct control or to upset existing suppression plans. Often accompanied by violent convection and may have other characteristics of a fire storm.

Bone yard: A mop up term. To "bone yard" a fire means to systematically work the entire area, scraping embers off remaining fuel, feeling for heat with the hands, and piling unburned materials in areas cleared to mineral soil.

Box canyon: A steep-sided, dead-end canyon.

Bucket drops: The dropping of fire retardants or suppressants from specially designed buckets slung below a helicopter.

Bucking: Sawing through the bole of a tree after it has been felled.

Burn patterns: The characteristic configuration of char left by a fire. In wildland fires burn patterns are influenced by topography, wind direction, length of exposure, and type of fuel. Definitions are scale-dependent: (1) They can be used to trace a fire's origin. (2) They are influenced by severity and intensity within a stand. (3) They describe the landscape mosaic.

Burn severity: A qualitative assessment of the heat pulse directed toward the ground during a fire. Burn severity relates to soil heating, large fuel and duff consumption, consumption of the litter and organic layer beneath trees and isolated shrubs, and mortality of buried plant parts.

Burning out: Setting fire inside a control line to consume fuel located between the edge of the fire and the control line.

Burnover: An event in which a fire moves through a location or overtakes personnel or equipment where there is no opportunity to utilize escape routes and safety zones, often resulting in personal injury or equipment damage.

Catface: Defect on the surface of a tree resulting from a wound where healing has not re-established the normal cross-section.

Cold trailing: A method of controlling a partly dead fire edge by carefully inspecting and feeling with the hand for heat to detect any fire, digging out every live spot, and trenching any live edge.

Command staff: A group of incident personnel that the Incident Commander or Unified Command assigns to support the command function at an ICP. Command staff often include a PIO, a Safety Officer, and a Liaison Officer, who have assistants as necessary. Additional positions may be needed, depending on the incident.

Containment: The status of a wildfire suppression action signifying that a control line has been completed around the fire, and any associated spot fires, which can reasonably be expected to stop the fire's spread.

Controlled: The completion of control line around a fire, any spot fires therefrom, and any interior islands to be saved; burn out any unburned area adjacent to the fire side of the control lines; and cool down all hotspots that are immediate threats to the control line, until the lines can reasonably be expected to hold under the foreseeable conditions.

Convective column: The rising column of gases, smoke, fly ash, particulates, and other debris produced by a fire. The column has a strong vertical component indicating that buoyant forces override the ambient surface wind.

Crown fire: A fire burning in both the underbrush and canopy of trees and/or brush.

Cup trench: A fireline trench on the downhill side of fire burning on steep slopes that is supposed to be built deep enough to catch rolling firebrands that could otherwise start fire below the fireline. A high berm on the outermost downhill side of the trench helps the cup trench catch material.

Demobilization: The orderly, safe, and efficient return of an incident resource to its original location and status.

Direct line: Any treatment applied directly to burning fuel such as wetting, smothering, or chemically quenching the fire or by physically separating the burning from unburned fuel. To cut direct line means to cut line while directly exposed to fire.

Dozer line: Fireline constructed by the front blade of a dozer.

Drip torch: Hand-held device for igniting fires by dripping flaming liquid fuel on the materials to be burned; consists of a fuel fount, burner arm, and igniter. Fuel used is generally a mixture of diesel and gasoline.

Duff: The layer of decomposing organic materials lying below the litter layer of freshly fallen twigs, needles, and leaves and immediately above the mineral soil.

Engine: Any ground vehicle providing specified levels of pumping, water, and hose capacity but with less than the specified level of personnel.

Entrapment: A situation where personnel are unexpectedly caught in a fire behavior-related, life-threatening position where planned escape routes or safety zones are absent, inadequate, or compromised. An entrapment may or may not include deployment of a fire shelter for its intended purpose. These situations may or may not result in injury. They include "near misses."

Escape route: A preplanned and understood route firefighters take to move to a safety zone or other low-risk area. When escape routes deviate from a defined physical path, they should be clearly marked (flagged).

Extreme fire behavior: Extreme implies a level of fire behavior characteristics that ordinarily precludes methods of direct control action. One or more of the following is usually involved: high rate of spread, prolific crowning and/or spotting, presence of fire whirls, strong convection column. Predictability is difficult because such fires often exercise some degree of influence on their environment and behave erratically, sometimes dangerously.

Faller: A person who fells trees.

Fine fuels (flash fuels): Fast-drying dead or live fuels, generally characterized by a comparatively high surface area-to-volume ratio, which are less than 1/4-inch in diameter and have a timelag of one hour or less. These fuels (grass, leaves, needles, etc.) ignite readily and are consumed rapidly by fire when dry.

Firebrand: Any source of heat, natural or human made, capable of igniting wildland fuels. Flaming or glowing fuel particles that can be carried naturally by wind, convection currents, or by gravity into unburned fuels.

Fire camp: A geographical site within the general incident area (separate from the Incident Base) that is equipped and staffed to provide sleeping, food, water, and sanitary services to incident personnel.

Fire front/head of fire: The part of a fire within which continuous flaming combustion is taking place. Unless otherwise specified, the fire front is assumed to be the leading edge of the fire perimeter. In ground fires, the fire front may be mainly smoldering combustion.

Fire interval: The number of years between two successive fire events for a given area; also referred to as fire-free interval or fire-return interval.

Fire management: All activities for the management of wildland fires to meet land management objectives. Fire management includes the entire scope of activities from planning, prevention, fuels or vegetation modification, prescribed fire, hazard mitigation, fire response, rehabilitation, monitoring and evaluation.

Fire pack (line pack): A one-person unit of fire tools, equipment, and supplies prepared in advance for carrying on the back.

Fire regime: Description of the patterns of fire occurrences, frequency, size, severity, and sometimes vegetation and fire effects as well, in a given area or ecosystem. A fire regime is a generalization based on fire histories at individual sites. Fire regimes can often be described as cycles because some parts of the histories usually get repeated, and the repetitions can be counted and measured, such as fire return interval.

Fire resources: All personnel and equipment available or potentially available for assignment to incidents.

Fire retardant: Any substance except plain water that by chemical or physical action reduces flammability of fuels or slows their rate of combustion.

Fire severity: Degree to which a site has been altered or disrupted by fire; loosely, a product of fire intensity and residence time.

Flanking fire suppression: Attacking a fire by working along the flanks either simultaneously or successively from a less active or anchor point and endeavoring to connect two lines at the head.

Flapper: Fire suppression tool, sometimes improvised, used in direct attack for smothering out flames along a fire edge; may consist merely of a green pine bough or wet sacking, or be a manufactured tool such as a flap of belting fabric fastened to a long handle.

Foehn wind: A warm, dry and strong general wind that flows down into the valleys when stable, high pressure air is forced across and then down the lee slopes of a mountain range. The descending air is warmed and dried due to adiabatic compression producing critical fire weather conditions. Locally called by various names such as Santa Ana winds, Devil winds, North winds, Mono winds, etc.

Fuel break: A natural or manmade change in fuel characteristics which affects fire behavior so that fires burning into them can be more readily controlled.

Fuel loading: The amount of fuel present expressed quantitatively in terms of weight of fuel per unit area. This may be available fuel (consumable fuel) or total fuel and is usually dry weight.

Fusee: A colored flare designed as a railway warning device, widely used to ignite backfires and other prescribed fires.

Geographic Area Coordination Center (GACC): The physical location of an interagency, regional operation center for the effective coordination, mobilization, and demobilization of emergency management resources. A coordination center serves federal, state, and local wildland fire agencies through logistical coordination of resources throughout the geographic area, and with other geographic areas, as well.

Gridding: To search for a small fire by systematically traveling over an area on parallel courses or gridlines.

Ground fire: Fire that consumes the organic material beneath the surface litter ground, such as a peat fire.

Hazard pay: A salary differential that compensates employees for exposure to hazards in the course of their duties.

Heavy fuels: Fuels of large diameter such as snags, logs, large limbwood, which ignite and are consumed more slowly than flash fuels.

Helibase: The main location within the general incident area for parking, fueling, maintenance, and loading of helicopters. It is usually located at or near the incident base.

Helispot: A natural or improved takeoff and landing area intended for temporary or occasional helicopter use.

Helitack: The utilization of helicopters to transport crews, equipment, and fire retardants or suppressants to the fireline during the initial stages of a fire. The term also refers to the crew that performs helicopter management and attack activities.

Incident action plan (IAP): An oral or written plan containing the objectives established by the incident commander or Unified Command and addressing tactics and support activities for the planned operational period, generally 12 to 24 hours.

Incident command: The ICS organizational element responsible for overall management of the incident and consisting of the incident commander or Unified Command and any additional Command Staff activated. They are usually stationed at the incident command post (ICP).

Incident command system: A standardized approach to the command, control, and coordination of on-scene incident management, providing a common hierarchy within which personnel from multiple organizations can be effective. Consists of command, planning, operations, logistics, and finance.

Incident commander: The individual responsible for on-scene incident activities, including developing incident objectives and ordering and releasing resources. The incident commander has overall authority and responsibility for conducting incident operations through a delegation of authority.

Incident complexity level: The incident level established by completing an incident complexity analysis considering the level of difficulty, severity, or overall resistance the incident or event presents to incident management or support personnel as they work to manage it; a categorization that helps leaders compare one type of incident or event to another. Type 5 is the least complex, while Type 1 is the most complex.

Indirect attack: A method of suppression in which the control line is located some considerable distance away from the fire's active edge. Generally done in the case of a fast-spreading or high-intensity fire and to utilize natural or constructed firebreaks or fuel breaks and favorable breaks in the topography. The intervening fuel is usually backfired; but occasionally the main fire is allowed to burn to the line, depending on conditions.

Initial attack crew (type 1 crew): Specially trained and equipped fire crew for initial attack on a fire, also called hotshots.

Kincentric: "An awareness that life in any environment is viable only when humans view the life surrounding them as kin. The kin, or relatives, include all the natural elements of an ecosystem." The term was coined by Enrique Salmón.

Ladder fuels: Fuels that provide vertical continuity between strata, thereby allowing fire to carry from surface fuels into the crowns of trees or shrubs with relative ease. They help initiate and ensure the continuation of crowning.

Leapfrog method: A system of organizing workers in fire suppression in which each crew member is assigned a specific task such as clearing or digging fireline on a specific section of control line, and when that task is completed, passes other workers in moving to a new assignment.

Limbing: Removing branches from a felled or standing tree, or from brush.

Long range spotting: Large glowing firebrands are carried high into the convection column and then fall out downwind beyond the main fire starting new fires. Such spotting can easily occur 1/4 mile or more from the firebrand's source.

Lookout: A person designated to detect and report fires from a vantage point.

McLeod: A combination hoe or cutting tool and rake, with or without removable blades.

Meal Ready to Eat (MRE): Self-contained military rations, to be eaten when fresh food is unavailable.

Mineral soil: Soil layers below the predominantly organic horizons; soil with little combustible material.

Mobilization: The processes and procedures for activating, assembling, and transporting resources that have been requested to respond to or support an incident.

Mop up: Extinguishing or removing burning material near control lines, felling snags, and trenching logs to prevent rolling after an area has burned, to make a fire safe, or to reduce residual smoke.

Mosaic: The intermingling of plant communities and their successional stages in such a manner as to give the impression of an interwoven design.

Nomex: Trade name for a fire-resistant synthetic material used in the manufacturing of flight suits and pants and shirts used by firefighters. Aramid is the generic name.

One lick method: A progressive system of building a fireline on a wildfire without changing relative positions in the line. Each worker does one to several "licks," or strokes, with a given tool and then moves forward a specified distance to make room for the worker behind.

Operational period: The time scheduled for executing a given set of operation actions, as specified in the IAP. Operational periods can be of various lengths, but are typically 12 to 24 hours.

Overhead: Personnel assigned to supervisory positions, including incident commander, command staff, general staff, branch directors, supervisors, unit leaders, managers, and staff.

Pack test: An aerobic capacity benchmark test that all wildfire personnel must pass. To walk 3 miles in 45 minutes, on flat ground while carrying a 45-lb. pack or weight vest.

Permafrost: A short term for "permanently frozen ground"; any part of the earth's crust, bedrock, or soil mantle that remains below 32° F (0° C) continuously for a number of years.

Piling and burning: Piling slash resulting from logging or fuel management activities and subsequently burning the individual piles.

Plume-dominated wildfire: A wildland fire whose activity is determined by the convection column.

Portable pump: Small gasoline-driven pump that can be carried to a water source by one or two firefighters or other conveyance over difficult terrain.

Prescribed fire: A wildland fire originating from a planned ignition in accordance with applicable laws, policies, and regulations to meet specific objectives.

Priming: Filling pump with water when pump is taking water not under a pressure head. Necessary for centrifugal pumps.

Pulaski: A combination chopping and trenching tool widely used in fire-line construction, which combines an axe blade with a narrow adze-like trenching blade fitted to a straight handle.

Reassigned: A resource on a filled request has been reassigned from one incident to the another, but the mobilization travel has not started.

Red flag warning: Term used by fire weather forecasters to alert forecast users to an ongoing or imminent critical fire weather pattern.

Retardant drop: Fire retardant cascaded from an airtanker or helitanker.

Sizeup: The evaluation of the fire to determine a course of action for suppression.

Slash: Debris resulting from such natural events as wind, fire, or snow breakage; or such human activities as road construction, logging, pruning, thinning, or brush cutting. It includes logs, chunks, bark, branches, stumps, and broken understory trees or brush.

Sling load: Any cargo carried beneath a helicopter and attached by a lead line and swivel.

Slopover: A fire edge that crosses a control line or natural barrier intended to confine the fire.

Snag: A standing dead tree or part of a dead tree from which at least the leaves and smaller branches have fallen. Often known as a stub, if less than 20 feet tall.

Spike-out: When personnel are self-sufficiently camping in a remote area near the fire.

Spot fire: Fire ignited outside the perimeter of the main fire by a firebrand.

Spot weather forecast: A special forecast issued to fit the time, topography, and weather of a specific incident. These forecasts are issued upon request of the user agency and are more detailed, timely, and specific than zone forecasts. Usually, on-site weather observations or a close, representative observation is required for a forecast to be issued.

Spotting: Behavior of a fire producing sparks or embers that are carried by the wind and which start new fires beyond the zone of direct ignition by the main fire.

Staging area: A temporary location for available resources in which personnel, supplies, and equipment await operational assignment.

Structure fire: Fire originating in and burning any part or all of any building, shelter, or other structure.

Succession: The process of vegetational development whereby an area becomes successively occupied by different plant communities of higher ecological order.

Swamper: A worker who assists fallers and/or sawyers by clearing away brush, limbs and small trees. Carries fuel, oil, and tools and watches for dangerous situations.

Tie-in: Act of connecting a control line to another fireline or an intended firebreak.

Torching: The burning of the foliage of a single tree or a small group of trees, from the bottom up.

Trench: A small ditch often constructed below a fire on sloping ground (undercut or underslung line) to catch rolling material.

Wet line: A line of water, or water and chemical retardant, sprayed along the ground, and which serves as a temporary control line from which to ignite or stop a low-intensity fire.

Wildland Urban Interface (WUI): The line, area, or zone where structures and other human development meet or intermingle with undeveloped wildland or vegetation fuels.

Work/Rest Ratio: An expression of the amount of rest that is required for each hour an individual is in work status. Current NWCG guidelines require one hour of rest for every two hours in work status.

Bibliography

Adams, John Quincy, Lewis Cass, and Pierre Menard. Indian Treaties. Message from the President of the United States, Transmitting Copies of Two Treaties with Indian Tribes. January 21, 1829.—Read, and Laid upon the Table. Vol. serial set no. 185. Washington, DC, 1829.

Anderson, M. Kat. *Tending the Wild: Native American Knowledge and the Management of California's Natural Resources*. University of California Press, 2013.

Banner, Stuart. *Possessing the Pacific: Land, Settlers, and Indigenous People from Australia to Alaska*. 1st ed. Cambridge, MA: Harvard University Press, 2007.

Birch, Joseph D., and James A. Lutz. "Fire Regimes of Utah: The Past as Prologue." *Fire* (Basel, Switzerland) 6, no. 11 (2023): 423-. https://doi.org/10.3390/fire6110423.

Catton, Theodore. *American Indians and National Forests*. Tucson: University of Arizona Press, 2016.

Dunbar-Ortiz, Roxanne. *An Indigenous Peoples' History of the United States (ReVisioning History)*. Beacon Press; Reprint edition (August 11, 2015).

Egan, Timothy. *The Big Burn: Teddy Roosevelt and the Fire That Saved America*. Mariner Books; Reprint edition (September 7, 2010).

Farmer, Jared. *Trees in Paradise: The Botanical Conquest of California*. Heyday; Reprint edition (March 1, 2017).

Gorges, Ferdinando. *America Painted to the Life. The History of the Spaniards Proceeding in America, Their Conquests of the Indians, and of Their Civil Wars among Themselves. From Columbus His First Discovery, to These Later Times.* London: printed by T.J. for Nath. Brook at the Angel in Cornhil, 1659.

Halsey, Richard W. *Fire, Chaparral, and Survival in Southern California.* Sunbelt Publications; Revised and Updated edition (January 28, 2008).

Hauser, Naomi, Barbara Branch, and Tina Palmieri. "1378. Fungal Infections in Burn Patients during Northern California Wildfires." *Open Forum Infectious Diseases* 9, no. Supplement_2 (2022). https://doi.org/10.1093 /ofid/ofac492.1207.

Jensen, Sara E., and Guy R. McPherson *Living with Fire: Fire Ecology and Policy for the Twenty-first Century.* University of California Press, 2008.

Keeley, Jon E., William J. Bond, Ross A. Bradstock, Juli G. Pausas, and Philip W. Rundel. *Fire in Mediterranean Ecosystems: Ecology, Evolution and Management.* 1st ed. Cambridge: Cambridge University Press, 2011.

Kobziar, Leda N., David Vuono, Rachel Moore, Brent C. Christner, Timothy Dean, Doris Betancourt, Adam C. Watts, Johanna Aurell, and Brian Gullett. "Wildland Fire Smoke Alters the Composition, Diversity, and Potential Atmospheric Function of Microbial Life in the Aerobiome." *ISME Communications* 2, no. 1 (2022): 8–8. https://doi.org/10.1038/s43705-022-00089-5.

Lowe, Jaime. *Breathing Fire: Female Inmate Firefighters on the Front Lines of California's Wildfires.* Macmillan Publishers, 2021.

Loya, Wendy, Anna L. Springsteen, Jennifer L. Barnes, and Scott Rupp. "Projected Vegetation and Fire Regime Response to Future Climate Change in National Parks in Interior Alaska." *Alaska Park Science* 10, no. 1 (2011): 22–25.

Madley, Benjamin. *An American Genocide: The United States and the California Indian Catastrophe, 1846-1873.* New Haven, CT: Yale University Press, 2016.

Marks-Block, Tony, Frank K. Lake, and Lisa M. Curran. "Effects of understory fire management treatments on California Hazelnut, an ecocultural resource of the Karuk and Yurok Indians in the Pacific Northwest."

Forest Ecology and Management 450 (2019). https://doi.org/10.1016/j. foreco.2019.117517

Mathews, Daniel. *Trees in Trouble: Wildfires, Infestations, and Climate Change.* Counterpoint Press, 2020.

Miller, Char. *Gifford Pinchot and the Making of Modern Environmentalism.* 1st ed. Washington, DC: Island Press/Shearwater Books, 2001.

Moore, Grace. "'They would put out that fire like a couple of matches burning': Climate Change and Reciprocity in George R. Stewart's Fire." *Occasion.* Fire Stories. Volume 13. August 12, 2022. https://shc.stanford.edu /arcade/publications/occasion/fire-stories/they-would-put-out-fire -couple-matches-burning-climate.

Morgan, R. Grace, James Daschuk, and Cristina Eisenberg. *Beaver, Bison, Horse: The Traditional Knowledge and Ecology of the Northern Great Plains.* 1st ed. Regina, SK: University of Regina, 2020.

Odion, Dennis C., and Chad T. Hanson. "Fire Severity in the Sierra Nevada Revisited: Conclusions Robust to Further Analysis." *Ecosystems* (New York) 11, no. 1 (2008): 12–15. https://doi.org/10.1007/s10021-007-9113-0.

Pyne, Stephen. *Between Two Fires: A Fire History of Contemporary America.* University of Arizona Press; 2nd ed. edition (October 15, 2015).

Pyne, Stephen. *Fire in America: A Cultural History of Wildland and Rural Fire.* University of Washington Press, 1982.

Pyne, Stephen. *California: A Fire Survey (To the Last Smoke).* University of Arizona Press, 2016.

Ray, Lily, Stuart F. Chapin, and Crystal A. Kolden. "A Case for Developing Place-Based Fire Management Strategies from Traditional Ecological Knowledge." *Ecology and Society: A Journal of Integrative Science for Resilience and Sustainability* 17, no. 3 (2012): 434–68. https://doi.org/info:doi/.

Rothman, Hal. *Blazing Heritage: A History of Wildland Fire in the National Parks.* Oxford: Oxford University Press, 2007.

Stewart, Omer C. *Forgotten Fires: Native Americans and the Transient Wilderness.* University of Oklahoma Press; Illustrated edition (February 1, 2009).

Vale, Thomas. *Fire, Native Peoples, and the Natural Landscape.* Washington, DC: Island Press, 2002.

Williams, Claire L., Lisa M. Ellsworth, Eva K. Strand, Matt C. Reeves, Scott E. Shaff, Karen C. Short, Jeanne C. Chambers, Beth A. Newingham, and Claire Tortorelli. "Fuel Treatments in Shrublands Experiencing Pinyon and Juniper Expansion Result in Trade-Offs between Desired Vegetation and Increased Fire Behavior." *Fire Ecology* 19, no. 1 (2023): 46-. https://doi.org/10.1186/s42408-023-00201-7.

Web Pages/Popular Sources:

Federal Register. "Viveash Fire Timber Salvage EIS-Santa Fe National Forest," March 16, 2001. https://www.federalregister.gov/documents/2001/03/16/01-6511/viveash-fire-timber-salvage-eis-santa-fe-national-forest.
CU Boulder Today. "Crowdfunding after the Marshall Fire Overwhelmingly Helped Wealthy Households," February 1, 2024. https://www.colorado.edu/today/2024/02/01/crowdfunding-after-marshall-fire-overwhelmingly-helped-wealthy-households.

Further Reading

Armstrong, Jeannette. "Keepers of the Earth." In *Ecopsychology: Restoring the Earth, Healing the Mind*, edited by Theodore Roszak, M. E. Gomes, and A. D. Kanner, 316–24. San Francisco: Sierra Club Books, 1995.

Cajete, Greg. *Native Science: Natural Laws of Interdependence.* Santa Fe, NM: Clear Light Publishers, 2000.

Cronon, William, ed. *Uncommon Ground.* New York: W. W. Norton & Company, 1996.

Debo, Angie. *And Still the Waters Run.* New Jersey: Princeton University Press, 2022.

Gutiérrez, Ramón A., and Richard J. Orsi, eds. *Contested Eden.* Berkeley, CA: University of California Press, 1998.

Heizer, Robert F., ed. *The Destruction of the California Indians.* Nebraska: University of Nebraska Press, 1993.

Hogan, Linda. *The Radiant Lives of Animals.* New York: Penguin Random House, 2020.

Hunter Austin, Mary. *The Land of Little Rain.* New York: Random House, 2003.

Jamail, Dahr, and Stan Rushworth, eds. *We Are the Middle of Forever: Indigenous Voices from Turtle Island on the Changing Earth.* New York: New Press, 2024.

Kimmerer, Robin Wall. *Braiding Sweetgrass.* Minneapolis: Milkweed, 2015.